THE FANTASY FOOTBALL
BLACK BOOK

2019 Edition
By: Joe Pisapia
@JoePisapia17

Featuring

Jake Ciely @allinkid The Athletic

Matt Franciscovich @MattFranchise EA Sports

Nate Hamilton @DomiNateFF Fantrax

Gary Davenport @IDPSharks Bleacher Report

Derek Brown @DBro_FFB The Quant Edge

Scott Bogman @BogmanSports InThisLeague.com

Chris Meaney @chrismeaney The Athletic

Edited by Tim Heaney @TeamHeaney RotoWire/ESPN

Facebook: Fantasy Black Book

Instagram @fantasyblackbook

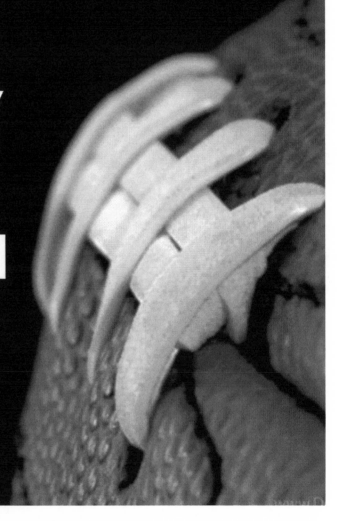

About the Authors:

Joe Pisapia *is the author of the #1 best-selling* **Fantasy Black Book Series** *and creator of the revolutionary player evaluation tool* **Relative Position Value** *(RPV). He currently hosts* **The Fantasy Black Book Podcast, The Pre-Snap NFL DFS Podcast** *and* **The On Deck MLB DFS Podcast** *for* **LineStarApp.** *Joe is also a senior fantasy columnist for* **Fantrax** *covering NFL and MLB. He's a former radio host for* **Sirius XM Fantasy Sports Radio,** *and* **FNTSY Radio** *where he won the Fantasy Sports Radio Show of The Year Award (FSTA 2016). He appears frequently on* **CBS TV NY on The Sports Desk Show.** *He's also worked for* **RotoWire, The Sporting News, FanDuel Insider** *and* **FantasyAlarm.**

The Fantasy Black Book Podcast

Available on iTunes, Google, Stitcher, iHeartRadio and everywhere you listen to podcasts.

Subscribe today! Click Below on eBook version for link!

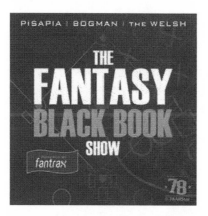

The Pre Snap NFL DFS Podcast by LineStar

Available on iTunes, Google, Stitcher, iHeartRadio and everywhere you listen to podcasts.

Subscribe today! Click Below on eBook version for link!

Jake Ciely *is an award-winning fantasy analyst and the Senior Writer covering NFL and MLB at* **TheAthletic.com**. *Jake is the creator of the expert* **FLEX Leagues** *and hosts the 2016 FSTA Fantasy Sports Radio Show of the Year,* **On Target**, *on* **FNTSY Radio**. *Jake is one of the industry's most accurate experts, finishing No. 1 in Fantasy Baseball in back-to-back years with a Top 5 average finish for his Fantasy Football ranking career. He is a yearly participant in both* **LABR** *and* **Tout Wars** *and was* **2017 LABR Mixed Champion**. *Get the Fantasy deal in seasonal, DFS and more from Jake on Twitter* @allinkid.

Matt Franciscovich *currently works for EA Sports, focusing on Madden NFL competitive gaming. Prior, he spent four football seasons working as a fantasy analyst for NFL Media, appearing on NFL Network and as a regular voice on the NFL Fantasy Podcast in addition to writing and editing articles for NFL.com, setting weekly rankings, and developing relationships throughout the industry along the way. During his five years as a fantasy football analyst, Matt has also contributed to fantasy football outlets like CBS Sportsline, numberFire and FantasyPros, and is proud to be contributing to the Fantasy Football Black Book for the second straight year.*

Gary Davenport, *considered by some (by which he means his mother) the fantasy football industry's leading expert on Individual Defensive Player (IDP) leagues, is a Senior Staff Writer at* **Fantasy Sharks**; *NFL and Fantasy Football Analyst at* **Bleacher Report**; *Contributing Writer at* **Rotoworld**, **The Athletic** *and* **Fantrax**; *and a Contributing Author and Associate Editor at* **Football Diehards**. *A seven-time FSWA Award finalist, Gary has been a finalist for the FSWA Football Writer of the Year Award each of the last three years. He won the award in 2017.*

Nate Hamilton *is a regular contributor in the fantasy football industry. He has provided advice & analysis on a daily basis since joining Twitter (@DomiNateFF) in August of 2013. He has produced content for many sites including: FantasyPros, The Fantasy Footballers, Fantasy Data, and currently, FantraxHQ. He is the co-host of The Fantasy Tilt Podcast with Keaton Denlay. Nate is a co-author of Amazon's #1 Best Selling "The Fantasy Football Black Book" with Joe Pisapia. He is a member of the Fantasy Sports Writer's Association (FSWA).*

Derek Brown *writes for* **The Quant Edge**, **Gridiron Experts**, & **Fantasy Data**. *He has made various guest spots on* **Sirius XM Fantasy Sports Radio** *and is an expert consensus ranker at* **FantasyPros**. *Born in Louisiana, he is a diehard Saints fan (Whodat).*

Scott Bogman *is Co-Owner and Co-Host of* **InThisLeague.com**. *He has been covering Fantasy Football, Baseball, Basketball and College Football for 5 years with ITL,* **FNTSY Network** *and* **Fantrax**. *He might have a bias towards player from the Pittsburgh Steelers, Texas Longhorns, Arizona Diamondbacks and Houston Rockets. You can reach Bogman through Twitter* @BogmanSports *or email* ScottBogman@gmail.com.

Chris Meaney *is a contributor for* **The Athletic**, *covering fantasy sports. Chris covered NHL, NBA, NFL and MLB as a producer, writer and host at* **FNTSY Sports Network**. *He was lead host of the daily live shows,* **"Fantasy Sports Today"**, **"The FanDuel Show"** *and* **"Home Ice Advantage."** *Chris has written for* **The Associated Press**, *the* **New York Daily News**, **The Fantasy Footballers**, **Fantrax**, **The Quant Edge**, **NBA Fantasy**, **Play Picks**, **LineStarApp** *and more. Follow Chris on Twitter* @chrismeaney.

About the Editor:

Tim Heaney *has cultivated award-winning and industry-recognized content in fantasy sports publishing for more than a decade, during which he's captured several industry-league titles and **Fantasy Sports Writers Association** honors for podcasting. The New York native started with **KFFL.com**, which eventually linked up with **USA TODAY Fantasy Sports**, where he contributed football and baseball analysis to **Sports Weekly** and on the web. Since 2016, he's worked for **RotoWire** as an editor, Senior Writer and podcaster (NFL and MLB), and he's written weekly football and baseball tips for **ESPN**. He competes annually in Jake Ciely's **FLEX Leagues** and baseball's **Tout Wars**. (He **won Tout's mixed auction** in 2018.) 2019 marks his second year as Editor of the **Fantasy Black Book**, and he even co-hosts the **@InThisRing** **pro wrestling podcast** with Black Book godfather Joe Pisapia! Join **@TeamHeaney** on Twitter.*

Click for link ↓

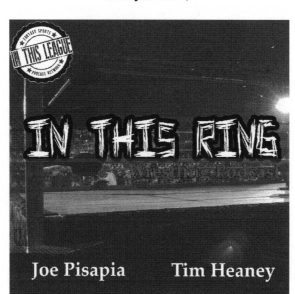

The 2019 Edition is dedicated to:

My two daughters who constantly inspire me to be the best father and man that I can be.

SPECIAL THANKS TO:
Brian Alspach
&
The Cover Art Team of @MatHouchens and Chad Greene

TABLE OF CONTENTS

Introduction

Chapter 1 Burning Questions for 2019

Chapter 2 Relative Position Value

Chapter 3 Draft Strategy 2019

      1. Standard
      2. PPR
      3. Superflex
      4. Best Ball

Chapter 4 Quarterbacks

Chapter 5 Running Backs

Chapter 6 Wide Receivers

Chapter 7 Tight Ends

Chapter 8 Kickers

Chapter 9 Team Defense/ST

Chapter 10 IDP (Why, How & Rankings)

Chapter 11 2019 Rookies & UDFA for Dynasty/Redraft, plus "Top 25 College Prospects"

Chapter 12 NFL DFS 2019

Chapter 13 Overrated/Underrated

Chapter 14 Being the Commish

Chapter 15 Making Moves

INTRODUCTION

Nine years ago, I started a book series: my thoughts, my system -- something unique and useful in a sea of copycat content. I never thought it would evolve into the #1-selling Football book last summer for nearly a month on Amazon.

Not just Fantasy, we're talking NFL here. The 2018 Fantasy Football Black Book was #1 over Tom Brady's "TB12" and Nick Foles' Cinderella story "Believe It". That's for one reason, and one reason alone: Fantasy players are coming back time and time again and having massive success with **The Black Book** Brand.

There's no major media machine behind this series, no global SEO or advertising team. It's just high-quality content, wrapped in a revolutionary system that's easy to use and yields consistent high-end results. The proof is in the success of the product that's grown from a literal one-man show to a team effort over that time. It's the American Dream. My passion for fantasy sports as a career that can feed my family. There have been numerous lows and countless struggles along the way, but the ultimate success of The Black Book continues to make it all worth it, and every year the goal is to be better that the last one.

So, what separates The Black Book from all the other publications? A few things. First, I care about YOU WINNING your leagues. Far too many fantasy sports analysts care about having *their* opinions trumpeted across platforms or causing a stir. They want to be "stars". All I care about is giving my readers a system based in reality (not merely projections or informed opinion) that can actually make a difference in every single league size, style and format.

I'm not the star here. YOU are! I want to empower you from the draft, to the waiver wire, to trades, and all the way to the championship. My job is to help make you the expert.

Some say that "draft guides" are outdated, and I agree! This isn't a "draft guide" or a rack magazine. It's a concept and a season-long companion to help readers maneuver through the fantasy season from start to finish. Fantasy football coverage is littered with "rankings" and "Top 100" lists. I call this lazy fantasy. Informed opinions are great, and we have plenty to offer here, but that's not enough!

That's where Relative Position Value (RPV) comes into play as the other separator between the Black Book and other fantasy football coverage. It's not enough to say Player X is better than Player Y.

We need to know: How much better? Where's the drop-off? How substantial is it from tier to tier? How does that transfer format to format? How can I use this information as a strategy? There have been other value-based drafting systems, but none have ever been as streamlined, thorough and effective as **RPV**.

The Black Book is a team. Our readers and analysts have created a community where fantasy sports is serious but still fun! Which is why we started playing fantasy in the first place. My goal is to form a better fantasy sports community. One that values the consumer, instead of taking advantage of them as many platforms do. My team reflects that goal. They're not only great analysts, but outstanding and entertaining individuals who know their football and care just as much about your teams and you do.

Welcome to the 2019 Fantasy Football Black Book! Welcome to #TeamBlackBook!

<u>NOW AVAILABLE FOR THE FIRST TIME!</u>

RPV CHEAT SHEATS FOR NFL!

Want all the RPV for every format on an easy to reference cheat sheet?

Send $5 to

PayPal Account <u>fantasyblackbook@gmail.com</u>

Write "Black Book Cheat Sheets" & <u>your return email address</u>
We'll send them in 24 hrs to you in a PDF format! (no refunds)

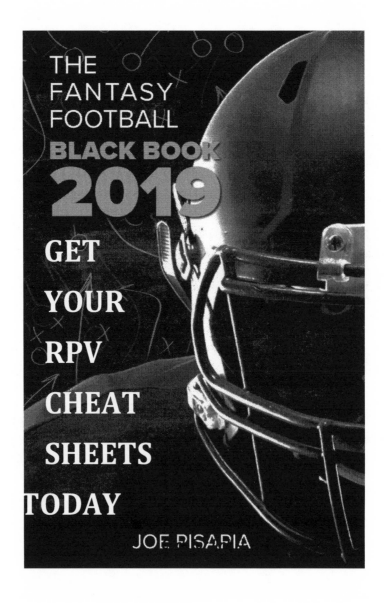

THIS IS YOUR YEAR.

THEFANTASYHEADLINERS.COM

YOUTUBE : THE FANTASY HEADLINERS

 #HEADLINERNATION

Click for link

Chapter 1

BURNING QUESTIONS FOR 2019

Joe Pisapia

Every year around the Black Book publication, I try to answer the 5 Burning Questions in fantasy. Then it occurred to me, that's not enough!

If the Black Book is going to be the People's Fantasy Source, then we have to ask the people what's on their minds! Of course, #TeamBlackBook responded with a slew of great questions, and I did my best to cherry-pick those I think might be on your fantasy football mind heading into 2019.

So, let's take a deep dive on what's on the mind of fantasy owners as we stand on the precipice of a new football season! And frankly, 5 questions seemed silly as a cap. So, let's blow this bad boy up!

Jay @GMenJay
How much do we knock Nick Chubb down now that Kareem Hunt is in town?

This has been one of the hottest topics this offseason. Hunt is suspended for the first eight games of the season. The Browns have a bye Week 7. That means Hunt is first eligible Week 10.

Neither the Browns nor fantasy owners have the luxury of looking that far ahead. The possibility of Hunt mucking with the last four weeks of Chubb (and potentially fantasy playoff rounds Weeks 14-16) is real, but you have to be relevant come November, first and foremost. I wouldn't let Hunt's presence affect my aggressiveness on Chubb, who was one of the best RBs in fantasy in the latter part of the season. Be grateful that other owners may be hesitant and take advantage of the discount.

If you want to stash Hunt on your bench, that's fair, but realize that may prohibit your waiver-wire flexibility over the first half of the season. Don't be shocked if folks who don't own Chubb draft Hunt and drop him a month into the season. Basically, my advice is play the long game with Chubb.

James Koutoulas @_JamesTheBrain
Are more fantasy owners fading the receiver position in favor of running backs this year? If so, why?

The Black Book is far more format-centric than any other "draft prep tool" out there. But generally speaking, there's a definitive upper-RB and -WR tier around which I would gladly build my roster in PPR leagues.

In standard formats, locking in the touches of the 1A class of RB is still valuable on a weekly basis, and I would still lean RB in that format early and often. Don't let the talent and depth of the WR1/WR2 class fool you. The back end of WR this year by the time you get to WR4 is weaker than years past and mostly inexperienced. Therefore, getting an elite WR in any format is a sound investment.

The "Zero" theory, whether it be RB or WR, is never a good approach. As we break down roster core building the draft strategy chapter, you'll see constructing roster strength and RPV advantage is what's key. Dismissing a position before a draft even starts is just bad fantasy. Being flexible and responsive to the board as the draft unfolds -- now that's good fantasy!

Kenny Infante @kendrickinfante
When do I draft Le'Veon Bell ... do I draft him?

I hear you. The Jets' wacky offseason was just so ... Jets. Adam Gase has failed many a talented running back in years past, but he's never had one as talented as Bell. A reliable running game is crucial to Sam Darnold's development. I don't trust Gase's crazy eyes, but I'm going to put my faith in Lev Bell's talent and commit to him as a mid-first-rounder in all formats. The later he falls, the more I like him.

Mike Smith @mikeysmith2
Is David Johnson still a top back?

Yes! The offensive system in Arizona last year was dreadful, and Kliff Kingsbury will not fail to utilize him. The O-line is still poor, but DJ will see plenty of touches trying to prop up a rookie QB, and touches are where it all starts. The best news is the discount you're getting on Johnson as a late first-rounder or early second-rounder, depending on league depth and format. He's a smart buy-low this year.

Fumble Na Net Podcasts NFL/NBA @fumblenanet
How to target interesting backup running backs? It seems like every year the winner is the one who finds the best replacements in that particular position...

The easy answer: Draft talent. For instance, the last two years, we were bullish on Marlon Mack, and eventually it paid off. Many lost patience and missed out on a difference maker in 2018. The other important consideration is opportunity. Does the back have health issues? Performance issues? Taking the handcuff for Ezekiel Elliott or Saquon Barkley when you own them is wasting a roster spot. If they go down, your season will likely not be saved by their replacement. However, looking at Dalvin Cook or Leonard Fournette's No. 2 as bench-worthy is far more appealing.

Andy Spiteri @gasdoc_spit
Can you trust spending a first-round pick on Todd Gurley?

This one will make or break fantasy seasons. The concern is real, but so is his potential productivity. It's safe to say the workload will be dialed back from the previous two seasons, regardless.

I think the best approach is situational. The later he falls, the easier it is to back him up with another solid RB. That's one positive scenario. In leagues with serious buy-ins and prize money, I'm more apt to play it more safely. In leagues for pride, I'd be likelier to take the risk.

In standard leagues, he's still a mid-to-late first-round value worth the risk. In PPR formats, he's easier to fade. So to answer the question: No, you can't "trust" Todd Gurley. That doesn't make him undraftable, though: It comes down to league situation and owner fortitude. The preseason could help give clarity here, but if you're drafting early, you have to weigh all the scenarios and proceed accordingly.

Greg Florez @gregflorez
How important is the waiver wire?

The waiver wire is extremely important. Misuse of FAAB can set you back. Some teams are too aggressive, overspending on players who can't return that value. While others get too relaxed and miss out on talent. The waiver wire should always be about acquiring talent. When David Johnson got hurt two years ago, remember all the wasted FAAB on poor RBs who couldn't fill that void? My best advice is be aggressive when talent and opportunity meet. Available touches don't equal production automatically. One great game doesn't mean a breakout season.

The draft is more important that the waiver wire. However, having depth from good waiver wire pickups can allow you to have leverage in trades and that can really turn a season around. The waiver wire is important, and it's important to use it wisely.

Charles Getter
Who leads the Eagles backfield in touches? Howard? Sanders?

If there's one backfield I want to stay away from in 2019, it's the Eagles. Miles Sanders is a nice young back, and Jordan Howard is absolutely serviceable. It's the usage that concerns me. HC Doug Pederson has a terrible history of killing fantasy running back value with inconsistent touches and undefined roles – enough so that I think you fade away from the group as a collective. I think Howard will lead the team in touches when all is said and done -- but not necessarily in fantasy points.

Marty Smith
Latavius Murray: Is he going to fill in for Ingram and be relevant in the Saints offense?

Murray will likely fill 75% of the role Mark Ingram vacated in New Orleans' offense. The Saints know what they have in Alvin Kamara, and in 2019, the gloves will be off with his usage. That being said, Murray is still going to be a useful back in fantasy formats. The deeper the league, the more valuable he becomes. Murray should also see enough goal-line action to make up for a lack of weekly touches. You can forget the notion of both finishing as RB1s as the Kamara/Ingram tandem did in 2017, but Murray will be a useful player in 2019.

//FFB @ffbflexicution
Are kickers and defense actually necessary in fantasy football?

Necessary? No. Especially kickers, if you ask Jake Ciely. I will argue that defense is, though, and IDP is a great way to take your league to the next level. Gary Davenport wrote a great argument for "Why IDP" in this year's book. I too was intimidated when I started out my first IDP league years ago, but it wasn't as tough as it seems, and the challenge can really spruce up an old league that's getting stale.

FF Evil Empire @FF_EvilEmpire
Which 2019 rookie WRs are going to shine and which are going to bust in year one?

The Chiefs' Mecole Hardman and the Colts' Parris Campbell have plenty of upside, but the Patriots have the greatest need and most potential available touches, so I'll say N'Keal Harry. He was probably the most complete receiver in the draft and has an easy path to becoming a relevant player. As the Pats have broken tradition by selecting big offensive names two years in a row, it's clear from Sony Michel's rookie year that they have every intention of using their new toys.

R Wilson @wilson27
Will the Chiefs offense ever recover from the loss of Hunt and Hill or are they done?

The Chiefs are far from done as long as Patrick Mahomes is under center. He may not throw 50 TDs again, but 35-plus is almost a lock, and he'll make the most of what's around him. That's what transcendent players do, and Mahomes is the kind of player that makes everyone around him better. The defense is a far greater concern; it was not a good unit last year, and I don't think the front office did enough this offseason to address that need. The good news there is that Mahomes won't be sitting out any fourth quarters.

Strong Style Ninja @iamstrongstyle
Will Kyler Murray be 2019 ROOKIE OF THE YEAR?

I say no. That's not a knock on Murray's size or skill, but that offensive line was the worst in the league last year and is looking as though it may repeat that feat in 2019. Putting a rookie QB behind a line like this is just not great for his development. Running for his life may give you fantasy points, but it may also lead to Murray getting knocked out of games.

Devin Bush is a Stiller @AlexVlahos1

With the evolution into RBBC instead of the feature back, does that make it so there will be more reliable fantasy RBs or just increase the value of the few workhorse RBs in the NFL?

When there's less of something, it becomes more valuable. As you'll see later on in the Black Book, the RPV bears out just how much more valuable those bell cows are in the days of RBBC. However, the flip side is that in PPR formats, teams that have secondary pass-catching backs can make great RB2/Flex options, and you can fade that top group in auctions and spread your budget around more evenly.

Chapter 2

RELATIVE POSITION VALUE (RPV)

Joe Pisapia

"The format and style of your league dictates the value of a player, not his talent."

There's nothing I hate more than lazy fantasy analysis. It's the worst.

There are a ton of well-educated and informed opinions out there across the fantasy sports landscape. In fact, many of them are in this very book!

But that's simply not enough. We live in the information age, where every owner in your league is spoon-fed quality information. The biggest misnomer in fantasy is mistaking information and opinion for strategy. They are NOT the same thing!

How many times have you seen: Fantasy Expert X's "Top 100", or Fantasy Expert Y's "Top 25 Running Backs" or Fantasy Expert Z's "Projections"? It's pretty much all that's out there. Lists. But what do they mean? How can you truly use rankings and tiers to your advantage without quantifying them in some way?

Well, we can. It's called **Relative Position Value (RPV)**.

Rankings are cute and good debate fodder. However, it doesn't matter that Player A is ranked two slots above Player B on some "experts' board". What REALLY matters is how much more productive Player A is than Player B -- and how much better they are than the other options at their position. Projections can be helpful, but not relied upon solely. When's the last time projectionists were held accountable (or held themselves accountable) for their many failures? The answer is hardly ever. Projections can have their place when you couple them with reality.

RPV compiles projections, previous season stats and three-year averages (when applicable) and weighs them to create a Black Book Point Total. That number is ALWAYS format-specific and is historically more reliable than projections alone, hence the success of the Black Book series. When it comes to rookies or young players, clearly we must rely more heavily on projections but use a cross section to do so.

Now, what happens next to that Black Book Point Totals? Although I won't give away how I weigh them, I happily will give away the RPV formula: It's how we are going to proceed with a better understanding of fantasy football throughout the rest of the Black Book. RPV may challenge your perspective -- or quite possibly affirm feelings you've always had but now can see in black and white.

Fair warning, for those who are new to the Black Book series, RPV will have you seeing fantasy value in a whole new light. While there are some other value-based drafting systems out there, NONE are as well-constructed, well-targeted and easy to comprehend as RPV.

Year over year, this chapter won't change too much, because RPV is the foundation of the Black Book series. However, NFL players run fundamental drills in training camp, so if you're returning to RPV, consider this getting in shape for the season and revisiting the basics that make you successful. Opinions are everywhere, but what fantasy players need is a way to quantify player value with actual proof.

Not only will RPV create player tiers, but it will define them. RPV is completely adaptable and adjustable to all league styles, depths and scoring systems. It's the single most useful player evaluation system available to fantasy owners and perhaps one of the easiest to grasp.

RPV IN THEORY

"RB isn't a position, BUT RB1 is!"

Considering a base of a 12-team league with two active RBs each week, a group of 24 backs is a good starting point to grasp the RPV concept. However, it's NOT how we're going to truly utilize the tool.

Over 17 weeks in 2018, Saquon Barkley led all PPR running backs with 385 pts for PPR scoring. Alvin Kamara ranked fourth with 354 pts. The 12th-best running back was Phillip Lindsay at 223, and the 24th was Aaron Jones with 171.

So, how much more valuable is each one of these guys compared to the other? Before we get ahead of ourselves, let's first see the formula in action.

The Fantasy Black Book formula is more complicated than the "basic" version I will present to you here. At the core, the way to determine the RPV -- or the percentage in which a player is better than the fantasy league average -- is:

(Individual Player Point Value – Fantasy League Average of the Position) ÷ Fantasy League Average of the Position = RPV

So, what is "Fantasy League Average"? Well, every league has a different number of teams and a varying number of active players at a given position. Some have 1RB/3WR/1FLEX, others play 2QB/2RB/3WR, and the list goes on and on.

The Fantasy League Average is whatever the average production is from a position based on the depth of your league. For example, if your league has 12 owners and starts 2RB every week, the RB pool is 24. If the top player scored 250 points and the 24th scored around 120, the fantasy league average is likely somewhere around 185 points. All players who score above this mark are "Positive RPV" players. The ones below are "Negative."

Fantasy sports is a simple game of outscoring your opponents as frequently as possible from as many active positions as you can. The more your team lives in the "Positive", the greater your chances are week-to-week. It's like playing the odds in Texas Hold'em. If you have a strong starting hand, the odds are in your favor. Sure, you may take some bad beats, but more often than not, the percentages will play in your favor.

Here's the trick! Even though there are 24 running backs, almost every team will likely have **one true RB1**, which means RB1 is its own unique scoring position. Rather than create a fantasy league average for 24 overall backs, it's more applicable to separate RB1s and RB2s into their own private groups and create an individual fantasy league average for each.

Now that we understand Fantasy League Average, let's get more specific. Last year, Saquon Barkley scored 385 pts. The Fantasy League Average (or FLA) at RB1 (top 12) was 301 pts.

Subtract that Fantasy League Average from Barkley's 385, then divide by that same FLA (301 pts), and you have a brilliant **Relative Position Value of +28% RPV**: [385-301] ÷ 301 = 27.9%.

That means Saquon was 28% more productive than the average RB1. That's substantial! That means something!

If we took the RPV of running back as a whole over the top 24, Barkley's RPV would jump to a whopping +57% RPV, because the Fantasy League Average would be just 245. BUT we don't do that, because he'll be stacking up, head-to-head, against other RB1s most weeks in theoretical terms against other RB1 slots on other rosters. Calculating RB1s and RB2s as their own positions gives a much more accurate depiction of a player's value. Hence, what makes RPV better than other value-based systems.

Are you in a 14-team league? Then use the top 14 to establish RB1 RPV. In a 10- team league? Adjust that way. The deeper the league, the more difficult it is to create an RPV advantage. The shallower the league, the less disparity you'll find (especially at WR). Therefore, you have more options to construct your roster in different ways. Have a wacky scoring system? Doesn't matter. RPV formula covers everything.

Below is the **Final RPV** for RB1s and RB2s from the end of 2018. You'll see not only the positive but also the negative side of RPV. The concept of not overdrafting or overspending on players that can't really supply you "positive" production is the path to success. You will also see as we go on how to create an RPV advantage!

2018 FINAL RB RPV for RB1 and RB2 (PPR scoring)

RB1 RPV   **RB2 RPV**

	Player	FPTS	RPV		Player	FPTS	RPV
1	Saquon Barkley	385.8	28%	1	Kareem Hunt	222.8	17%
2	Christian McCaffrey	385.5	28%	2	Kenyan Drake	206.2	8%
3	Todd Gurley	372.1	24%	3	Chris Carson	201.4	6%
4	Alvin Kamara	354.2	18%	4	Derrick Henry	201.3	6%
5	Ezekiel Elliott	329.2	9%	5	Nick Chubb	194.5	2%
6	James Conner	280	-7%	6	Tevin Coleman	193.6	2%
7	James White	276.6	-8%	7	Adrian Peterson	189	0%
8	Melvin Gordon	275.5	-9%	8	Jordan Howard	180	-5%
9	David Johnson	246.7	-18%	9	Marlon Mack	178.1	-7%
10	Joe Mixon	243.4	-19%	10	T.J. Yeldon	173.1	-9%
11	Tarik Cohen	233.9	-22%	11	Lamar Miller	172.6	-9%
12	Phillip Lindsay	230.2	-24%	12	Aaron Jones	171.5	-10%

The first obvious takeaway from last year was that the RB1 RPV was incredibly top-heavy. The bottom of the tier wasn't bad; in fact, those low-end RB1s were quite productive. The elite became super-elite, though, and that meant we ended up having "haves" and "have nots".

RB2 was much more forgiving. It only bottomed out at a -10% RPV, as opposed to the -24% RPV of RB1. RPV is not only a great tool to use in drafts but also analyzing what's happening around the league.

So, how can the fantasy player exploit RPV?

By having a high-end RB1 and then drafting ANOTHER RB1 as your RB2, you have "frontloaded" the position and created an area of strength.

The BIGGEST mistake fantasy owners make in any sports in "filling their roster for positions", instead of filling their roster with talent and strength.

When you fill your roster for positions, you get a mediocre .500 team. When you fill your roster with strength, you have an advantage over the rest of the field. As long as you can responsibly fill the other positions and avoid negative RPV as often as possible, that roster strength can carry your season.

With more NFL teams adapting backfield committees, the true starting running backs are worth more than ever in standard formats. That especially goes for the RB1s who get goal-line carries and the bulk of touches. In PPR, you can build the same strength of front-loading WR1s as you can with RB1s, then make up ground later by buying running backs in bulk with upside. The tough sell there is the difference between definitive running back touches as opposed to expected wide receiver catches. One is frankly more reliable on a weekly basis.

The same could be said for Superflex/2QB leagues. By "frontloading" elite QB play, you simultaneously create a team RPV strength and weaken the pool for the other owners. RPV shows you how stark the value can be position-to-position. Some will bottom out at -10% while others will be -20%. With middle-tier receivers, you'll see little advantage to be gained.

RPV is the ultimate tool to truly define talent and, even more importantly, where the drop-off in talent lies. Rankings are biased. RPV is honest.

Obviously, every league will be different. Flex players and OP (offensive player) slots will change values a bit, but the RPV theory holds in **EVERY LEAGUE and EVERY FORMAT**! It just needs to be adjusted according to each league's specifications. In the Black Book, I've done much of the work for you, but you must be sure to adjust the RPV for your league(s) quirky scoring wrinkles if you are going to truly achieve ultimate success.

Now that we've outlined RPV, let's dive deeper.

RPV IN PRACTICE (Draft and Trades)

Last year, so many folks asked, "How does the Black Book determine its RPV?"

The Black Book takes a combination of 3-year averages (when applicable/available), previous season stats and the upcoming season projections, creating a hybrid point total for each player that then gets utilized within the RPV equation.

For rookies, clearly there is no track record from which to work to create that number. Therefore, I use a composite of projected stats from a few choice entities, their college statistical profile and their potential use in their new team system in order to create each rookie's point total for the RPV formula.

With so many new styles of fantasy football, it's crucial to understand the value of each position in your league.

For example, I prefer PPR leagues (points per reception) that play a lineup consisting of QB, RB, RB/WR, WR1, WR2, WR3, TE, K, 5 IDP and an OP slot (which can be a QB) or a second mandatory QB spot.

If a quarterback is the most important skills entity in *real* football, I want my fantasy experience to mirror that truth. The RPV for this kind of league is different than a standard league. Teams play 2 QBs every week, therefore QBs become the equivalent of the RB1/RB2 RPV I just laid out in the last section.

Another big adjustment: Since I technically only have to start 1 RB, the talent pool is adjusted back into a "one large group of running backs" theory. Possession WRs and big playmakers garner attention. This is a perfect example of why a tool like RPV is so necessary. If I were to use the standard old rankings from a website or a magazine in this format, I would get crushed.

Now more than ever, there is no "one ranking system" that will be useful to you in any format. Ignore these Top 100 lists and nonsense like that – and instead focus on the true value and weight of the player in *your* league. That's why RPV works.

The last best thing about RPV is the fact it strips away a lot of the hype and noise surrounding the athletes, as well as the fictional computer projections that can be misleading and downright destructive.

RPV is about understanding a player's value -- his ACTUAL value. Not what his value may be projected to be while you sit in last place wondering where you went wrong. The best way to evaluate a player is through a mixture of career averages, previous statistics and projections that are then weighed against the other players of the same position. NOT PROJECTIONS ALONE!

Using only last year's numbers will give you a great team … for last season. Using just projections will give you a great team … in theory. RPV will give you a great team in REALITY!

You can choose to be great at one spot or two, but if you are below-average at other places, your overall RPV will even out. You may find yourself managing a middle-of-the-road team. Being above-average in as many places as you can, even without a top-flight star, you will find yourself consistently out-producing your opponents. If you use RPV correctly, you may even find yourself above average in most places and great in others, which makes you the one to beat. It's the ability to adapt, adjust and understand that separates us. RPV is the difference-maker.

RPV can not only tell you how much better a player is than the average for his position, but it can also tell you how much better he is than the next guy available at his position on the draft board. Understanding these RPV relationships is a key technique in maximizing your positional advantage.

To illustrate this point and its application, let's take a draft-day example. It's your turn to pick and you've got openings to fill at WR and TE. The top available players on the board at each position look like this:

WR

Player A: +15% RPV

Player B: +10% RPV

Player C: +8% RPV

Player D: +7% RPV

Player E: +5% RPV

TE

Player F: +8% RPV

Player G: -2% RPV

Player H: -2% RPV

Player I: -4% RPV

Player J: -6% RPV

At first glance, you might be inclined to take Player A, who is a +15% better than the average at his position. All other things being equal, however, Player F is probably the better choice.

Even though he is only +8% better than the average, the drop-off between him and the next-best player at his position is 10 percentage points. That's a significant dip. If you take Player A now, Player F almost definitely won't be on the board when your next pick rolls around, and at best you'll be stuck with an average or below-average tight end.

If you take Player F now, however, you'll be on the right side of that 10% RPV advantage over the teams who haven't drafted a TE yet. You'll also probably lose out on Player A at WR, but you will still most likely get someone from the above list (Player C, D or E) -- all of whom are trading in the same RPV range and, more importantly, still in the positive. It may not sound like a big deal with mere percentage points, but it adds up the more you rise above or fall below the average RPV threshold.

By picking this way, you end up with a strong advantage at one position while remaining above average at the other. The alternative is to be above-average at one position and decidedly average or worse at the other. That's the reason so many fantasy owners fail. Usually they base these decisions on the *name* of the player instead of his Relative Position Value. The same can be said when evaluating trades. You must look at what advantage you're gaining and potentially losing in each deal.

The owner who does that effectively has a distinct advantage. Remember, don't marginalize your strength!

Chapter 3

DRAFT STRATEGY

Joe Pisapia & Nate Hamilton

This year, I decided to dive deeper. If the Black Book is truly going to be the best tool out there, then each league format needs its own specific draft strategy section. Not a "blurb," not "general strategy", but a true look at building a roster core.

You'll see lots of magazines with their mock drafts, but really that's not super helpful at the end of the day. Instead, Nate and I decided to do 4 rounds of "Core Building" from each draft slot in the hopes of showing not only where we think the value lies in each format, each pick -- but to also present a cohesive voice of how to approach your draft slot.

Now obviously every draft will be unique. What we want to do it give the reader an approach to be prepared for that inevitability.

As you read on each draft is broken down into thirds in terms of approaching draft slots. We'll also discuss each format in shallower and deeper leagues and how the draft pool affects certain positions. There will certain players who miss the first four rounds, and we'll justify why that's the case.

We want to prepare you better than everyone else does in the fantasy football industry for ALL of your drafts! Standard, PPR, Superflex, Best Ball … EVERYTHING!

Successful drafts are built with a great knowledge of the player pool, RPV and the ability of an owner to be flexible. I'm not a fan of mock drafting. I feel it sometimes leads folks into a false sense of security, and other times people are just trying out concepts, and that's not going to prepare you for a draft with money on the line.

The only thing mocks are helpful for is training your ability to be flexible and react as runs happen. The discipline of when to go with the pack and when to run the other direction is crucial, and RPV is extremely useful in those instances. Remember, it's all about building roster strength, not just filling open roster positions.

AUCTION LEAGUE STRATEGY

Most drafts are of the snake variety, which saddens me, as I am a fan of auctions. It allows for the most prepared owners to excel.

You may think, "Hey where are the dollar values?" That's not a strategy. Dollar values for players are a suggestion: You can find them on any site, and they'll all be similar.

I want to give you an **approach**. The biggest mistake people make with auction leagues is following artificial and arbitrary dollar amounts many publications will put out.

Winning leagues with salaried players is about (1) Getting proven big-time, RPV-advantage talent, and (2) finding cost-effective, low-priced talent on the back end. The "stars and scrubs" philosophy is effective because you are paying a premium for proven talent and getting premium production.

If you're a student of the fantasy game, you'll know where the values sit in single-digit-priced players. Plus, the waiver wire will be viable to make up ground inseason and fill any holes. Injuries always present new talent on a weekly basis nowadays. However, that talent is rarely STAR-LEVEL.

Therefore, you should invest heavily and without apology for the big-time RB/WR/QB talent when you can in the draft. Solidifying those guys is paramount! The worst thing you can do is let a David Johnson go for that one extra $1. You'll regret it later.

Also, the best in-draft strategy I can suggest is never, EVER nominate a player you want on your team when it's your turn early on in a draft. Every time you bleed money out of the room from other owners, that's less money they have to fight you on players that you want on your team. It sounds like small potatoes, but if you do that consistently in the early going, it'll pay late dividends.

Moreover, I would avoid starting to bid on any player you truly want until the first time you hear "going twice". There's an intimidation factor at play in auctions that's equal parts football knowledge and in-draft gamesmanship. Many owners get frustrated when this happens. They go from thinking they have a player to not having them. Some can recover, but most get thrown off their game. Then they panic. Then they either back off or make a bad inflated buy.

There's no reason to artificially inflate salaries of players you like by bidding on them in the early going. Wait. Be patient. Then pounce. And please, forget what the websites and magazines tell you is an "appropriate salary" for a player. The "appropriate salary" is what gets you the player you believe in on your roster!

The upcoming draft sub-chapters will take you through the values, but more importantly the "Core Building". To carry this over from snake to auction is simple. You'll see in each format which team cores we prefer in each format and why. That will help you budget and attack similar strategies with dollars rather than draft picks.

STANDARD SCORING STRATEGY

Nate Hamilton

4-Round Draft Strategy

	Round 1	Round 2	Round 3	Round 4
Team 1	Ezekiel Elliott	Phillip Lindsay >	A.J. Green	Sammy Watkins
Team 2	Saquon Barkley	Sony Michel	Travis Kelce	Kenny Golladay
Team 3	Christian McCaffrey	Keenan Allen	Devonta Freeman	Kenyan Drake
Team 4	Alvin Kamara	Antonio Brown	George Kittle	Lamar Miller
Team 5	Melvin Gordon	Derrick Henry	T.Y. Hilton	Robert Woods
Team 6	Le'Veon Bell	JuJu Smith-Schuster	Chris Carson	Cooper Kupp
Team 7	Todd Gurley	Dalvin Cook	Amari Cooper	Brandin Cooks
Team 8	Joe Mixon	Mike Evans	Aaron Jones	Damien Williams
Team 9	Davante Adams	Odell Beckham	Zach Ertz	Kerryon Johnson
Team 10	DeAndre Hopkins	Nick Chubb	Adam Thielen	Mark Ingram
Team 11	Julio Jones	David Johnson	Stefon Diggs	Josh Jacobs
Team 12	James Conner >	Michael Thomas	Marlon Mack >	Patrick Mahomes

UPDATE as of 7/20 With the Tyreek Hill news of no suspension, Hill should be slotted in place of Odell Beckham and all other WR get bumped back in order respectively.*

It's the format I first experienced back in the very early 2000s. The format that I loved and had no intention of ever letting go. The format that was ... well ... safe. Standard scoring is easy to understand. There isn't much else to think about outside of yards and touchdowns. It's the perfect format for beginners in fantasy football and for the old school, "run up the middle" running back truthers.

In standard scoring, touches are king. Since you do not get additional points for receptions, you'll want to stack your team with players who touch the ball early and often. This is why traditionally, you'll notice a lot more running backs tend to be drafted earlier in this format. There is a clear difference in workload for a running back than even the best wide receivers. To put that into context, your typical "workhorse" RB will see around 20-plus touches a game. A wide receiver may only have 7 receptions on a good day.

As it was so famously said to my favorite comic book hero growing up: "With more touches, comes more opportunity for fantasy points." Or at least that's how I remember it. Either way, you want to seek out players who get the ball a bunch every game. They will add points to your roster (almost) every time they touch the ball (20-plus times). They will also see more scoring chances as they will handle most (if not all) of the goal-line duties.

2019 Player Pool Approach

Every season, there is an elite group of running backs that gets drafted in the first 5-6 picks of every fantasy draft, and this year is no different. For the reasons listed above, the running back position is the priority for the top picks in drafts. One difference you may see in 2019 and going forward is the contrast in running back and wide receiver draft picks. Just because you find yourself in a standard league doesn't necessarily mean wide receivers and pass-catching backs will fall in average draft position.

Over the years, the NFL has become more focused on the passing game, and as a result, wide receivers have become more valuable earlier in fantasy drafts. The output of pass-catching backs in college and, in turn, the NFL are at a much grander level than we've ever seen. This type of player would have fallen further in fantasy drafts in the past but has gained so much value that this mold competes with the volume running backs earlier and earlier every year. As the NFL changes, we (the fantasy community) must adapt and reinvent ourselves. Sadly, I won't be surprised to see standard point leagues fall to the gauntlet of time and *snap* … cease to exist.

Where are you drafting?

Picks 1-4: It should be no surprise that 4 of the top running backs were drafted in these spots. These 4 RBs have common attributes: Each gets a ton of volume on the ground and through the air in each respective offense. All 4 were in the top 5 in targets and receptions among running backs in 2018. This just reiterates how important volume is when it comes to the top draft picks. If you have the benefit of a top-4 pick, you may feel more comfortable straying from RBs for the next few rounds before you pick your second.

Picks 5-8: The middle set of picks offers a harder choice between a running back and a wide receiver. Because this draft was done under the standard format, running backs still ruled all 4 of these picks. If you find yourself in this position, you'll want to weigh your options from a volume/opportunity standpoint. Because you don't earn more points for receptions, wide receivers fell outside of the top 8 picks in this draft format. If you have a middle-round pick, you don't have the benefit of closer picks. You'll find yourself struggling to draft players from the same position on back-to-back picks, and as a result, you should look for roster balance earlier than others.

Picks 9-12: Here come the wide receivers -- 3 of these 4 picks, to be exact. Just as deciding what to do with the middle picks is difficult, having picks closer to the turn may force you to go against the strategy with which you're most comfortable. The elite tier of running backs is often gone by the time you get to the end of the 1st round. Your first 2 picks are close together, so a lot of the time, you'll want to get your hands on a top-3 WR and pair him with the best player available after the turn. It often gets tricky, even for running back truthers, to avoid taking a WR

-- possibly 2 WRs -- with their first two picks. These picks become the catalyst for breaking trends for the rest of the draft.

How a 10-Team League Changes Your Approach: With fewer slots between your next pick, your approach may naturally change. There is less urgency to balance your roster before the top players at each position are taken. You could stock up at a certain position (preferably RB) as you will have more opportunities to acquire quality assets in the other positions later than usual. Doing this would also force your leaguemates to go after the position on which you stock up. So, while they are filling the void you already filled, you will be selecting other roster positions from an expanded pool.

How a 14-Team League Changes Your Approach: In my experience with deeper leagues, it's vital that you keep roster balance in mind when drafting. If you fill 1 position on back-to-back picks, you'll quickly find yourself drafting whatever is left in the other positions out of desperation. That is not how you want to be drafting. You want to be in control of your selections, not reacting to missed opportunities. Look ahead. Count how many picks until your next pick and see if you'd be happy with your next selection before you make your current pick.

If You Can Pick Your Draft Slot: I would prefer a top-5 pick in this format. I feel it is more crucial to lock up a top-5 RB given the scoring structure in standard leagues. You'll wait a while before your next pick, but at least you'll have close to back-to-back picks every couple of rounds to snag guys within the same value tier.

Players who missed making the core and why: Derrius Guice & Leonard Fournette

Both of these running backs have the potential of being top-10 at the position, but there is just too much uncertainty surrounding them. Guice is working back from injury, and the Redskins have locked up Adrian Peterson (who just had over 1,000 rushing yards in 2018) for the next 2 years. They also added Stanford running back Bryce Love with the 112th overall pick in this year's draft. The insurance the Redskins feel they need at the position speaks volumes to the lack of trust in Guice's health.

Fournette also has injury concerns, but his off-field issues could be the main reason for his drop in ADP. Fournette was recently arrested this spring for driving with a suspended license. The relationship between Fournette and the Jaguars doesn't appear to be solid. There are too many questions for him moving forward to spend a 4th-rounder or better on him.

How You Can Ruin Your Draft

I'm going to upset a lot of "Zero RB" truthers here, but I truly believe passing on RBs until the mid-to-late rounds in standard scoring formats will hinder your team. Sure, you can get lucky and end up with some late-round RB gems, but in this format, it's best to lock up volume-driven players early and take chances later. Remember, receptions don't get you extra points here, so filling your roster with high-end wide receivers and secondary backs will put you at a disadvantage more times than not. It's not a coincidence that you see more RBs in the top 24 fantasy players in standard leagues than PPR.

PPR SCORING STRATEGY

Nate Hamilton

4-Round Draft Strategy

	Round 1	Round 2	Round 3	Round 4
Team 1	Saquon Barkley	Zach Ertz >	Stefon Diggs	Damien Williams
Team 2	Ezekiel Elliott	Travis Kelce	Amari Cooper	Kenyan Drake
Team 3	Christian McCaffrey	Joe Mixon	Cooper Kupp	Calvin Ridley
Team 4	Alvin Kamara	T.Y. Hilton	Dalvin Cook	Tyler Lockett
Team 5	Le'Veon Bell	Adam Thielen	Julian Edelman	Chris Carson
Team 6	Melvin Gordon	A.J. Green	Nick Chubb	O.J. Howard
Team 7	DeAndre Hopkins	Keenan Allen	Marlon Mack	Patrick Mahomes
Team 8	Davante Adams	Antonio Brown	Derrick Henry	Tarik Cohen
Team 9	Julio Jones	Mike Evans	George Kittle	Phillip Lindsay
Team 10	Todd Gurley	JuJu Smith Schuster	Sony Michel	Robert Woods
Team 11	Michael Thomas	David Johnson	Aaron Jones	Kenny Golladay
Team 12	James Conner >	Odell Beckham Jr	Devonta Freeman >	Brandin Cooks

UPDATE as of 7/20 With the Tyreek Hill news of no suspension, Hill should be slotted in place of Odell Beckham and all other WR get bumped back in order respectively.*

In PPR (point per reception) leagues, running backs still hold a ton of value because of the type of back we see in today's NFL. Pass-catching backs have become the "standard" for which NFL organizations look to add to their rosters. As a result, running backs still make up the majority of selections in the first round, and PPR drafts are looking more and more like standard drafts than in the past.

Everything stated above applies in the first few rounds. Once we get into the middle rounds, it becomes clear that WRs are the focus. In PPR drafts, you may not feel so bullish on locking up your RBs early as you want to maximize your value with top-end wide receivers. After all, you do get an additional point for each reception, and they don't call them "receivers" for nothing. Even the top tight ends are drafted earlier in this format as we have seen 100-plus targets allotted to the few elite at the position.

It's important to remember that volume is king. Even if a wide receiver doesn't get the yardage or touchdowns, he can still be a valuable asset with reception volume. A perfect example of this is Jarvis Landry. In 3 of his 5 years in the league, Landry had over 100 targets and 80 receptions yet finished with under 1,000 receiving yards. Still, he's been a mid-round value finishing as a top-20 WR in each of the last 4 seasons and a top-10 option in 2 of those seasons.

This goes for all strategies: Do your homework. Look up the settings of your league and study them. What is the point system? Do you get more points for 3rd-down conversions? Does the league have a tight-end premium? Don't be afraid to reach out to your commissioner and ask questions. You want to understand all of the details for each league you are in before you draft. Proper knowledge will likely change your approach. Not all leagues are the same, and your strategy shouldn't be either.

2019 Player Pool Approach

You will definitely want to use target/reception volume as a tiebreaker when deciding between running backs throughout the draft. Most of the top RBs in today's NFL have healthy volume in those categories anyway, but it's important to keep in mind for the middle-to-late rounds.

In 2019, we seem to have more value picks than usual. I think we are quick to forget players who were injured last season. Most fantasy draft ranks reflect production from the previous season, and the casual fan may not think to scroll down further on the list and draft someone like an A.J. Green or Cooper Kupp ahead of some players listed ahead with a lower ceiling.

Yes, injuries should be a concern and are often the reason for a fall in ADP, but pay attention to the injury itself. Is it recurring for that player? Is it a type of injury that causes many people to struggle during rehab? If not, I would treat them as they were before the injury occurred and draft them appropriately.

Lastly, pay attention all situational changes for teams. If an elite, high-volume player has been traded or has suffered a preseason injury that can linger, that often leads to a healthy uptick in volume for the surrounding players of that team. Evaluate who could benefit most in those situations, and don't be afraid to reach on those guys.

Where are you drafting?

Picks 1-4: This is a point-per reception league, but that doesn't mean you should abandon the top running backs in the game. There is more depth at WR, especially in PPR, where you should take a top RB with these picks and supplement with a volume WR in the late 2nd round.

Picks 5-8: This area of draft position is the tipping point. It happens a bit sooner than standard formats, where you begin to see the top WRs coming off the board. Even if the top 2 WRs get taken, don't panic. This is where you can get a great value on a RB who has fallen because of the PPR format bias. If one of the top 5-6 RBs is there, I'd go after him. If not, then grab one of those top 2 WRs here.

Picks 9-12: Once the top RBs and top 2 WRs are gone (presumably), it's time for some math. Since you are close to the turn, you are lucky enough to grab a quality player at RB and WR to begin your roster. I suggest you take a look at the next X number of players available and see how many quality WRs versus RBs are left. This way, you can begin with the position that has fewer top assets left and then pick from the best of the other position with your turn pick.

How a 10-Team League Changes Your Approach: Although there will be less urgency to balance roster spots early with 10 teams, you may want to use the lack of urgency to your advantage. If you can, get yourself a top RB with your first pick but then load your roster with pass catchers as you will have more time to draft a solid RB2 for your roster. Running backs are important for your team, but you must follow the supply and demand of each draft.

How a 14-Team League Changes Your Approach: Similar to what I said in the Standard chapter, you will want to balance your roster fairly quickly before you get into the middle-to-late rounds. Having more teams means more picks between your turns, which means the talent pool drains more rapidly. If you don't grab a top 3-4 tight end, then it may be best to punt the position and grab a late-round sleeper. You can wait on QB as well – and you should be. Stock up on WRs and RBs until the talent pool is "meh" and then fill out the rest of your roster.

If You Can Pick Your Draft Slot: I would love to have a pick closer to the turn in PPR drafts. I feel like I can still get a top RB in that position and complement it with a top WR before they disappear. Also, the RBs fall a bit further in these drafts, calming the urgency to draft your second and third RBs. I love drafting RBs as I feel it creates a solid foundation for your fantasy team, but in this format, it's nice to sit back on the position a bit more.

How You Can Ruin Your Draft

Running backs are still a vital piece of your roster in PPR. Do not overreact to the WRs coming off the board at a faster pace in this format. You could find yourself in a situation where you draft a bunch of WRs and are left picking at RB scraps. When this happens in drafts, you often end up trading some of the top WRs you drafted for RBs you could have taken instead. This could leave your team feeling flat if you trade out of desperation.

SUPERFLEX/2QB STRATEGY

4-Round Draft Strategy

Joe Pisapia

	Round 1	Round 2	Round 3	Round 4
Team 1	Saquon Barkley	Adam Thielen >	Matt Ryan	Phillip Lindsay
Team 2	Ezekiel Elliott	A.J. Green	Deshaun Watson	Damien Williams
Team 3	Christian McCaffrey	Joe Mixon	Cam Newton	George Kittle
Team 4	Alvin Kamara	Keenan Allen	Travis Kelce	Philip Rivers
Team 5	Le'Veon Bell	Mike Evans	Ben Roethlisberger	Zach Ertz
Team 6	Melvin Gordon	Antonio Brown	Drew Brees	Aaron Jones
Team 7	Todd Gurley	Aaron Rodgers	Dalvin Cook	Amari Cooper
Team 8	Davante Adams	Andrew Luck	T.Y. Hilton	Josh Jacobs
Team 9	DeAndre Hopkins	JuJu Smith-Schuster	Russell Wilson	Marlon Mack
Team 10	Julio Jones	Odell Beckham Jr.	Nick Chubb	Devonta Freeman
Team 11	Patrick Mahomes	David Johnson	Derrick Henry	Stefon Diggs
Team 12	James Conner >	Michael Thomas	Sony Michel >	Baker Mayfield

UPDATE as of 7/20 With the Tyreek Hill news of no suspension, Hill should be slotted in place of Odell Beckham and all other WR get bumped back in order respectively.*

NOTE: This draft was based on 1/2pt PPR along with Superflex to level the playing field and compromise the value between RB/WR.

Finally, after years of living in the recesses of the fantasy world, Superflex leagues are finally starting to emerge as a more common practice.

The QB is the most crucial position in real football, yet he was a second-class citizen in fantasy based upon supply and demand. It's not hard to find 12 worthy QBs to start, leaving many talented point-getters on the sidelines of the waiver wire while fantasy owners fought over back up running backs and fifth-string receivers in the late rounds of drafts.

NO MORE! If you've never played in a league that utilizes multiple QBs with an OP (Superflex/Open Player/Offensive Position) spot, it's time to get on board. It opens up multiple strategies, philosophies and the ability to overcome crucial injuries to skill position players that would normally sink you in other leagues.

Draft strategy in this format has a lot to do with draft position. However, I still prefer to solidify two QBs in the first five rounds and create an RPV advantage on the rest of the league. As highlighted in the Quarterback Profiles chapter, having an elite QB1 and then a low-level QB1/high-level QB2 serving as a QB2/OP/Superflex is a distinct advantage on a weekly basis. While some teams are playing with a WR or low-end RB with questionable targets or touches, a

QB is a lock for at least an opportunity to produce. QBs also tend to stay healthier over the length of a season than, say, running backs, thanks to the rules of the NFL.

This doesn't mean you take a QB back to back in Rounds 1 and 2. On the other hand, it does mean you should make them a priority and consider drafting a third QB on your roster.

Why? Well first of all, if you're relying on the QB position as a strength on your roster, you are going to need an extra for two bye weeks. When you're playing head-to-head, every week counts, and having even a mediocre QB who can throw up 15 points potentially over those byes could be the difference between a win and a loss. That could mean the difference between making and missing the playoffs.

The second reason: You also simultaneously weaken the player pool at the position. Don't necessarily reach for that third QB, but a wise play would be to have one in-house before the season starts.

The draft should also be dictated by the scoring. Is it ½ point PPR, full PPR, standard (non-PPR)? Whatever it is, judge accordingly.

For this chapter, we split the difference with ½ point PPR scoring. I'd still prefer to get my elite RB and WR early, then shift the focus hard to QB. The argument can be made to take an elite QB in the early first round, but that's more for a 10-team league strategy or an owner who's not afraid to play the wire for more RB help as the season unfolds.

2019 Player Pool Approach

There's a clear group of elite level QBs this year in Patrick Mahomes and Andrew Luck. After that, QB1 is deep, and any pairing of the next 20 quarterbacks will work. As you go down the list, of course you're assuming more risk, but discounts on Carson Wentz and Jameis Winston could return big fantasy production.

Overall, it's a great year to participate in this format. This depth should point you in the direction of solidifying a true elite RB and WR in the first two rounds, then pivot accordingly, trying to get two QBs over the next 2-4 rounds. The good news is that if you truly desire to own Mahomes or Luck, there some decent RB selections like Sony Michel and Devonta Freeman to make up ground. As always, be aggressive on YOUR guys. If you're properly prepared, you can build a strong core no matter where you go your first two picks. s

The depth at WR this year is once again strong, so if you were to prioritize, there's more ground to be made up later at WR than RB/QB.

Where you're slotted in the draft will impact your best way to control the player pool.

Where are you drafting?

Picks 1-4: The top running backs should still be your targets at the top of this draft. In a 10-team league, I can justify Mahomes and Luck at the top, because there are more RBs available in the player pool. In 12-team leagues, getting the true bell cow with TD upside and PPR appeal is your best approach. You could just as easily take Ezekiel Elliott and go back-to-back Matt Ryan/Ben Roethlisberger or take a QB and the best RB/WR/TE on the board.

Picks 5-8: The middle of drafts typically is a tough spot to make work, but taking the best player on the board in the early going is the best advice. You'll have to be on the lookout for position runs, but this is the draft area where the scoring comes into play the most. In this ½ point PPR, the riskier RBs still should be valued just a hair above the elite WRs. However, in a full PPR Superflex situation, you can certainly be more aggressive on WRs.

Picks 9-12: Ah, the turn! Some folks hate it, but I think it's a great opportunity to build strength. The trap here is filling positions over building roster strength. You need to think about how you're going to build a weekly advantage, not fill spots. Filling spots is for the middle rounds. In a standard Superflex, I'd want to take a strong RB, but in any PPR style the WR are the better return on investment. You can also be the first to drive the QB market, which I support. If not, you can wait until the 3-4 wraparound, where you can double up at QB easily with the low-end QB1/high-end QB2 types. The world is your oyster down here.

How a 10-team league changes your approach: In a 10-team version, I offer the concept of mandatory two QBs played on each roster. This ups the ante considerably and challenges the league as a collective. If you don't, I'd be more aggressive on the elite QB and content to wait on WR.

How a 14-team league changes your approach: If a shallow league means we should be more aggressive on the elite QB, then the deeper Superflex means be more aggressive on the QB position as a whole. Having 32 NFL teams means 28 QBs potentially starting in that 14-team league in a given week -- even before bye, injuries and other issues. Having two strong options is essential. Then fade WR or QB accordingly depending on the rest of the scoring system.

If You Can Pick Your Draft Slot: Picks 4 and 5 gave the best combination of balance and strength across the board, which allows the rest of the draft to basically fall into your lap.

Players who missed making the core: Leonard Fournette, Rams receivers (Cooper Kupp, Brandin Cooks, Robert Woods), Calvin Ridley, Tyler Boyd, Chris Carson, Julian Edelman, Kerryon Johnson, Kenyan Drake

We decided to be aggressive on Josh Jacobs after the Isiah Crowell injury and Marshawn Lynch retirement. Even if Lynch came back, Jacobs would be the guy sooner or later. Fournette has too many issues making him a risky "core" player. The Rams receivers are great and will fly off the board Round 5 of this draft. The rest of those RB probably will as well. It wasn't personal. It was just the math of QBs bumping them back a few rounds.

Favorite Team Core: TEAM 4 -- I love the balance of this squad with a high-end RPV player at QB, RB, WR and TE. It wasn't a case of trying to fill positions -- but rather filling them appropriately with high-end talent at the appropriate value. Getting a second QB in Round 5 will be a piece of cake for this squad. Kamara-Allen-Kelce-Rivers is about as strong and reliable a start as you can have in 2019.

Least Favorite Team Core: TEAM 7 -- A team with infinite upside -- and equal potential for disaster. In for a penny, in for a pound: Once you take Gurley, you may as well play for first, but I prefer a core with fewer questions. Rodgers had his issues in 2018, Cook has been hurt for 2 years, and Cooper continues to lack consistency.

How You Can Ruin Your Draft

The trap is worrying about positions early on instead of concerning yourself with building a strength on your roster. Superflex/OP leagues are just another opportunity to build that strength in a different way. Be careful of overvaluing younger, hyped QBs like Baker Mayfield and big stars like Russell Wilson and Tom Brady. They're all still great selections, but Matt Ryan will outscore them all likely again, and boring guys like Philip Rivers and Kirk Cousins will practically keep pace. If you overpay for Wilson, Mayfield, etc., you'll miss out on key RB/WR talent.

BEST BALL STRATEGY

Nate Hamilton

Best Ball leagues have become increasingly popular for many fanatics of the fantasy football industry. This format is designed to consume in much higher quantities.

What would be your first thought if someone told you that they were in 50-60 fantasy football leagues? Crazy, right? In Best Ball, this is a common occurrence. The reason one can be in so many leagues is due to all of the maintenance that is typically applied to your fantasy teams throughout the season is eliminated.

What is Best Ball?

Have you ever thought, "I wish I didn't bench player X this week" … or, "I don't have the time to shop waivers and make lineup adjustments"? Many people feel this way, and so "Best Ball" was born.

In this format, all you have to do is draft. Once the draft is complete, you have no other responsibilities other than checking in to see if you've won that league at the end of the season. No roster moves need to be made, no trading, no waiver wire. Simply set it and forget it.

How? You draft an expanded roster, typically 25 players or so. Best Ball takes your best players and constructs your best possible lineup from your expanded roster each week. Best. (Wasn't sure if I said it enough).

Just because you don't have to maintain your rosters doesn't mean there isn't any work or thought that needs to go into Best Ball. In fact, you should put extra effort and thought into your draft process since that is all you have in these leagues.

The old saying "you don't win your leagues at the draft" couldn't be further from the truth here. First of all, the results of your draft help you set the foundation of team in all formats, and in Best Ball it sets the tone for the entire season. As with any setup, your draft approach should change.

There are different aspects to consider in Best Ball drafts than any other.

What's Different?

You will want to treat this draft no differently for the first 4 rounds than what is noted in the Standard and PPR strategy chapters (depending on the scoring format of the Best Ball league you are in). After that, your mindset should shift to accommodate the intricacies of the beast that is Best Ball. Remember, once the draft is over, you do not make any roster moves.

You are now locked into the 25 or so players you have selected for the entire season. If your players get injured, benched or just isn't playing up to the standards you would like, you're stuck with them, so it is important that you take that into consideration when drafting.

Depth: Cover your bases for alternatives at each position. If your roster construction is set for 1 QB to start any given week, you'll want to have at least 2-3 on your team. You must plan for injury and underperformance. You shouldn't just draft Patrick Mahomes and think you're set at the position. If he goes down, you are stuck with zeroes from that position all year.

High Risk, High Reward: Take chances. I encourage you to spend draft capital on hit-or-miss players. It's just another thing that is great about Best Ball. If you draft a player who will get you 25 points one week and 3 the next, you benefit from the monster weeks and are not negatively impacted by their down weeks. However, you shouldn't stuff your roster with these players, which could lead to some low-scoring weeks across the board for your roster.

Balance is Key: This logic could be applied to any format. The reason it's so important in Best Ball is because the flexibility is limited. Since you cannot make additional moves with your team post-draft, you'll want to balance your team. One of the best ways to do so is to draft solid, reliable, consistent players and counter with the high-risk, high-reward players noted in section above. This will protect you from those low-performing weeks by giving your team a safe floor from a performance perspective.

Now that you have a better understanding of Best Ball leagues and a good foundation on how to approach this format, go and be free. Join a ton of Best Ball leagues this season!

My preferred platform for Best Ball is Fantrax.com. Feel free to reach out to me on Twitter (@DomiNateFF) and ask me how you can join a Best Ball draft on Fantrax!

Chapter 4

QUARTERBACKS

SINGLE-QB RPV

	Player	RPV
1	Patrick Mahomes	24%
2	Andrew Luck	10%
3	Aaron Rodgers	7%
4	Matt Ryan	4%
5	Deshaun Watson	2%
6	Cam Newton	-2%
7	Ben Roethlisberger	-5%
8	Russell Wilson	-6%
9	Baker Mayfield	-7%
10	Drew Brees	-7%
11	Carson Wentz	-9%
12	Jared Goff	-10%

SUPERFLEX/OP/2QB RPV

	Player	RPV
1	Philip Rivers	15%
2	Kirk Cousins	13%
3	Tom Brady	9%
4	Jameis Winston	7%
5	Kyler Murray	6%
6	Mitchell Trubisky	-2%
7	Josh Allen	-3%
8	Dak Prescott	-4%
9	Jimmy Garoppolo	-8%
10	Lamar Jackson	-11%
11	Sam Darnold	-13%
12	Matthew Stafford	-14%

RPV ANALYSIS, POSITION OVERVIEW & PLAYER PROFILES

Joe Pisapia

2019's RPV shows how significant of a difference maker Patrick Mahomes can be. He's more than double the RPV of No. 2 Andrew Luck, and that's taking 2018 regression into account. If you miss out on the appropriate value of one of the top five QBs in the early rounds, it's best to let the position come to you. I would preach being patient to the point of scooping up two QBs toward the end and playing matchups on a weekly basis. That way, you're maximizing the single QB position on a weekly basis, rather than chasing the elite group, which is likely a losing battle. Keeping pace with solid QB production is fine, as long as you have the RB/WR talent to lead your roster.

In leagues with multiple QBs in play, here's the quick math on how to create an RPV advantage. The fantasy league average of the QB1 position this year is 327 points. That's taking the top 12 QB on this list, their 2019 projections, 2018 performance and three-year averages (when available) into account, then creating their average total between them.

Example: Patrick Mahomes' 405 Black Book Total for 2019 makes him a +24% RPV QB1.

RPV is 405 (Black Book expected player points) *minus* the 327 Fantasy League Average of QB1 (FLA), *divided* by 327 FLA … which equals .24, more easily seen as +24% advantage over all QB1s.

The key is to remember that QB2/Superflex/OP is its own position on your roster. Having Mahomes then waiting to take Sam Darnold at -13% is marginalizing the good work Mahomes is doing. However, if you were able to solidify Drew Brees as your QB2/Superflex/OP, his Black Book Total is now compared to the QB2 group. In QB1, Brees was a -7% RPV. But, when we you take his 303 projected Black Book Points and compare them to the Fantasy League Average of the QB2 group (258 points), Brees jumps to a plus +17% RPV advantage.

THIS is how you create an RPV advantage. THIS is how you create roster strength. THIS is how leagues are won. As you read on, the same concept is true for RB and WR in formats that favor that position. You can build roster strength in many different ways, but the best practice is always to tailor to the scoring format (standard, PPR etc.).

The quarterback position is all a numbers game. The majority of fantasy leagues still start just one active QB every week, although Superflex/OP leagues are without a doubt on the rise. The QB position is in a fascinating place heading into the 2019 season. Results from last year's rookie class were a mixed bag, and some of them are still a work in progress. The aging once-elite QBs have gotten another year older, and the aging lower tier could be on its last legs. Luckily, two QBs emerged as a clear leaders of the field, and single-QB formats should have no trouble getting production out of the 12th-14th QB off the board. Keep up with the same strategy: Wait, and let the market come to you.

Multiple-QB leagues are a different story. Owning one of the top guys is more crucial than ever because health is a real question for many QB1s in 2019. That QB1 group consists of guys either coming off of injuries, showing some wear and tear, or carrying some questions surrounding their supporting cast. Meanwhile, the QB2 group is a comprised of veterans hanging on by a thread or second-year signal callers still finding their way. For success in 2019, having two QB1s on your roster filling the QB and OP/Superflex position respectively is a huge Relative Position Value advantage. Especially when you consider the potential fallout of many secondary quarterbacks at the position. Attacking the position early and often is key. Drafting a "top guy" then waiting too long on the secondary QB market will just bring down the elite-level advantage you started with and marginalize your overall bottom line. If you miss out on the high-end talent, doubling up with a pair like Matt Ryan and Ben Roethlisberger should still be a viable approach for this season.

THE ELITE

1. **Patrick Mahomes, KC:** Historic. There are so many adjectives to describe Mahomes' 2018 season, but historic I think is the best one: 5,000 yards passing, 50 TDs and 12 INT, with two more rushing touchdowns and 270 yards on the ground. He was top-three in basically every important measureable QB category. He had 10 300-yard games while posting 25 or more fantasy points in nine of his 16 starts and 30 points or more 4 times. Basically, he had four games when he basically won you the week singlehandedly. How's that for a close to a fantasy season? There were two games when he didn't throw for at least 2 TDs, but he had a rushing TD in each of them. One could fill a book with all the incredible Mahomes feats from last year, but that was last year. Another season of 5,000 yards would be asking a lot. A reasonable expectation is 4,800 yards and 40 TDs, which would still probably keep him as the No. 1 overall QB with relative ease. There will be plenty of single-QB leagues that see him over-drafted with stunning authority. That will be a mistake. As great as he was last year and as talented as he is, Ben Roethlisberger threw for more yards last year, and Andrew Luck is a good bet for 40 TDs in 2019. In other words, perspective is important, and the ratio of supply and demand favors the supply in those leagues. As a first-rounder in leagues where you can start more than one QB, Mahomes is worthy of a No. 1 overall pick debate.

2. **Andrew Luck, IND:** I'm the first to admit: Last year I had zero shares in single-QB leagues based solely on the amount of decent QB1 options available and the risk involved with Luck. Although I missed out on a great return season, I couldn't be more excited that Luck returned to his old form and is now right back into the conversation for best quarterback in the league. Over his first three starts, Luck was still getting his footing, but from September 30 onward, he averaged 19 fantasy points per game. Seven of his 16 starts were 300-yard games, and his 39 TDs were his best mark since 2014. One of the biggest reasons for Luck's return to dominance was a vastly improved offensive line. A sack % that was high as 7% in 2016 fell to a league-low 2.7. Luck remaining upright more often is a good thing. Who would have guessed it? At 30, this is Luck's prime, and he's one of the best keeper-league assets around. The running game is still complementary at best, so expect basically another season of 4,500 yards passing and a run at 40 TDs. His receiving corps is basically the same, with one addition of Devin Funchess (which isn't anything to get excited about). However, as long as the offensive line stays healthy, Luck will once again make the most of the weapons he has again in 2019.

TOP TALENT

1. **Aaron Rodgers, GB:** Last year was not a vintage Rodgers season. His 25 TDs marked his lowest total for a full season in his career. We all know the relationship between Rodgers and now former head coach Mike McCarthy was strained, to put it mildly. There were conflicting stories about Rodgers being unhappy with the playcalling, meanwhile equal reports that he was changing plenty of those plays himself. Matt LaFleur will no doubt be an easily influenced young coach, who will allow Rodgers to run the joint his way. It's difficult to say if that's a positive or a negative, though. Rodgers was as efficient as ever with just two interceptions last year, but his "big games" seemed to be few and far between. He threw for just four 300-yard games and had only two three-touchdown games (none of which came after Week 5). If you can believe it, he actually had seven weeks with one TD or less. That is NOT what folks were looking for when paying a draft premium for a QB. The supporting cast hasn't changed, and the 36-year-old Rodgers is likelier to be a slightly lesser version of what we've known over his Hall of Fame career. Now that he's closer to the pack at the top of the tier, rather than the leader of it, it would be wise to not overpay for him in single-QB leagues in 2019. Consider him very good, with some great moments, rather than merely "great" at this stage of his career.

2. **Matt Ryan, ATL:** While everyone was buzzing about Patrick Mahomes or celebrating the triumphant return of Andrew Luck, Ryan was the second-highest-scoring QB in many fantasy formats. His 4,924 passing yards and 35 TDs were third overall in the league in each category. This was the second time in three years that Ryan nearly passed for 5,000 passing yards and threw for 35 or more TDs. His seven picks matched his career-best from his MVP season. The lack of a running game may have frustrated some fans, but it was money in the bank for Ryan owners who reaped the benefits of this Falcons air attack. He has a premier WR in Julio Jones, an emerging star in Calvin Ridley and some nice complementary pieces as well. He will go rounds later than the likes of Aaron Rodgers and looks like a safer bet with frankly more fantasy upside. He had eight 300-yard games last year and 10 weeks with 20 or more fantasy points. Ryan is durable, productive and incredibly undervalued.

3. **Deshaun Watson, HOU:** Perhaps our expectations were slightly too high in 2018. After all, Watson was still coming back from ACL surgery, and his magical 2017 run ended at peak buzz for the rookie QB at the time. Logging 19 touchdowns in just six starts was going to be a tough act to follow. In 2018, Watson threw for 26 TDs and rushed for five more. The problem was five of those scores came in one game. Watson never threw for more than two TDs in any other game all season. With just five 300-yard games, Watson scored fewer than 20 fantasy points seven times. On the plus side, Watson still has a premier wide receiver (DeAndre Hopkins) and consistency playing in the same offense two straight years. A healthy Will Fuller would also help. Watson is a clear notch behind the elite quarterbacks, but he's still young enough to enter that tier in the years ahead. More consistent offensive line play would help, but really, Watson needs to show a higher floor in 2019.

4. **Cam Newton, CAR:** Newton nearly made the Red Flags list, but all news regarding his offseason shoulder surgery have been positive, and all signs point to him having a regular training camp. He's settled into a 3,500- yard, 25-TD QB over the last two seasons. Had he not missed two and a half games at the end of the year, he could've had room for more. While he will continue to run, 500 yards will be about his max at this stage in his career. Newton will always toss in a

handful of rushing TDs every year, which will continue to help his fantasy value. As for the prospect of him developing further as a passer, I think you can comfortably say that's never going to happen. Newton is what you see. His 2015 season will likely be a career outlier as he now approached his 30s. Christian McCaffrey's emergence resulted in a career high 67% completion rate. Low risk, high percentage passes help take pressure off Newton in the pocket as well, which is a good thing for his health. The shoulder surgery will suppress his stock in early drafts. The later you draft and more preseason games prove his health, that discount will disappear. He's a reliable 20-plus-point QB most weeks, with a strong floor and a ceiling for more.

5. **Ben Roethlisberger, PIT:** There will be folks who will fade Roethlisberger after losing Antonio Brown and Le'Veon Bell this offseason. That will be unwarranted. Big Ben didn't play with Bell last year and has said goodbye to Plaxico Burress, Santonio Holmes and now Brown without missing a beat. JuJu Smith-Schuster will slide right into the No. 1 role, and James Washington has all the makings of an emerging stud. With the running game in flux, Roethlisberger threw for his first 5,000-yard season, so expect another run at that number in 2019. His 5,129 yards passing and 34 TDs were both career highs, and his eight 300-yard games were one shy of his best mark. At 37, he's not a great long-term investment, but in redraft leagues, you can count on a floor of 250 yards and two TDs most weeks. He's also thankfully bucked the bad road splits now for two straight years that plagued him the three previous seasons.

SOLID OPTIONS

1. **Russell Wilson, SEA:** It was disappointing to see Wilson's yardage total decline for a second straight year. In 2016, he accumulated a career-best 4,219 yards. In 2017, that mark fell to 3,983, then ultimately just 3,448 in '18. His rushing yards also fell of year over year, from 586 to 376. Now, part of that gaudy 586 was Wilson running for his life with a dreadful offensive line. Last year, that unit improved, as did the running game. The good news is that Wilson seems to have settled into the 35-TD range and threw a career low seven INTs last year. As nice of a QB as Wilson is, he had just one 300-yard game and isn't a "game changer." He posted fewer than 20 fantasy points in 10 weeks, including three in single digits. He also only exceeded 25 points twice. Wilson isn't going to win you weeks on his own, but he's still a solid fantasy QB. Don't confuse his monster contract with monster stats.

2. **Baker Mayfield, CLE:** There's reason for optimism in Cleveland! There's also plenty of room for hype. Be cautious of the hype. There's no denying Mayfield is the franchise quarterback the Browns have searched for the last two decades. The addition of Odell Beckham to go along with Jarvis Landry and an emerging David Njoku is worth getting excited over. However, Mayfield is still a work in progress. Sure, the abundance of weapons will help bump up his stats, but Mayfield isn't as polished as some of the veterans on this list quite yet. He only had five fantasy games of 20 or more points and was under 15 points seven times. Mayfield did make a giant step forward when the Browns made Freddie Kitchens offensive coordinator. Under his playcalling, he threw for 19 TDs and eight INTs. Reaching 30 TDs this year seems realistic, as does a run at 4,000 yards. He could leap into the top grouping sooner than later, but for now,

it's better to avoid overpaying for Mayfield in single-QB leagues. In Superflex, he should be an early target and a perfect pairing with a safe veteran like Mathew Stafford.

3. **Drew Brees, NO:** Had Brees made and won the Super Bowl last year, I think he might have hung up his cleats. He'll be 40 this year, and although he dropped 32 TDs last year, he also fell under 4,000 passing yards for the first time since 2005. Yeah, it's been a while. Still, Brees is as efficient as he's ever been, throwing just five INT's and leading the league in completion percentage for the second straight season (74.4). He's still a better QB in the dome, as always: 21 of his 32 TDs came at home. He also averaged 321 YPG at home compared to just 217 on the road. Those splits make DFS the best scenario for Brees ownership. You'll get a lesser version on the road, but five of his eight home starts were 300-yard games. That means there's probably six weeks of the season when Brees' monster games will carry your fantasy team to victory nearly on his own. You just have to make sure your roster can support those road weeks. Drafting a second QB for those games isn't insanity depending on whom you can pluck at the end of the draft. This HOFer is near the end, but he's still a fantasy stud when used properly.

4. **Carson Wentz, PHI:** After Wentz's Pro Bowl 2017 season ended in injury, folks were cautiously optimistic about him returning to dominance in 2018. After his campaign ended early due to injury, folks are now just plain cautious. I must admit, Wentz was right on the border of making the Red Flags class, but instead I want fantasy owners to embrace an opportunity. Like Andrew Luck last year before him, Wentz will carry a heavy discount in drafts. Outside of an awful three-INT performance versus the Saints, Wentz had a solid year. He was on pace for close to 4,000 yards and 30 TDs. With the myriad of injuries he's suffered, expect his 299 rushing yards two years ago to be a distant memory. Regardless, Wentz has QB1 upside and is still just 27 years old. Despite starting just 11 games, Wentz had five 300-yard performances and six weeks with 19-plus fantasy points. He could be a steal in Superflex leagues in 2019 as your second QB should his draft stock slide.

5. **Jared Goff, LAR:** Look, I know the last memory you have of Goff is that atrocious Super Bowl performance, but Bill Belichick has embarrassed many a young QB in his illustrious career. The open man still alludes Goff at times, but Sean McVay has been able to remake this offense in such a way that Goff can still be productive from a fantasy perspective. Todd Gurley's health is certainly a huge concern, but a healthy Cooper Kupp will make all the difference in the world should Gurley miss time again. You could see that Kupp's absence made Goff uncomfortable down the stretch. The Gurley injury just compounded that fact. He posted 8, -1, 10, 16 and 23 fantasy points the last five games of the year, respectively. Goff threw for a career-high 4,688 yards and 32 TDs. He threw for an incredible eight 300-yard games. To be fair, Gurley's presence in the receiving game and his yards after the catch supported these big stats. A season without Gurley still likely would hold 28 TDs and 4,200 yards in this offense. Four of his 12 picks came in one miserable game versus the Bears in Chicago's cold, but other than that, Goff protected the football and played well in 2018 for fantasy owners. There's some risk here for 2019 -- but also plenty of value.

6. **Philip Rivers, LAC:** Every year, Rivers falls too far in drafts. Every year, I end up with a ton of shares of Rivers. Every year, I am pleased with this trend. Look, there are flashier names on the board, but Rivers will get you 20 points a week or more 50% of the time, play all 16 games and drop 30-plus TDs and 4,300 yards like clockwork. He had five 300-yard games last year and at 37 looks to be right in line for another strong season. Mike Williams continued growth and a

healthy Hunter Henry should make you excited to own Rivers at his usual discount. In Superflex, if you don't want to pay for a premium QB, Rivers is the perfect part of a duo of No. 1A guys.

7. **Kirk Cousins, MIN:** I think we can all agree: Things didn't go well for Cousins in his first year with the Vikings. Maybe it was adjusting to a new team, new city or the pressure of a big contract. Whatever it was, it was not what fantasy owners or the Vikings hoped for and perhaps expectations were set too high. Cousins completed 70% of his passes, threw for 30 TDs (just 10 INT) and threw for almost 4,300 yards. It was a better statistical season than Tom Brady, yet because the Vikings missed the playoffs, Cousins' 2018 season carries a negative stigma. Cousins still had five 300-yard games and two great WRs to help him. If Dalvin Cook can stay healthy, he'll take pressure of Cousins to be "perfect." For perspective, he had a near identical season statistically to Tom Brady (if not better) and was branded a "disappointment". Why? Because he failed to get the Vikings where they wanted to be. Brady wins another Super Bowl, so his stock is fine. Focus on the numbers, not the narrative.

8. **Tom Brady, NE:** To be fair, Brady was a fringe QB1 by the end of last season. A healthy Carson Wentz or a 16-game season of Baker Mayfield could have surpassed Brady on the board. Brady lost his No. 1 red-zone target in Rob Gronkowski (unless he unretires and returns midseason, which is not out of the realm of possibility). Julian Edelman is another year older and beaten; questions remain about what Demaryius Thomas has left in the tank after his torn Achilles and declining productivity; and the running game has become a clear shift of focus for the Patriots. Yet, do any of us really think Brady won't cross 4,000 yards and 28 TDs? So, he's 42. So, what? No one outworks or out-prepares Brady. However, in fantasy terms, I would prefer him as a QB2 in Superflex than as my QB1 in single-QB formats at this stage of his career. However, if you don't have the stamina to draft a risky Wentz or believe Baker Mayfield is ready for primetime, Brady will continue to be a safe low-end QB1 in 2019. Just make sure you build some "boom" in your roster, because Brady had 10 games with fewer than 20 fantasy points in 2018. He's a floor player at this stage of his career, more than an explosive ceiling asset. The running game will continue to be a greater focus as the Pats try and keep Brady fresh for the playoffs.

SUPERFLEX QB2

1. **Jameis Winston, TB:** Sometimes being bold is rewarded. Bruce Arians has a track record of being an offensive guru and has come out of retirement to take over an offensive roster with legitimate talent at QB, WR and TE. He didn't do so because he was bored; he did so because he sees potential. Therefore, you should see the same potential in the Bucs offense this year. Arians is the perfect antidote to the Dirk Koetter (or enema, depending on your outlook) and the right personality to get the best out of Winston. The Bucs offense had the most passing yards in the league last year, but it also had the most picks. If Arians can get Winston to make better decisions and restore the confidence he lost last season being yanked in and out of the job, 2019 could be his best season. Winston is in a make-or-break contract situation, and with the money on the line, I expect him to be money. If he can limit the turnovers, watch out. He's best paired with a reliable QB1.

2. **Mitchell Trubisky, CHI:** Trubisky's first full season started out strong but faded in the final two months. Trubisky missed two weeks with an injury, and one could attribute the dropoff to health. Matt Nagy has a great offensive mind, and if Trubisky can find a bit more consistency in 2019, a career year is within his grasp. He had three games of more than 30 fantasy points and

four games with single-digit performances. That's a problem. A healthy, full season should offer something like 500 rushing yards, 3,500 passing yards, 27 passing TDs and five rushing TDs. He could leap into QB1 territory, but he has to prove those single-digit stinker outings are a thing of the past.

3. **Josh Allen, BUF:** From Nov 25 onward, Allen averaged 23 fantasy points per game. Yes, he never threw for more than 231 yards in any one of those contests, but he did rush for 90-plus yards in four of them. It may not be the artistry of watching Aaron Rodgers, but who cares? This is fantasy! Points matter. What they look like as they tally up is inconsequential. We can't expect Allen to rush for 90 yards in every game and play 16 games in the NFL, but eight rushing TDs in 10 games is still eight rushing TDs in 10 games. Even if that stays flat and the volume of a full season gives him 20 passing TDs and 3,000 yards, the fantasy points are going to be there. New WR John Brown gives him a legitimate deep threat, but more importantly Cole Beasley could be the slot safety blanket that could help Allen improve that 52% completion rate. Remember, it's about points, not style points.

4. **Dak Prescott, DAL:** I went out on a limb last year saying Prescott would be a useful fantasy QB in 2018. After a sluggish September, that take was looking pretty bad. Then the Cowboys started to roll and rolled all the way into the playoffs. Prescott had some good days and some not so good ones, but as a QB2, he was a decent value. With Ezekiel Elliott as the focal point of the offense, Prescott's point total will be capped most weeks. His third straight year with six rushing TDs makes up for his lack of 300-yard-game potential. Amari Cooper's presence helped Prescott reach a career-high 3,800 passing yards and 1,200-plus yards in November and December last year. Prescott is a quintessential second QB in Superflex.

5. **Jimmy Garoppolo, SF:** We never got a chance to see what Jimmy G could do last year, so we're back to square one again, speaking in hypothetical terms. The three-week sample size was a mixed bag, but I think indicative of what we can expect from him in 2019. Outside of George Kittle, the rest of his offensive weapons are equally theoretical. If you drafted an elite QB1, then you can take the gamble on Kyle Shanahan getting the most out of Garoppolo in 2019. A reasonable expectation is 3,500 yards with 25 TDs and 12 INTs. The totals should be fine. It's the consistency in which they arrive on a weekly basis that's anyone's guess.

6. **Lamar Jackson, BAL:** The bad news is that Jackson had just one game of 200 passing yards in his seven starts. The good news is that Jackson averaged 80 yards rushing over those same games. There's no denying Jackson is a special athlete. The question is how good of a quarterback can he be. New OC Greg Roman spent the offseason working with Jackson on his mechanics and building an offense that will work off of his strengths. Unfortunately, Jackson is working at a disadvantage with his below-average wide receivers. Rookie Marquise Brown has been compared to DeSean Jackson, and the two could make an explosive pair at some point. His impact is too difficult to gauge in 2019, though. Jackson is a QB2 until further notice. He'll have QB1 games and could be a DFS darling some weeks. His rushing TD upside is undeniable. The rest of the skill set is a work in progress for now.

7. **Sam Darnold, NYJ:** After starting hot out of the gate, Darnold took quite a few lumps in his rookie year. Like most young QBs, he struggled with turnovers, throwing 14 INTs in his first 8 games. In Week 10, Darnold had a respite with an "injury" and settled down nicely on his return down the stretch. Over his final four games, Darnold threw six TDs and just one INT. There's a lot of hope that Darnold builds off this strong finish, and bringing in a premium all-purpose

weapon like Le'Veon Bell to this offense takes a ton of pressure off the young QB. The receiving corps, led by Robby Anderson, added Jamison Crowder this offseason. A new slot receiver coupled with an All-Pro RB means expectations will be higher in 2019. A line of 3,500 yards and 25 TDs is well within his grasp. It's all about limiting mistakes. If Darnold stops killing his own drives, the Jets could be a surprise team in 2019.

8. **Matthew Stafford, DET:** Year 1 of Matt Patricia's reign as head coach produced the worst Stafford season in some time. It was so bad that Stafford didn't reach 4,000 yards for the first time since his rookie year, and his 21 TDs were the lowest in six years. Golden Tate moved on, but Kenny Golladay is a serious talent, and Marvin Jones is still around to help. If Kerryon Johnson's workload increases in his second year, that should help Stafford bounce back to the 4,200-yard/25-TD range, making him a safe QB2. His career average of 270 YPG gives you hope that last year's 236 YPG was a casualty of a team in transition.

9. **Andy Dalton, CIN:** Thumb ligament surgery ended Dalton's 2018 season prematurely. New HC Zac Taylor is bringing in a fresh offense, which could be a good thing for the veteran QB. It could also be a disaster. That inherited learning curve puts the usually vanilla Dalton into mystery box for 2019. There's no shortage of weapons for him, though, alongside A.J. Green. Tyler Boyd emerged as a legitimate No. 2 WR, and a healthy Joe Mixon is a difference maker. Dalton has only thrown for 4,000 yards in a season twice in his career, so it's not like he's winning you any weeks on his own. However, as a decent QB2 in Superflex, you can get by with him since there's no imminent in-house threat to his starting role.

10. **Eli Manning, NYG:** Manning's lack of mobility in the pocket led to him being sacked 47 times last year and killed plenty of offensive momentum for the Giants. The addition of elite running back Saquon Barkley last year, yielded the highest completion percentage of his career (66). It's easy to dump it off to Saquon and watch him add to your yardage totals. 2018 was Manning's best season by most statistical measures in three years but still not an exciting one from a fantasy perspective. Even after the departure of Odell Beckham, his weapons are better than folks are giving them credit. Golden Tate and Sterling Shepard make a better duo than most teams have heading into the year, and Evan Engram has yet to reach his full potential. The Giants line is still mediocre, though, and the organization was not aggressive in the draft on that front. Manning is a serviceable low-end QB2, with the emphasis on serviceable.

RED FLAGS

1. **Derek Carr, OAK:** The weekly output from Carr is about as predictable as a Raiders draft. There will be a strong narrative heading into 2019 that Carr will magically be transformed with Antonio Brown now the No. 1 target. Sure, it helps to have a talent like Brown, as well as a young, exciting back like Josh Jacobs. However, the QB pool is deep enough that there's no reason to purchase Carr to find out what impact they'll have on his stats. Carr did improve slightly in the second half. He didn't throw a single pick between Weeks 8 and 16. He only had four weeks with multiple TDs over that span as well. Don't confuse the possibility of being better with the guarantee of improvement. They are NOT one in the same.

2. **Marcus Mariota, TEN:** There were plenty of reasons to be frustrated with the Titans offense last year, most notably Mariota. After a great run in 2016, Mariota has been unable to build on that

success for two seasons. I give him credit for playing through a myriad of injuries, but at some point, we have to come to the realization that the juice hasn't been worth the squeeze and "potential" goes by the wayside when you log so many weeks of lackluster fantasy production. A commitment to the run game featuring Derrick Henry may further suppress any residual upside he still carried. Don't sleep on the fact the organization brought in Ryan Tannehill via trade this offseason, as Mariota plays out the final year of his rookie deal. This is the fork in the road for Mariota as a Titan. Considering the track record of disappointment, you'd be better served letting another owner find out what he can do. If he loses the job midseason to Tannehill via injury or performance, it would hardly be shocking.

3. **Josh Rosen, MIA:** Congratulations Rosen! You went from the worst O-line in the league to the second worst! Rejoice! Last spring, Rosen was ranked anywhere from the top QB in the 2018 draft class to the fourth (which is ultimately where he was drafted). After a dreadful rookie year with the Cardinals that was doomed before it began, Rosen now finds himself in Miami with a new system and a new team. He'll certainly start Week 1 for the Dolphins, who brought in Ryan Fitzpatrick as a backup. Rosen's ceiling is Eli Manning 2.0. Manning never had an embarrassment of riches in terms of offensive talent around him in his prime, but he did have excellent coaching and a high football IQ. Rosen has similar polish, but the line questions and middling weapons surrounding him are not encouraging for success in his 2019 campaign. A change of scenery is nice and all, but it's going to take more than that to make Rosen a fantasy asset.

4. **Nick Foles, JAC:** Separate Cinderella from his glass slipper for a moment. Foles had a terrific game last year against the Falcons, in which he threw for four TDs and 471 yards. The other three games he started, Foles threw for three total TDs. The Jaguars came apart at the seams last year. Leonard Fournette's injuries and off-field issues are piling up, and they don't have a true No. 1 WR. This Foles signing has the potential to be one of the largest free-agent blunders of all time, and there's absolutely no reason to get be involved with this offense from a fantasy perspective.

5. **Joe Flacco, DEN:** The Ravens wanted to turn the page last year at the quarterback position, and no matter how respectable Flacco was, it was only a matter of time before they did. Statistically speaking, Flacco was in line for a year reminiscent of his 2016 season. That year he threw for 4,200 yards, 20 TDs and 15 INTs. That's probably your "Flacco ceiling." The Broncos drafted Drew Lock, but there's little chance he starts over the first half of the season barring an injury to Flacco. The Broncos see themselves as a contender and Flacco as the QB who can manage them to the playoffs. That doesn't mean he's irreplaceable, but he has a longer leash in 2019 than he did last year. In fantasy terms, he's nothing more than a bye-week/QB3 in Superflex.

ROOKIES

1. **Kyler Murray, ARI:** The NFL scouting world is divided on Murray. Some say he's too small. Others will argue he's just another young QB changing our perspective of what an NFL signal caller looks like. Frankly, it's where he ended up that will ultimately make or break his career, and the Cardinals deserved to be picking first. Sure, David Johnson and Larry Fitzgerald are still around, but the line ranked dead-last at the close of 2018. That's the biggest issue. Russell Wilson is the often times comp for Murray, and he too spent some time running for his life in 2017. The difference is, Wilson had a few years under his belt by then, and Murray is a rookie. This poor offensive line will not allow Murray the proper umbrella to shade him from the harsh reality of the NFL. The fact the Cardinals took a big swing on a polarizing and undersized WR Andy Isabella instead of addressing the offensive line tells you that it doesn't matter who the coach or QB is in 2019. The Cardinals don't have their priorities in the right place, and that's why Murray should be a pass in redraft single-QB leagues.

2. **Dwayne Haskins, WAS:** The arm slot could use some work, and the sample size isn't huge, but Haskins is a gifted athlete who seems to have the right demeanor for life in the NFL. Playing for Ohio State, Haskins won't flinch under the spotlight, and landing with Jay Gruden is outstanding for his developmental path. Haskins threw for 50 TDs and 8 INTS last year but still lost the Heisman to the flashier Kyler Murray. There's a very good chance Haskins plays sooner than later, and opening the season as the Washington starter isn't an impossibility by any stretch. Haskins has the most 2019 appeal of this QB class and the best three-year window as well in dynasty leagues because of his head coach. Case Keenum was brought in and could still start the season as the QB. However, for a team in the standings looking up, the future will start sooner rather than later for Haskins.

3. **Daniel Jones, NYG:** Giants fans were not thrilled about the selection of Jones. Playing for Duke, he didn't face a whole lot of top talent and had some clunkers at times. The good news is he moves in the pocket better than old man Eli Manning. But then again, who doesn't? Jones will sit for the next year or more. As a fantasy asset, he's best left aside for now, as the G-men are committed to Manning for the next two years.

4. **Drew Lock, DEN:** The Broncos let the QB market come to them, and Lock could be the latest in a long line of misfires for Denver at the position. Lock has a strong arm, but the highlights you'll see of him are in an extremely secure pocket. The Broncos offensive line is mediocre, and Lock will sit behind Flacco for at least the 2019 season. He's more of a fantasy dart throw than a sure thing: His upside is Jay Cutler; the downside is, well, the ghosts of Broncos QBs past.

5. **Jarrett Stidham, NE:** Stidham is the latest in the New England middle-round "project QBs." After transferring from Baylor to Auburn, there were high expectations for Stidham, but he and the Tigers ultimately fell short of those. It would take a natural disaster for him to start over Brady anytime soon, but in dynasty leagues, he's worth being aware of for the fact the Patriots have turned Ryan Mallett and Jimmy Garoppolo into trade bait over the last few years. The same can be said for them in the dynasty trade arena, where Stidham could gain some positive traction and be worth dealing for picks or other talent in two years if you have the roster space.

Chapter 5

RUNNING BACKS

STANDARD LEAGUE SCORING RPV

RB1			RB2			RB3		
	Player	RPV		Player	RPV		Player	RPV
1	Ezekiel Elliott	21%	1	Nick Chubb	11%	1	David Montgomery	20%
2	Saquon Barkley	20%	2	Josh Jacobs	8%	2	Kerryon Johnson	17%
3	Christian McCaffrey	12%	3	Devonta Freeman	6%	3	Ronald Jones II	13%
4	Alvin Kamara	10%	4	Marlon Mack	4%	4	Kenyan Drake	9%
5	Le'Veon Bell	5%	5	Sony Michel	0%	5	Miles Sanders	7%
6	Melvin Gordon	1%	6	Phillip Lindsay	-1%	6	Lamar Miller	4%
7	Todd Gurley	-3%	7	Damien Williams	-1%	7	Jordan Howard	-7%
8	James Conner	-11%	8	Chris Carson	-2%	8	Latavius Murray	-8%
9	David Johnson	-12%	9	Aaron Jones	-3%	9	Tevin Coleman	-10%
10	Joe Mixon	-14%	10	Derrius Guice	-7%	10	LeSean McCoy	-12%
11	Derrick Henry	-14%	11	Mark Ingram	-7%	11	Darrell Henderson	-13%
12	Dalvin Cook	-15%	12	Leonard Fournette	-9%	12	Tarik Cohen	-13%

½ & FULL-POINT PPR LEAGUE SCORING RPV

RB1			RB2			RB3		
	Player	RPV		Player	RPV		Player	RPV
1	Saquon Barkley	22%	1	Josh Jacobs	10%	1	Kenyan Drake	17%
2	Christian McCaffrey	18%	2	Damien Williams	7%	2	Kerryon Johnson	12%
3	Ezekiel Elliott	12%	3	Derrick Henry	5%	3	James White	7%
4	Alvin Kamara	11%	4	Marlon Mack	3%	4	David Montgomery	7%
5	Le'Veon Bell	6%	5	Devonta Freeman	2%	5	Tevin Coleman	5%
6	Melvin Gordon	-2%	6	Mark Ingram	0%	6	Ronald Jones II	2%
7	Todd Gurley	-5%	7	Phillip Lindsay	-1%	7	Tarik Cohen	1%
8	Dalvin Cook	-7%	8	Aaron Jones	-2%	8	Lamar Miller	-3%
9	James Conner	-11%	9	Sony Michel	-3%	9	Darrell Henderson	-10%
10	Joe Mixon	-15%	10	Chris Carson	-5%	10	Jerick McKinnon	-11%
11	David Johnson	-17%	11	Derrius Guice	-7%	11	Miles Sanders	-12%
12	Nick Chubb	-20%	12	Leonard Fournette	-9%	12	Latavius Murray	-14%

RPV ANALYSIS

Joe Pisapia

To refresh everyone, RPV is created off a few things: previous season's stats, then 2019 projections and three-year averages when available. With young players, projections are what we have to weigh more heavily, and that's why I trust Jake Ciely, who handles those for the Black Book. These are all compiled and then produce a Black Book Point Total. The top 12, then next 12 etc. are grouped together as RB1, RB2 and RB3. Finally, The RPP formula is used on each RB grouping to determine the RPV for each individual player.

RB1 and RB2 are their own respective positions. As you'll see, the names and RPV% of the players varies between the different formats. Format AND talent dictate a player's value, not merely talent alone. By drafting two RB1s on your roster, you'll create an RPV advantage over most teams. Should you miss out on the elite RB1s, doubling up at RB early can offset that deficit. This is especially true in standard scoring, where it's difficult to make up ground at the position. In PPR formats, you have more room to maneuver with players such as James White, who become quite useful in this format. Sure, you can draft a bunch and try to play matchups to maximize your weekly RB roster productivity, but having a true top-talent bell cow is still the preferred approach.

POSITION OVERVIEW & PLAYER PROFILES

Jake Ciely

When it comes to running backs, I have and always will be team #BellCow RB. Unless I'm drafting near the end of the first round (which is rare, because I mostly play auction, as should you -- sorry, sidebar there), I'm definitely taking a bell cow running back in the first round. Yes, there is risk with any and all running backs in getting hurt, but the same can be said for any position, as we've seen starting with a duo of Odell Beckham and A.J. Green blow up, or a few years ago when both Jordy Nelson and Dez Bryant unexpectedly went down.

The injury debate aside, there is too much value in having a player with a guaranteed floor of double-digit points and the ceiling for plenty more. In fact, Davante Adams was the only receiver to score double-digit points in every game last year, and that was in half and full PPR, not non-PPR. ZeroRB can work ... any strategy can work, but there is significantly more risk with ignoring a bell cow running back than getting your piece of the action.

Outside of the bell cow part, when it comes to constructing your bench of running backs, you're going to have one who's a mediocre option for depth (a RB3/flex or so). After that, go pure upside. Forget about the Frank Gores of the world. You want to load up on the Ryquell Armsteads: running backs who would become bell cow, or close to it, with just one injury or situation change in front of them. If you're smart in your depth, you could end up overwhelmed with RB2 riches by midseason. Maximize that bench.

THE ELITE

1. **Saquon Barkley, NYG:** There's no doubt about Barkley's talent ... whether it ends up wasted for years in New York is another thing. Only Todd Gurley had more FPPG than Barkley did, and Barkley doesn't have the knee concern. Even behind a putrid OL, Barkley averaged 5.0 YPC and had 91 receptions for 721 yards. The Giants will need him even more with Odell Beckham gone, and they focused on retooling the line.

2. **Ezekiel Elliott, DAL:** You can argue that Elliott is the safest of all elite running backs. Elliott averaged 25 touches per game last year and is set to do the same in 2019, even if the passing game improves. After all, Elliott had 77 receptions in his 15 games, and the 381 touches and 2,002 yards actually points to a positive touchdown regression. Scoring just nine times with those numbers is shocking given the performance and Elliott's ability.

3. **Christian McCaffrey, CAR:** Can we put the size concerns to rest? Though, we might have a "McCaffrey got *too* big" concern this year. Honestly, none of it matters, as CMC is one of the most dominant running backs and had 107 receptions last year. That's more than Antonio Brown had and would have been the seventh-highest figure for wideouts. There is a case for McCaffrey to be the first back in full PPR with 187 receptions in his first two seasons, plus 1,098 rushing yards and 13 total TDs last year.

4. **Alvin Kamara, NO:** Kamara was a top-five running back already, and now Mark Ingram is off in Baltimore. The Saints did sign Latavius Murray, but he's even less of a threat to Kamara than Ingram was. Kamara did see a stark drop in YPC (6.1 to 4.6), but the carries jumped from 120 to 194, and he had nearly the same targets and receptions (101/82 to 105/81) in one fewer game. Kamara is locked into the lead role for the Saints and is as explosive as they come. Another season with 1,500/15 as the minimum is a guarantee.

TOP TALENT

1. **Le'Veon Bell, NYJ:** Bell returns to the NFL, and you are warranted in being concerned over his absence. While Bell is still in his prime, 100% healthy and as determined as they come, taking an entire year off and nearing two years since playing a game concerns us all ... plus, the Jets offensive line was one of the worst. Fortunately, the Jets improved their OL (some), and Bell is among the best ever at waiting to find a lane and exploding through gaps. Bell has averaged 4.5 YPC and 8.5 YPR (Yards Per Reception) since 2014, and with 350 touches, Bell will be back in the top five.

2. **Melvin Gordon, LAC:** If not for injuries, Gordon would be one of the best picks in fantasy. Gordon, when healthy, is a fantasy stud with 18.0, 16.1 and 20.5 FPPG (half PPR) the past three seasons, which includes some time of being banged up. The Chargers offense is also one of the better groups, and the defense is now among the best. Combine those facts, and you have a strong workload and offense to work in for Gordon, which could see him repeat his career-best 5.1 YPC and 20.5 FPPG. Again, the only downside to Gordon is health.

3. **Dalvin Cook, MIN:** It took Cook longer than we wanted to get back to 100%, but once he did, Cook showed that his skill/ability is among the best. Cook was RB6 in both points and FPPG from Weeks 12-16, averaging 5.6 YPC with 20 for 159 receiving and four total touchdowns. The Vikings were clearly confident enough in Cook's health to let Murray leave and merely draft

Alexander Mattison for insurance. A full season of a 100% healthy Cook means a top-10 finish is in store.

4. **James Conner, PIT:** While Conner didn't see Bell's workload, he did have the sixth-highest running back snap percentage, averaging over 70%. Conner is the lead, and the Steelers and Mike Tomlin lean on their lead more than most. Jaylen Samuels is best left to the passing game, and Benny Snell is merely a backup plan for Conner. In just 13 games, Conner finished as RB6 thanks to 13 touchdowns (12 rushing) with a 4.5 YPC and often overlooked 55 receptions for 497 yards. Conner is a true RB1 despite any concerns fantasy owners might have.

5. **David Johnson, ARI:** You can't fault Johnson too much for his down season. The Cardinals offense was terrible, and the team clearly misused him, often asking Johnson to run straight up the middle. With Kliff Kingsbury and Kyler Murray in town, things are going to get interesting, and we know DJ has the talent to get his desired 1,000/1,000 season. Truthfully, he has the talent for 2,500 total yards, and as long as Murray doesn't bomb, Johnson is primed to be the bounceback running back of the year … and even so, he was still RB10 in a down year.

6. **Joe Mixon, CIN:** Mixon's breakout season was in full effect last year, sending him to top-10 value despite him missing two games. In fact, Mixon fell short of a 4.0 YPC average in just two games, while rushing for 100-plus four times, including three of the final four games. Sure, you can argue that those games came after Andy Dalton's season ended, but you can also argue that defenses keyed on Mixon more with subpar quarterback play. With the passing game bouncing back in 2019 with an also healthy A.J. Green, Mixon's next-level breakout season could be on tap given his great all-around ability.

7. **Nick Chubb, CLE:** People often forget Chubb was mentioned in the same breath as Todd Gurley before blowing out his knee in college. Chubb proved that his talent has gone nowhere with a breakout season of his own, even though he barely saw any touches before Week 7. From that point on, only six running backs had more fantasy points, and it would have been five if not for Derrick Henry's insane finish. Don't worry about Kareem Hunt's return. If healthy, Chubb won't cede many touches to Hunt, as he's simply too talented to "mess with success."

SOLID OPTIONS

1. **Damien Williams, KC:** Sure, we can worry about Williams reverting to his Dolphins days or getting hurt. But why? Let's focus on the fact that Andy Reid loves his lead running backs, and that the Chiefs offense is terrific. Let's also focus on the fact that Williams scored 10 touchdowns from Week 14 through the playoffs (six games) with an absurd 22.4 FPPG and 5.2 YPC in the final five games. Given the situation at receiver, Williams could see even more consistent work and touches in 2019, which means a top-five finish isn't out of the question.

2. **Derrick Henry, TEN:** Henry scored nearly 50% of his fantasy points (47.6) in three weeks (14-16). Think about that before you go overboard in your drafts. In fact, Week 14 accounted for 24.5% of his points alone. Now, the positive side is that the Titans finally realized Henry can and deserves to be a workhorse, plus Matt LaFleur is gone. While the Titans offense is still a bit concerning and Henry won't do much in the passing game, Henry is certainly worthy of top-15 status and sees a small boost in non-PPR scoring… especially now that he started embracing running like a bull and has stopped trying to dance too much.

3. **Marlon Mack, IND:** Speaking of elusiveness, Mack is quite good at eluding would-be tacklers but was a bit too dance-happy as a rookie. Fortunately, he settled in during year two with 4.7 YPC and 1,011 total yards and 10 touchdowns in 12 games. He's not going to see heavy passing-game use, but the Colts plan to utilize Mack more in 2019. With a modest uptick there along

with his improved NFL knowledge and the Colts offense being back with Andrew Luck 100%, Mack could be knocking on the RB1 door.

4. **Derrius Guice, WAS:** Guice tore up his knee in the preseason, which put him ahead of Cook's schedule from 2018. That meant he could have been the midseason Cook (back near 100%) by Week 1, but reports vary on Guice's progress. If he is near 100% for Week 1, Guice is more talented than the man he replaced in college, Fournette. That gives him RB1 upside, even if Chris Thompson is also 100% and with Adrian Peterson in the fold. The Redskins drafted Guice to be their lead and a bell cow (or extremely close to it), and the real question is only how good his knee is for 2019. He could be an enormous value or waiver wire bust.

5. **Devonta Freeman, ATL:** Freeman has a No. 1 finish to his name. That was just 2015 and in only 15 games ... and Freeman is still *only* 27 years old. Freeman is an O.G. dual-threat running back, barely topping 1,000 rushing yards in 2015-16 but putting up 73/578 and 54/462 as a receiver those seasons. Tevin Coleman is now gone, to boot, and with Ito Smith and rookie Qadree Ollison behind him, Freeman should eat this season ... if, like many, he can stay on the field. Freeman insists on running headfirst, and with his injury history including a good amount to the head, you can't trust Freeman as more than a mid-level RB2. If he somehow played 16, even 15, games, Freeman would be a third-round steal, but those are slim odds.

6. **Aaron Jones, GB:** Jones has one of the bigger bust potentials for the RB2 group, as injuries have held him back, and the Packers drafted a running back that can handle the lead better than Jamaal Williams can. Jones is explosive, elusive and a real threat in open space. It's hard for the Packers not to give him more opportunities with that talent, but the addition of Matt LaFleur and interest in keeping Jones healthy could easily push Jones into the complementary (40%) role with more use in the passing game.

7. **Phillip Lindsay, DEN:** Lindsay was one of the biggest surprises of 2018 and unfortunately ended the season on a sad note with an injured hand/wrist that needed surgery. It's supposed to involve a 3-to-4-month recovery timeline, which would give Lindsay plenty of time to be ready for training camp, etc., but that's far from a given. As for Lindsay, he should lead the Broncos backfield again this year, and while the team likely hopes to get more from Royce Freeman, Lindsay's 5.4 YPC, 1,037 yards and nine TD rushing proved he's not "too small." Add in his receiving numbers, and a healthy Lindsay should be right back in the RB2 mix.

8. **Chris Carson, SEA:** Carson proved that draft capital doesn't mean much when one running back is outperforming the other and the head coach prefers that same player (see: not Rashaad Penny). With Doug Baldwin done, the Seahawks will be as run-heavy as ever, and Carson had 247 carries for 1,151 yards in 14 games last year. Carson also had six games in which he topped 100 rushing yards, including the final three weeks of the season. While a healthy Penny should command a decent amount of the passing-game work, Carson is as strong as any other mid-to-low RB2.

9. **Sony Michel, NE:** While Carson's work is a bit concerning with a healthy Penny, Michel's is even more so given James White and newly drafted Damien Harris. Plus ... it's the Patriots. Michel finished as RB28 in 13 games, so RB2 numbers are certainly likely, as the Patriots were actually one of the run-heaviest teams last year, and that was before Rob Gronkowski retired this offseason. The issue is always the same with Patriots backs, though: the weekly roller coaster ride of top-15 RB numbers or waiver-level production.

10. **Mark Ingram, BAL:** Even with Lamar Jackson taking a step forward, the Ravens will still be one of the run-heaviest teams in the league, if not the leading team. Ingram has only played three full seasons but has averaged 4.7 YPC since 2014 and had 50-46-58 receptions in 12-16-16 games from 2015-17. Of course, that's with Drew Brees, but it should also ease any concerns about Ingram sharing too many touches with whomever the Ravens keep in addition to the rookie

Justice Hill. Ingram deserves to be a mid-level RB2 on his ability, guaranteed touches and the Ravens' run effectiveness.

UP & COMING

1. **Josh Jacobs, OAK:** The negatives are nitpicking for sure, as Jacobs is everything you want in a running back and breakaway speed can be overrated if the secondary can't tackle you anyway. Jon Gruden has rarely rostered a true No. 1 talent at running back, and yet he gave Cadillac Williams 290 carries in 14 games one season and then another 225 in 14 games the next season, despite that injury concern. Gruden also gave Tyrone Wheatley more than 200 carries twice and Earnest Graham 222 in 10 starts (15 games). Jacobs is going to dominate this backfield, don't you worry, and he's a legitimate RB1 as a rookie with that work and talent mix.

2. **David Montgomery, CHI:** Montgomery is a high-quality running back, and those making Carlos Hyde comparisons aren't far off. He's not exactly Hyde for me, but putting him in the realm of a good RB2 for fantasy who can be a threat in all facets makes sense. The Bears already said they see a higher ceiling for Montgomery than Jordan Howard, and people overlook that Howard saw 250 (270 touches) last year. Montgomery is more explosive and better in the passing game, so even if he only sees Howard's touches and nothing more, that puts Montgomery as a near lock for RB2 numbers.

3. **Miles Sanders, PHI:** Sanders' style fits well for the Eagles, and he's "what they have been looking for" as a solution. Still, we know Doug Pederson is the king of committee backfields. On the positive side, Sanders has a good all-around skill-set, giving him the potential to be an every-down option. The negative is, again, we're dealing with the Eagles and Pederson. There may be some inconsistency, and Sanders is an RB2 in the mold of a Patriots option. The ceiling is the Sanders breaks the Pederson mold, gets around 20 touches a game and is a top-15 option.

4. **Darrell Henderson, LAR:** Henderson is the definition of "big play waiting to happen." Gurley's knee is a major concern, and Henderson has so much athleticism and elusiveness that top-10 numbers aren't out of the question if he gets the lead work with Gurley sidelined. Even if Gurley stays on the field, Sean McVay already said he's been looking for an explosive change-of-pace piece, and Henderson could have Tarik Cohen-like value at the least.

5. **Devin Singletary, BUF:** Singletary deserves a chance to at least share a backfield, if not lead it. The question of whether he becomes a three-down threat will be answered quickly, and that will depend on Singletary improving his receiving production (has the skill for it) and his patience/understanding to sometimes take what's there. Marlon Mack was similar coming out of college. As you'll see in the LeSean McCoy writeup below, the backfield is crowded, but if McCoy and one of Frank Gore or T.J. Yeldon isn't on the team for Week 1, Singletary could sneak into the RB2 conversation.

6. **Justice Hill, BAL:** Hill has the look of a passing-game running back but isn't an elite pass-catcher. When Hill is decisive, he flashes potential, but too often he shows hesitation. Without developing more in that area, Hill is likely going to mix in as a third option, possibly seeing a Wendell Smallwood-like role on the right team. Fortunately, he has a higher ceiling than Kenneth Dixon and Gus Edwards, especially if the Ravens use him as the main pass-catcher. Dixon could even get cut, which would make Hill an upside bench PPR value.

7. **Damien Harris, NE:** Harris is a well-rounded running back who could serve as the lead option in a backfield duo. While he's a good passing-game option, Harris is probably best used in a time share with a more explosive complement, keeping him in that RB2 timeshare range. In that vein, the Patriots drafted him. Sony Michel is the lead, and James White is the pass-catcher. Harris is

the "does everything well" backup, and he won't have much value without a Michel injury. Though, we know that's certainly likely given Michel's past.

8. **Alexander Mattison, MIN:** Mattison has all-around quality, but his best ability is being a "no-nonsense" runner. Mattison keeps grinding late into games and topped 30 carries several times. He's also an adept pass-catcher, but he's not elusive and is willing to take too many hits. Mattison replaces Murray as the next man up with RB2 value if Cook misses time. But Mattison lacks the upside of Cook in the passing game, which would point to Michael Boone, Ameer Abdullah or someone else stealing that work.

9. **Benny Snell, PIT:** Snell is a heavy runner in a good way with physicality but also the poor way with his legs and feet. Snell found the end zone often in college, but he's more of a grinder that will need volume to sustain; think Jordan Howard as mentioned. He's purely a stash if the league is deep enough and a waiver "run to grab" option if Conner misses time.

RED FLAGS

1. **Todd Gurley, LAR:** It's Todd Gurley. You don't need any insight on him … outside of something we'll never know: just how concerning is that knee? Gurley is a threat to be the best fantasy running back in the game. He's done it already. Heck, he was last year, even with missed time. However, when we see Gurley unable to get back on the field late last year and in the playoffs, you have to be concerned. Talent-wise, Gurley is No. 1. Injury-concern-wise, he's also tops (almost), and it means he's a tough sell in the first round.

2. **Leonard Fournette, JAC:** Two years in the league; two seasons cut short due to injuries. When we said Gurley was almost tops injury wise, he couldn't be No. 1 because it's Fournette. Injuries date back to college for him, and it's unfortunate given his ability. He's a better pass-catcher than we saw with LSU's dated offense, and while he's far from a great receiver, a season similar to Elliott's isn't out of the question … if he could stay on the field. Now, Fournette is also more of a volume runner than Zeke, but he's also had a much worse OL in front of him. Fournette has shown his elusiveness with broken tackles and a career 8.4 YPR. If … and that's the biggest if you can find … Fournette played a full season, his talent is top-five-level.

3. **Jordan Howard, PHI:** Howard is an everyman running back, as in, nearly every man (NFL running back) can do what he does. Howard doesn't have one exceptional ability, and he's a straight-line runner that takes what is given and often, not much more. That's why the Bears were willing to move on, and now Howard is with the Eagles and behind Sanders, and definitely behind anyone in the passing game. With that limitation, his best hope for reliable numbers is a Sanders injury or Sanders being a massive disappointment. Howard is a handcuff of sorts, but an uninspiring one.

4. **LeSean McCoy, BUF:** There is a non-zero chance that McCoy isn't even on the team come Week 1 … or earlier. Forget the Avengers spoilers jokes; McCoy was miserable last year with 3.2 YPC and just five double-digit scores and three TDs. The Bills backfield is currently crowded, and even as the lead, McCoy has little value at this point of his career. It was a fun ride, but it's over.

5. **Adrian Peterson, WAS:** Peterson had more left in the tank than anyone thought, but make no mistake: If Guice is healthy, this is his backfield. Of course, that's a big question, and Peterson was RB17 with 1,250 total yards and eight touchdowns, despite being on a poor offense. The weak passing game actually had Peterson see more attention than some other running backs, so it's impressive that at his age, Peterson still had 4.2 YPC. Peterson could end a wasted fantasy

pick if Guice is near 100%, as the touches will be slim, but we saw Cook struggle for more than half the season last year. Peterson could at least be a first-half RB2 if Guice isn't himself.

6. **Kareem Hunt, CLE:** Talent-wise, Hunt is one of the 10 best in the league ... possibly even top-five. The 10-game suspension obviously changes everything, as does the fact that Chubb is arguably as talented. As long as Chubb plays to his ability and is healthy, Hunt returning isn't going to cut into Chubb's work more than a few touches. This is similar to Carlos Hyde behind Damien Williams in KC, and the Browns made a business decision. Your fantasy decision is likely to pass on Hunt given the tied-up bench spot for the majority of the season.

SERVICEABLE

1. **Kerryon Johnson, DET:** Johnson is exceptionally explosive, and his games against the Patriots and Dolphins showed the Lions that they may have something special. At the same time, it's Matt Patricia running things from the Bill Belichick School of running back use. So, while we can pine for more touches, the Lions brought in C.J. Anderson and still have Theo Riddick in the mix. Oh, they also drafted Ty Johnson, who looks to be the future Riddick on this team but also points to Johnson never seeing a workhorse role. He's a great fringe RB2.

2. **Kenyan Drake, MIA:** The Dolphins hate the Drake. Yes, we know that and know that the joke has been driven into the ground. Well, Adam Gase is gone (though not far), which means Drake could get his chance to break out with a lead-back workload. Even with inconsistent work, Drake still finished as RB18. While the Dolphins offense will struggle, so will the defense, meaning more opportunities for the offense, and Drake had some nice passing-game numbers with 73 targets for 53/477/5.

3. **Tevin Coleman, SF:** Coleman disappointed is his opportunity to be the go-to option, finishing RB19 with 199 touches for 1,076 yards and nine TDs, losing work to Ito Smith and others. Coleman is reunited with Kyle Shanahan, who can maximize his upside, but the 49ers are now flush with options, including Jerick McKinnon, Matt Breida and possibly even a healthy Raheem Mostert. Coleman could actually put up similar numbers on fewer touches as the majority lead of a timeshare now that he's back with Shanahan, but he could also fall behind McKinnon ... or even Breida if he disappoints again.

4. **Ronald Jones II, TB:** Jones was a big disappointment after being drafted early by the Buccaneers and looking to be their future at the position. Jones never got going in 2018 and was vastly outplayed by Peyton Barber. The Buccaneers did next to nothing in addressing the position this offseason, which could be seen as a vote of confidence in believing Jones still has plenty to offer. On the other hand, Bruce Arians likes pass-catching running backs, and Jones struggles there and in pass blocking. Jones is a nice upside gamble as an RB3/4 for the ceiling being in the top-20 range, but he still has the same bust potential we saw in 2018.

5. **Tarik Cohen, CHI:** Cohen is more valuable in PPR, jumping to RB11 while being RB19 in non-PPR. Read that second finish again and keep in mind that even in non-PPR, Cohen can carry flex value. The reason it's flex is two-fold. We already covered that the Bears appear enamored with Montgomery and his potential. Secondly, Cohen's high level of inconsistency is magnified in non-PPR. Even in PPR, he's best served as a flex RB or as your RB2 if you start receiver-heavy.

6. **Lamar Miller, HOU:** If it feels like we've wanted more from Miller forever, you wouldn't be wrong. With the Dolphins, it was, "Imagine Miller with more touches." With the Texans, it's been, "Well, he's less effective with more touches, so just the same ol' low-end RB2 ... meh."

D'Onta Foreman struggled to return from his Achilles injury, but it sounds as if the Texans are going to give him the chance to unseat Miller as the lead. The team also rolled the dice late on Cullen Gillaspia and undrafted Karan Higdon. So while neither appears much of a threat, the Texans clearly are just as uninspired by Miller's performance as his fantasy owners are.

7. **James White, NE:** Every year owners "reluctantly" draft White, and then he continues to put up big numbers in PPR … when healthy. As mentioned with Michel, the Patriots backfield is always going to have multiple options with each filling a role. The good news is that the pass-catching role is White's and White's alone. As long as White plays another 16 games, a top-20 finish is guaranteed. Of course, there will be a few down weeks, but getting a top-20 RB in the middle rounds means you can deal with a few off-weeks given the extreme return value.

8. **Jerick McKinnon, SF:** McKinnon may go from the most over-drafted running back to one of the best values. Sure, we'll never know if the McKinnon "haters" were right in that he couldn't handle a workhorse role thanks to the injury, but with the Coleman signing, now McKinnon looks to be an afterthought. McKinnon was RB24 in 2017 with just 202 touches (43 receptions), mixing in for the Vikings. He's still explosive and dangerous. Shanahan should get the best out of McKinnon, and forming a Bears-like duo with Coleman (as the Cohen option) wouldn't be a shock.

9. **Latavius Murray, NO:** Honestly, if the Saints use Murray the same way they used Ingram, Murray would turn out to be one of the best middle-round RBs. Time and again, Murray steps in when asked and produces right around 4.0 YPC with a little passing-game work … and he's reliable, playing 62 games the past four years. The only reason Murray isn't an RB2 is the question of use, not effectiveness and not the Saints offense. You'd be wise to own Murray if you go WR-heavy.

ONES TO WATCH

1. **Rashaad Penny, SEA:** Penny is the proof that draft capital doesn't matter much when you can't stay healthy and also aren't performing (ahem, Ronald Jones II). Pete Carroll doesn't seem too fond of Penny and has made it clear that he likes Carson. At the same time, Penny is still an extremely talented running back and superior to Carson in the passing game. Carroll also said, "both will have a role in 2019," for whatever that's worth. Penny is a worthy flier in half and hull PPR alone, and if Carson misses time, Penny could surprise with lead carries.

2. **Ryquell Armstead, JAC:** Armstead is your hammer. If you want a lead running back who's "no-nonsense" and going to produce the hard yards, you want Armstead. Basically, he runs like Derrick Henry should. The lack of passing-game ability and high-level elusiveness will keep him as the lead/power option in a timeshare if on his own. That's a distinct possibility given Fournette's injury risk. Armstead is one of the top backups to grab in the middle rounds that could turn into a top-20 RB rather quickly.

3. **Royce Freeman, DEN:** Freeman was supposed to be the breakout running back for the Broncos, but Phillip Lindsay took care of that. Freeman performed admirably in his opportunities with a 4.0 YPC and five touchdowns. Freeman will never be a major factor in the passing game, and his real appeal was to be a better version of Howard with a complementary pass-catcher alongside him. As mentioned, Lindsay took over, which means Freeman is mainly a short-yard/goal-line/power option that will be volatile thanks to his reliability on touchdowns.

4. **Dion Lewis, TEN:** The fact that Lewis had a worse season than with the Patriots is telling. Early in the season, it appeared the Titans would go full 50/50 split with Henry and Lewis. However, one of Lewis' three great games was in Week 1, and then he rarely performed outside of Weeks 7 and 9. In fact, he averaged just 3.3 YPC and without games one and seven, it's worse. This is Henry's backfield now, and Lewis is in the pass-catcher role, which isn't as valuable as some teams given the offense and Marcus Mariota's play. Nevertheless, 59/400 receiving is a solid mark, and if Henry got hurt, Lewis would be an RB2.

5. **Carlos Hyde, KC:** Hyde is a nice all-around running back, and while he's not a natural pass-catcher, he can be a three-down threat … when healthy. The problem is that Andy Reid loves to lean on his lead, and the signing of Hyde points to an insurance role versus regular work. Of all backups, though, few have as much upside as Hyde does if Williams were to get hurt.

6. **Austin Ekeler, LAC:** Ekeler is best utilized with a limited workload. While Gordon has missed time, Ekeler shows some of the upside we see weekly, but similar to Lamar Miller, he often ends up producing similar numbers on more touches (less efficiency). The good news is that Ekeler more than doubled his carries and mildly dropped his YPC from 5.5 to 5.2. He also averaged 10.4 YPR after 10.3 the previous year on 12 fewer receptions. Ekeler is a real threat for the Chargers and in fantasy as a half or full PPR flex option … when healthy.

7. **Ito Smith, ATL:** We'll get to the next piece of the Falcons backfield soon, and that piece is the reason Smith doesn't rank higher. Smith is a solid pass-catcher and showed as much with 32 targets for a terrific 27 receptions but just 5.6 YPR. Smith also averaged just 3.5 YPC, though two of his three games with double-digit carries came with 6.5 and 5.5 YPC. There is some upside with Smith, and Freeman is an enormous injury risk, making Smith a late-round stash.

8. **Chris Thompson, WAS:** We know how good Thompson can be. Similar to Theo Riddick, Thompson is mainly a passing-game weapon but one that already produced RB2 numbers based just on that. What we don't know is how healthy Thompson will be, how much the Redskins will share touches if everyone is healthy, or if Thompson can even stay on the field. Thompson has plenty of upside, finishing as RB26 in just 10 games in 2017 and RB32 in 2016.

9. **C.J. Anderson, DET:** Anderson was expected to have value as the complement to McCaffrey last year, possibly similar to Kamara and Ingram in New Orleans. CJA barely saw the field and got axed after Week 10. Once Gurley's knee became a concern, the Rams picked up Anderson and proved he still had plenty of ability left … even if it looks like some of that was pounds to give. Anderson reeled off three straight games with 123-plus rushing yards with a low of 5.3 YPC. The Lions gave LeGarrette Blount work last year, even before Kerryon Johnson went down. That's going to be Anderson's role, as once again, it's Patricia and the Patriot Way of using a player's best skills when needed, and Anderson brings more steadiness.

BENCH DEPTH

1. **Matt Breida, SF:** Breida shared work and missed time last year, yet still finished as RB25 with 814/3 rushing and 27/261/2 receiving. He also improved his YPC from 4.4 to 5.3 and was the best 49ers running back. If you argued that Breida should be their top option for 2019, it would be hard to say you're wrong based on performance, but the 49ers signed McKinnon and Coleman in back-to-back seasons. Breida looks locked into the No. 3 role unless there's a surprise roster move or injury, but if McKinnon did get hurt, Breida could sneak in some Flex/RB4 value again.

2. **Nyheim Hines, IND:** The Colts are ready to turn Mack into a feature back, and Hines is simply a poor man's Cohen at this point. That doesn't mean he's worthless, though, because while Hines

showed that pure rushing isn't a strength with just 3.7 YPC, his performance through the air -- 81 targets for 63/425/2 -- gives him enough PPR value to warrant a late-round pick.

3. **D'Onta Foreman, HOU:** Achilles injuries normally end careers, and Foreman looked slow and nothing like himself upon his return last year. Foreman is still a powerhouse, and, if he hadn't been hurt, likely would have pushed aside Miller for the lead role. That possibility isn't out of the question, but it's appearing like a longshot given how much explosiveness that injury takes away from players. If Foreman can even get back to 90%, he could be the power to Miller's elusive passing-game work, but even so, it would likely be a 50/50 split.

4. **Jaylen Samuels, PIT:** Samuels is best served in the passing-game role, as a former hybrid Move TE/H-Back. Yes, Samuels gave us some excitement when James Conner was hurt, but a lead running back isn't his best role, and the Steelers will lean on Conner once again. However, unlike the years of Le'Veon Bell seeing 90% of the snaps, it should be more around 70% these days with Samuels turning into a lower-level half and full PPR option. He'll likely even keep that role, possibly with slightly more touches (40% instead of 25%), if Conner got hurt again.

5. **Kalen Ballage, MIA:** Ballage didn't see much work until late in the season with just eight carries before Week 15 and then 28 over the final three. There is no certainty in this backfield, especially with the coaching changes. However, Drake has shown the ability to be a lead and will get the first crack at it. Ballage is a bigger running back (6'1", 227) with enough athleticism to surprise defenders and even fantasy owners if he takes over and puts up RB2/3 numbers. That's the ultimate lottery ticket result, but Ballage is worth that gamble.

6. **Rex Burkhead, NE:** Remember when Burkhead crept into the fifth round of drafts last year? Let that be a testament to how dicey it can be trying to gamble on frustrating backfields, even when another injury looks to clear up the situation. That said, it was understandable, as Burkhead appeared to be the lead dog early on, but an injury derailed his season, and once everyone was healthy, he only hit double-digit touches twice from Week 13 through the Super Bowl. Burkhead wouldn't even be draftable if not for the upside of this backfield if Michel or White were to get hurt and Burkhead started seeing a dozen touches per game.

7. **Peyton Barber, TB:** Barber is another version of Howard in that he's a fine backup plan, but he doesn't bring enough to the table to be the "guy you want". Just look at last season. Barber averaged a pedestrian 3.7 YPC with 20 receptions for 92 yards (4.6 YPR). Meh. Barber had 108 carries for 423 yards (3.9 YPC) in 2017, and he's just an average player. There is nothing wrong with that as your backup, but Jones has a much higher ceiling. The downside to Jones was addressed, and that's why Barber is still worth drafting in case he leads the Buccaneers backfield again, and Arians does prefer backs that can actually catch and block. Don't be surprised if undrafted Bruce Anderson makes the roster and surprises too.

8. **Duke Johnson, CLE:** The Browns insist Johnson has a role and is extremely valuable to the team. After all, Johnson is one of the best pass-catching running backs in the league. However, how many touches will Johnson see each week with Chubb turning into one of the best running backs in the game, and that's before Hunt's return later in the season. It's hard to see value you can trust with Johnson without a team change or injury to Chubb.

9. **Elijah McGuire, NYJ:** In the new-look NFL, McGuire was supposed to be the Jets' version of Tarik Cohen. He's not as small as you might think for that role, but he struggles with early-down and between-the-tackles rushing. Fortunately, he's dangerous in space and therefore the passing game, evidenced in his 10.4 and 10.2 YPR his first two seasons. Unfortunately, limited playing time and injuries have McGuire with a career 36 receptions, and now Le'Veon Bell is in town. There's not much here unless Bell were to get hurt … or Adam Gase is a crazy person, which is possible.

10. **Doug Martin, OAK:** Isaiah Crowell was the original backup plan for Jacobs, but once he was out for the season, the Raiders brought back Martin. Last year was Martin's best performance since 2015, but Jacobs should see the vast majority of the work, and Martin might not even be Gruden's top change-of-pace, passing-game weapon. Martin may be more of a Damien Harris/Benny Snell type, whereas he steps in if the lead gets hurt, but the touches will be limited otherwise.

11. **Jamaal Williams, GB:** Williams has received opportunities to seize control of the Packers backfield when Aaron Jones has missed time, but yet again, we look to have another Howard-type player on our hands. Williams has 3.6 and 3.8 YPC in his two seasons and is a decent but not great weapon in the passing game. Williams has all the moves and the look of a feature back, but he's just too slow at executing and could easily be the team's No. 3 for 2019.

12. **Dexter Williams, GB:** It's been a long time since Notre Dame produced an NFL starting running back, but Williams can break that trend. Williams likely won't be the lead initially, but if given the opportunity, the talent is there to be a consistent RB2 with upside for more, especially with the aforementioned disappointment that is Jamaal Williams. Dexter Williams is the definition of "hit the hole and he's gone," which means he might even push Jones to a complementary role.

13. **Giovani Bernard, CIN:** It's hard to get excited about Bernard these days for two reasons. First, Mixon has proven to be one of the better all-around backs in the league. Secondly, the Bengals drafted a Bernard duplicate in Mark Walton last year and again with Trayveon Williams this year. Actually, the Bengals doubled down with Rodney Anderson, so let's just call this running back "Bengals pass-catching backup." Whether it's Bernard, Williams or Anderson, the backup will have deep PPR value as a one-week fill-in if desperate or with RB2 upside if Mixon misses time. That RB2 value would only go for the lead, and the early signs point to Williams, but keep a close watch.

14. **Trayveon Williams, CIN:** The reason Williams seems like the best option is that while he's not the most creative in his running style, his durability, reliability and passing-game work will give him opportunities, even as a backup.

15. **Theo Riddick, DET:** Riddick is holding on to his fantasy life by his fingertips, but thankfully, we've talked about how there are defined roles in the backfield. The passing-game work is Riddick's, who will even line up in the slot at times. Kerryon Johnson is a receiving threat as well, but if back near 100%, Riddick is going to still contribute for one more season. After all, he still had 75 targets for 61/384 last year, which was his first time without a receiving touchdown since his rookie season.

16. **Chase Edmonds, ARI:** Johnson is going to monopolize the Cardinals backfield, but the options behind him are lacking, and the most talented option is clearly Edmonds. Even with that terrible offense and play-calling, which sent Edmonds up the middle just like Johnson, Edmonds was still able to produce 208 yards on 60 carries. That number would go up as the team's lead and with better use, and Edmonds has the receiving ability to be a three-down option, and the Cardinals roster construction would point to them believing the same.

17. **Jordan Wilkins, IND:** Wilkins had a shot to be the top Colts running back with Mack hurt early last year, but he didn't do much in Week 1 against the Bengals, and while he looked better against the Redskins, it was the last time Wilkins had double-digit carries. His mention in the running backs is only because if Mack were to get hurt again, he would be half of the committee with Hines, given Hines' limitations, and would have Flex RB value in the Colts offense.

18. **Justin Jackson, LAC:** Jackson has more all-around ability than most realize, and he proved that with a nice game against the Chiefs when needed. However, Melvin Gordon is one of the best running backs in the league, and Ekeler is a proven threat in the passing game. Jackson is a nice backup plan for either option, but he'll never be a workhorse. The upside is if Jackson can get

30-40% of the touches each week -- with an injury as mentioned -- and that would put Jackson in the RB4 conversation.

19. **Qadree Ollison, ATL:** Ollison is another big boy late in these rankings, and he didn't complain when the role became a timeshare. Defenders struggle to tackle him below the waist and turns into a bull with momentum. However, Ollison doesn't have a ton of agility, lacking in elusiveness and passing-game work, but he does have nice speed for his size (6'1", 228; 4.58, 40). Ollison could threaten Smith's backup role and even become the lead with a Freeman injury and barrel into RB2 value.

20. **Mike Weber, DAL:** The Cowboys drafted Tony Pollard as well, but Weber profiles as the better Ezekiel Elliott handcuff with Pollard possibly even seeing return-game work. Weber has amazing vision. He's a highly skilled running back that lacks a bit in athleticism, but his intelligence and precision make up for it.

21. **Darwin Thompson, KC:** Thompson always gives everything he has. Too often, however, that can't overcome poor choices, likely due to inexperience, which also shows up in the passing game. Thompson is a developmental pick, but he has the potential to surprise in a few years ... or since it's the Chiefs, he could be the 2019 version of Damien Williams if Williams and Hyde both get hurt.

22. **Frank Gore, BUF:** Gore appears to be the safest of the Bills trio in front of rookie Singleton. Gore keeps churning along, McCoy doesn't near his contract value and T.J. Yeldon brings nothing special to the table.

Chapter 6

WIDE RECEIVERS

STANDARD SCORING RPV

WR1

	Player	RPV
1	Davante Adams	18%
2	DeAndre Hopkins	14%
3	Julio Jones	9%
4	Michael Thomas	4%
5	Tyreek Hill	3%
6	Odell Beckham	0%
7	JuJu Smith-Schuster	-1%
8	Antonio Brown	-3%
9	Mike Evans	-8%
10	Keenan Allen	-10%
11	A.J. Green	-10%
12	Adam Thielen	-12%

WR2

	Player	RPV
1	T.Y. Hilton	12%
2	Amari Cooper	10%
3	Stefon Diggs	7%
4	Brandin Cooks	6%
5	Robert Woods	0%
6	Kenny Golladay	-0%
7	Cooper Kupp	-2%
8	Tyler Lockett	-2%
9	Alshon Jeffery	-6%
10	Julian Edelman	-8%
11	Chris Godwin	-8%
12	Sammy Watkins	-8%

WR3

	Player	RPV
1	Sterling Shepard	7%
2	Mike Williams	7%
3	D.J. Moore	5%
4	Corey Davis	4%
5	Allen Robinson	0%
6	Tyler Boyd	0%
7	Calvin Ridley	-1%
8	Jarvis Landry	-2%
9	Will Fuller	-5%
10	Robby Anderson	-6%
11	Christian Kirk	-8%
12	Courtland Sutton	-9%

WR4

	Player	RPV
1	Golden Tate	6%
2	Robert Foster	5%
3	Michael Gallup	4%
4	Dede Westbrook	1%
5	Marvin Jones Jr.	0%
6	Dante Pettis	0%
7	Curtis Samuel	0%
8	DeSean Jackson	-2%
9	DaeSean Hamilton	-2%
10	Parris Campbell	-3%
11	N'Keal Harry	-4%
12	James Washington	-5%

½ & FULL-POINT PPR SCORING RPV

WR1

	Player	RPV
1	DeAndre Hopkins	12%
2	Davante Adams	10%
3	Julio Jones	8%
4	Michael Thomas	6%
5	Tyreek Hill	5%
6	Odell Beckham	3%
7	JuJu Smith-Schuster	-1%
8	Antonio Brown	-2%
9	Keenan Allen	-4%
10	Adam Thielen	-7%
11	Mike Evans	-10%
12	A.J. Green	-12%

WR2

	Player	RPV
1	T.Y. Hilton	12%
2	Amari Cooper	11%
3	Stefon Diggs	4%
4	Tyler Lockett	2%
5	Kenny Golladay	1%
6	Brandin Cooks	-1%
7	Cooper Kupp	-2%
8	Julian Edelman	-4%
9	Robert Woods	-5%
10	Alshon Jeffery	-5%
11	D.J. Moore	-6%
12	Chris Godwin	-7%

WR3

	Player	RPV
1	Jarvis Landry	7%
2	Corey Davis	5%
3	Allen Robinson	4%
4	Mike Williams	3%
5	Calvin Ridley	2%
6	Tyler Boyd	1%
7	Robby Anderson	0%
8	Christian Kirk	-2%
9	Sterling Shepard	-3%
10	Marvin Jones Jr.	-4%
11	Courtland Sutton	-6%
12	DaeSean Hamilton	-8%

WR4

	Player	RPV
1	James Washington	6%
2	N'Keal Harry	5%
3	Emmanuel Sanders	3%
4	Golden Tate	2%
5	Larry Fitzgerald	1%
6	Sammy Watkins	0%
7	Robert Foster	-1%
8	Dante Pettis	-2%
9	Will Fuller	-2%
10	Dede Westbrook	-3%
11	Marquez Valdes Scantling	-4%
12	Curtis Samuel	-6%

STANDARD WR RPV ANALYSIS & POSITION OVERVIEW

Joe Pisapia

"All he does is catch touchdowns." This was once the knock on HoFer Chris Carter. Well, that worked out pretty well. In standard format leagues, a receiver who gets red-zone targets and continuously converts them is fantasy gold. In 2019, the WR3 group is particularly talented. Perhaps the most potential breakouts since 2014 that came with a rookie class of Odell Beckham, Mike Evans and others. Should you miss a run at WR, you can potentially make this up significantly with the multiple selections from the WR3 class, who have potential to outperform their ADP.

½ & FULL-POINT PPR RPV ANALYSIS & POSITION OVERVIEW

Joe Pisapia

As a reminder, when you select a player from the WR2 class as a WR1 you're behind in RPV. Each group of 12 is compared to that specific group. Conversely, select two players from the WR1 class, and the second becomes the WR2 on your roster. You'll benefit from an RPV advantage. In PPR formats, from Pick 6 onward in the draft, it's highly acceptable to create a strong RPV advantage by taking two WR1s back-to-back as the cornerstone of your team. The NFL game is more wide-open than ever, and in PPR leagues, there are many more RBs that can be useful than in standard leagues. That means you can address the RB position after Round 2. That doesn't mean Zero RB. That never was or is a smart strategy, despite the love it got a few years ago. While elite receivers will see consistent targets, elite RBs still touch the ball more frequently.

As I said in the standard league paragraph, that WR3 group with Calvin Ridley, Tyler Boyd, Mike Williams etc. offers a ton of upside. Should you be an early RB drafter, you can make up some group by purchasing WRs in bulk between the low-end WR2s and solid WR3s. The danger lies in waiting too long to address the position. Not only will you be dealing with negative RPV issues, but the WR4 group is a mix of unproven and aging-out talent. That's not the best group to be relying on week to week, especially in PPR.

PLAYER PROFILES

Matt Franciscovich

THE ELITE

1. **DeAndre Hopkins, HOU:** Two years ago, Hopkins was fantasy's WR1 in standard scoring and WR2 in PPR. In 2018, he racked up a career-high 115 catches on 163 targets for 1,572 yards and hit double-digit TDs for the second consecutive season with 11. His chemistry with quarterback Deshaun Watson only grew stronger last year, and because of that, Nuk's ceiling is once again sky-high. Hopkins' elite body control and ability to make tough catches makes him a relevant WR1 no matter who his quarterback is. But as long as Watson is healthy, this stack could be unstoppable for fantasy purposes.

2. **Davante Adams, GB:** In his first year as Green Bay's No. 1 target (following Jordy Nelson's departure), Adams posted career highs across the board: 111 receptions, 169 targets, 1,386 yards, 13 TDs and 329.6 PPR fantasy points, good enough for No. 2 at the position for the season behind only DeAndre Hopkins. Adams took a huge step forward and has emerged as an elite NFL and fantasy wide receiver. The latter has something to do with Adams scoring double-digit TDs in three straight seasons now. When Adams and a healthy Aaron Rodgers get into a groove, statistical eruptions will follow. Fantasy managers can feel confident taking Adams to anchor the WR1 slot.

3. **Julio Jones, ATL:** The Falcons' powerhouse of a No. 1, Jones led the NFL in receiving yardage in 2018 with 1,677, marking his fifth straight year with at least 1,409 yards. But Jones began the year with a seven-game touchdown drought, which was one of the concerns on him coming into the season, since he only scored three times in 2017. While he did finish with eight TDs, five of them came during the last four weeks of the NFL regular season, including Week 17. Still, Jones' track record of yardage production plus durability over the last five seasons makes him worthwhile of being a WR1 for your squad.

4. **Michael Thomas, NO:** In his third NFL season, Thomas securely hauled in a ridiculous 125 of 147 targets, resulting in an unprecedented 85% catch rate. He's an absolute target hog, averaging 148 looks over the last two years, with over 100 receptions in each, making him a PPR manager's dream. He's also scored nine touchdowns in two of the last three seasons, though he has had a stretch of seven games without scoring in 2017 and a few droughts last year. But he still boasts upside, given the sheer level of opportunity Thomas gets on a weekly basis, and he remains the focal point of Drew Brees' passing offense.

5. **Tyreek Hill, KC:** Hill is capable of big things on the field, and in the fantasy stat sheets. But his behavior off the field has hurt his overall value. Just because he's not suspended now, doesn't mean he's a safe asset when you consider multiple issues that seem to plague him off the field. However, he's a lock for 1,200 yards again and double digit TD's in that high octane Chiefs offense. As a keeper, there's still plenty of risk here, but in redraft you're looking at a strong #1 WR.

6. **Odell Beckham, CLE:** OBJ managed to play in 12 games last season before a quadriceps injury put him on the shelf. Despite the missed games, and the fact that he was playing with shell of a quarterback Eli Manning, Beckham still managed to post over 1,000 receiving yards, notching five 100-yard outings and six TDs -- a true testament to his elite talent. Looking ahead, OBJ finds himself in Cleveland with an exciting crew of young talent around him including second-year QB

in Baker Mayfield and a loaded corps of receivers like BFF Jarvis Landry. There is reasonable concern that the target share may be an issue, but the Browns would be misguided to not feature the dynamic superstar receiver in their offensive plans on a weekly basis. Beckham warrants top-five wideout consideration in all formats.

7. **Antonio Brown, OAK:** The most consistent and most elite wide receiver in terms of fantasy football production for the last six seasons, Brown probably will take a statistical step back with his move to Oakland. He's no longer in the conversation as a No. 1 overall pick in PPR drafts, nor will he be the first WR off the board. But he's still a top-10 fantasy wideout, and an argument could be made for him as top-five, despite heading into his age-31 season. He's amassed at least 1,200 yards in six straight seasons and has scored double-digit touchdowns in four of his last five campaigns, including a league-leading 15 last year. Brown has finished as a top-five fantasy receiver in five straight years, but those were all with Pittsburgh. The new environment brings some uncertainty, but he remains an elite option in all fantasy formats.

TOP TALENT

1. **Mike Evans, TB:** The WR6 in standard scoring in 2018, Evans was one of only six wideouts to eclipse the 200-fantasy-point mark for the season. His 139 targets came in at just three more than he had seen the previous year, when he was labeled a fantasy bust with 1,000 yards and five touchdowns. He bounced back nicely with an 86/1,524/8 line catching balls from both Ryan Fitzpatrick and a struggling Jameis Winston along the way. Ironically, Evans posted three scores in each of his first three games of the season with Fitzmagic at the helm, but the big wideout needed 12 more games to score another three touchdowns (two of his eight TDs came in Week 17 after the majority of fantasy leagues had already crowned a champion). Entering his age-26 season, the 6-foot-5 beast is one of the more physical receivers in the NFL, especially in the red zone. He remains one of the best receivers in the league and in fantasy, and with new Tampa Bay head coach Bruce Arians calling the shots, Evans' late-second- or early-third-round ADP could end up being an absolute steal.

2. **JuJu Smith-Schuster, PIT:** In his second year in the NFL, JuJu broke out for the fantasy football owners who were fortunate enough to roster him. He posted a 111/1,426/7 line in the Steelers' pass-happy offense, and that's alongside the absurd production of Antonio Brown. He posted eight 100-yard games and provided extreme consistency for his owners, finishing the year as the WR9 in standard and WR8 in PPR. With Brown out of the picture, JuJu is set up to be Pittsburgh's No. 1 receiver, and Ben Roethlisberger's contract extension with the team ensures this duo will be set to pop off for at least one more year. He's being regarded as a potential top-five pick at receiver this year, but some concerns can be found in his playing style in terms of being that No. 1 guy, having to produce without AB drawing double coverage on a weekly basis. Time will tell, but considering Smith-Schuster is in line for somewhere around 150 targets at the least, he's a solid second-round pick.

3. **Adam Thielen, MIN:** What a season Thielen enjoyed in 2018. He was Kirk Cousins' go-to guy in Minnesota, and his incredible production ranked him as the WR7 in both standard and PPR scoring for the year. Thielen soaked up 155 targets, which he converted into a 113/1,373/9 line (all career bests). His sticky hands led him on an incredible run with at least 100 yards in eight straight games to start the season, during many of which he also found the end zone. Seemingly

always underrated, Thielen is now on the radar as a viable low-end WR1 in all fantasy formats. Early ADP data show the 28-year-old getting drafted as a top-10 WR in the third round, and there's no reason to believe he will not return that value this season.

4. **A.J. Green, CIN:** During the Bengals' Week 2 game against the Ravens, Green exploded for three touchdowns in the first half of the game. He proceeded to score just two more touchdowns in the six games to follow before getting shut down for the season with a toe injury. He's entering his age-31 season, but Green deserves some optimism that he can still produce at a high level with offensive-minded Zac Taylor, former Rams quarterbacks coach, now the head coach in Cincinnati. Still, the age and injury track record over the last three seasons (ended season on injured reserve in 2016 and 2018) will keep Green in the WR2 tier going forward rather than the WR1 conversation where he's lived the majority of his career.

5. **Keenan Allen, LAC:** The No. 1 target for Philip Rivers, Allen has finally strung together two consecutive stellar seasons. Though Allen's 2018 campaign was a bit of a step down from the previous season, he still finished as the WR14 in standard and WR12 in PPR with a 97/1,196/6 line. Simply put, Allen is a physical mismatch who demands targets in the Chargers' pass-happy offense and has a seasoned veteran QB slinging to him. He's coming off draft boards as the WR11 in the early going, and you could make the argument for Allen to be top-five at his position. There are some injury and durability concerns, but Allen is a glorious pick in Round 3 (if his value remains there).

6. **T.Y. Hilton, IND:** With Andrew Luck back under center (finally), Hilton bounced back with a 76/1,270/6 line to wrap 2018 as fantasy's WR15. He posted five 100-plus-yard games and two multi-TD games on the season. He reportedly did all of this while playing through ankle sprains, showing his toughness. The Colts offense is trending upward, and there's a ton of hype surrounding the team's star players for fantasy purposes. We know what Hilton is capable of, and his early ADP of WR10 is reflecting that excitement amongst fantasy managers. You'll have to pay a hefty price if you want him on your squad this year, but he's going to be worth it.

7. **Stefon Diggs, MIN:** Coming off of a career year with a 102/1,021/9 line, early ADP data shows Diggs as a top-15 fantasy receiver, and he's a total stud skill-set wise. Every summer, he draws a ton of hype, his ADP creeps up, and he produces well when he's healthy, but he has yet to elevate himself to the next level, as a surefire WR1. Notoriously inconsistent on a game-to-game basis, over half of Diggs' TDs last year came in Week 11 or later. He's also never played a full 16-game slate in his four years in the NFL due to injury woes. So, while his overall production will likely rank him among the top 15 WRs in fantasy at the end of the 2019 season, don't bank on him delivering beyond WR2 value weekly.

8. **Amari Cooper, DAL:** A midseason trade from the Raiders to the Cowboys might turn out as the best thing that ever happened to Cooper and the Dallas offense (and of course any fantasy managers that bought low on him before the trade). Up until Week 9, his first game with Dallas, Cooper had found the end zone just once all year. He promptly scored in that Week 9 game and legitimately found his groove with Dak Prescott in a Week 12 matchup against Washington where he dropped 180 yards and two TDs on eight receptions. Two games later he racked up 217 yards and THREE TDs on 10 catches. There's no doubt his fantasy arrow is pointing straight up heading into this season. His WR14 ADP in the Round 4 vicinity feels like a perfect storm for a guy who could see upwards of 120 targets as the top target in the Dallas passing attack.

9. **Cooper Kupp, LAR:** Kupp tore his ACL in Week 10 last season, ending his year with a 40/566/6 line. His absence greatly affected the efficiency of the Rams offense, a signal that Kupp is truly a game-changing kind of receiver that QB Jared Goff relies on week in and week out. He is a player you can set and forget in your fantasy lineup as a high-end WR2. In terms of his health, the goal is for Kupp to be fully healthy for the Rams' Week 1 opener. We likely won't see much of him in

the preseason, though he's still returning WR19 ADP in early mocks. If he is indeed fully healthy and ready to rock by Week 1, that value is unbeatable.

10. **Brandin Cooks, LAR:** The WR13 last year in both standard and PPR formats, Cooks was boom-or-bust from a week-to-week basis. When QB Jared Goff has solid options all around him, there are going to be games where not everybody gets to eat. Two of Cooks' five regular-season touchdowns came in Week 17, so they weren't fantasy-relevant outside of DFS. Despite Cooper Kupp's season-ending injury, Cooks didn't have a strong end to his campaign from a fantasy standpoint. Still, any receiver with the absurd speed and burst that Cooks possesses in a high-octane offense like the Rams is going to be a coveted fantasy asset. He's being drafted in the Round 5 area according to early ADP data, and that feels about right for a WR you can feel comfortable flexing every week.

11. **Robert Woods, LAR:** In his second year with the Rams, Woods posted career bests across the board, leading his receiving corps with 130 targets that he converted into an 86/1219/6 line and was fantasy's WR10 in standard and WR11 in PPR. There's clear chemistry between Woods and QB Jared Goff and that was on display during some of Woods' biggest games. With Cooper Kupp coming off an ACL injury and Brandin Cooks on the outside to open up the top, Woods has solidified himself as a consistent producer compared to Cooks, whose value is volatile week to week. Woods feels like a steal as early ADP data shows him coming off draft boards in Round 5 as the WR17. He should outproduce that value easily as long as he's healthy.

12. **Kenny Golladay, DET:** In his second season in the NFL, Golladay led the Detroit Lions in receiving with a 70/1,063/5 line and finished as the WR21 in standard scoring. He's lived up to his "Babytron" moniker (credit to JJ Zachariason of numberFire for the nickname), making incredible catches all over the field. The scary (in a good way) part is that Golladay is primed to be even better this season. He'll enter the year as Detriot's de facto No. 1, and early ADP data has him going as the WR17, somewhere in Round 5. He'll be a value there, if he does indeed produce at a higher level than he did a season ago, which is a virtual lock as long as he stays healthy.

SOLID OPTIONS

1. **Allen Robinson, CHI:** The former Jacksonville Jaguar came into the 2018 season with some sleeper hype after missing all of the previous season with a torn ACL. But on a new Bears offense, A-Rob finished only as the WR41 in standard scoring despite leading the receiving corps in yardage. Given his track record, Robinson could improve on his 55/754/4 line as Chicago's young offense continues to hone its identity with Mitchell Trubisky under center. Though Robinson will be competing for targets with Anthony Miller, Riley Ridley, Taylor Gabriel, Trey Burton and Tarik Cohen, the big-bodied Penn State product should produce low-end WR2 numbers at worst.

2. **Julian Edelman, NE:** Coming off yet another Super Bowl victory (and Super Bowl MVP award), Edelman has an early ADP of WR20, near the end of Round 5. That seems kind of ridiculous considering he'll be 32 years old, and his quarterback will be 42 entering the season. But when has Edelman ever let you down in terms of fantasy production, when healthy? The Patriots WR depth chart is as thin as it ever was, and Edelman will soak up targets as he always has. He should remain a consistent WR2 as long as he's on the field.

3. **Alshon Jeffery, PHI:** Jeffery started last season in Week 4 as he was recovering from offseason shoulder surgery, yet he still managed to finish as the WR26 in standard scoring. He led the Eagles receiving corps with 843 yards and scored six times. Jeffery could be a sneaky pickup in drafts this year, as he's really only competing with tight end Zach Ertz for target share (along with Nelson Agholor and DeSean Jackson, with an outside threat from rookie J.J. Arcega-Whiteside). When he's fully healthy, Jeffery has potential to be in the low-end WR2 conversation, and that's where he will be entering 2019.

4. **Sammy Watkins, KC:** Watkins only played 10 games during the regular season last year for the Chiefs, but he came up for air with 114 yards on four receptions in the AFC Championship against the Patriots. That performance revived some optimism that Watkins might still be a thing for fantasy purposes. Though Watkins' foot injury issues will always be a looming concern, plus now that Tyreek Hill is playing a full season original offseason projections need to be scaled back.

5. **Mike Williams, LAC:** When Williams was given a chance to shine last year, he took major advantage. On a Chargers team loaded with talent, the 2017 first-round draft pick was a red-zone monster, especially in a memorable Week 15 game against the Chiefs in which he posted three total touchdowns on nine targets and a game-winning two-point conversion; Kansas City simply couldn't cover the 6-foot-4, 218-pound specimen in and around the end zone. He was one of only three wideouts to score six TDs from inside the 10-yard line (Davante Adams, Michael Thomas) and planted his flag as Philip Rivers' go-to No. 2 receiver opposite Keenan Allen. Williams caught a tough break in missing his entire rookie year due to injury, but he displayed what he's capable of when given the opportunity last season. There's nowhere to go but up for the talented Clemson product, and 2019 could be a breakout campaign. His early ADP often finds him going outside the top 50 overall picks, a value he should have no problem outperforming.

6. **Tyler Lockett, SEA:** Lockett expanded his horizons in 2018. He saw an identical number of targets (71) as he did the previous year, yet he dropped a 57/965/10 line compared to 45/555/2 in 2017. With an average of 10.3 standard FPPG, Lockett finished as the WR11 in standard scoring. With WR1 upside once again, Lockett is one of the best deep-ball receivers in the league, so he doesn't need to rely on volume to produce. His Round 6 or 7 ADP feels like a bargain at this point, though it may be tough for him to repeat double-digit touchdowns.

RED FLAGS

1. **Will Fuller, HOU:** Fuller is a stud fantasy asset when he's on the field, but he's played in just 17 games over the last two seasons due to various injuries, hence this designation. His most recent injury was an ACL tear last year, and it seems like he's tracking well in his rehab. His speed supplies major fantasy upside, but proceed with caution and have some insulation at WR if you take a chance on Fuller on draft day.

2. **Larry Fitzgerald, ARI:** The veteran receiver fell off a statistical cliff a season ago, posting a 69/734/6 line after three straight campaigns of at least 100 receptions and 1,000 receiving yards. That onus did not fall entirely on Fitz himself, but more so the dullness of a Cardinals offense led by rookie QB Josh Rosen and head coach Steve Wilks for most of the year. Arizona landed top QB draft prospect Kyler Murray and have a new head coach in place in Kliff

Kingsbury, who coached 2018 NFL MVP Patrick Mahomes at Texas Tech. While Fitz should not be completely dismissed in drafts, his advanced age (he'll be 36 at season kickoff) has become a perennial concern to his value in 2019, even with the injection of youth (again) behind center.

3. **Anthony Miller, CHI:** A rookie last season, Miller played through a shoulder injury he suffered in Week 3, which required surgery back in January, so he's likely to be limited in preseason training activities. Miller is an exciting young talent with a ton of potential in the Bears' offense as an explosive slot man, but the shoulder injury has landed him in this concerning group heading into draft season.

4. **DeSean Jackson, PHI:** D-Jax is back with his old squad for the 2019 campaign. He came out of the gate hot last year, scoring three TDs in his first two games with Ryan Fitzpatrick slinging bombs, but after that magical run, Jackson fell off. He also suffered an Achilles injury, which at age 32 isn't great for his outlook going forward. The Eagles were optimistic enough to ink him to a three-year deal, but fantasy managers should remain cautious, despite the fact that Jackson will likely begin the year as the team's No. 2 receiver opposite Alshon Jeffery.

UP & COMING

1. **D.J. Moore, CAR:** Moore made an immediate impact as a rookie, posting a 55/788/2 line in his first year in the NFL. Not necessarily a TD magnet, Moore put up consistent production and proved more valuable in a PPR format. But heading into 2019, Moore projects as the Panthers' WR1, which should open up the door for more opportunities to score, among other things like soaking up targets. His early ADP in late Round 7 feels like a huge value considering his production is almost guaranteed to increase by default this year.

2. **Calvin Ridley, ATL:** Ridley set the fantasy football world on fire in his first month in the NFL. In his first three games, Ridley scored six TDs (including a three-TD game with 146 yards) and skyrocketed to the top of the WR rankings for a couple of weeks. He eventually leveled out but was a key contributor to the Falcons pass game all season, opposite Julio Jones. As a rookie, he amassed an impressive 64/821/10 line, and while he may not reach double-digit TDs two seasons in a row (though, there's a chance he does), he's likely to see more growth in his second year. Early ADP data shows Ridley going frequently as the WR25 in Round 7, but his draft stock may creep higher if he makes waves in camp. Either way, he should return solid WR2 numbers at worst.

3. **Courtland Sutton DEN:** At 6-foot-3, 218 pounds, Sutton has the size and athletic ability to become a main contributor for Denver. With veteran Demaryius Thomas gone and Emmanuel Sanders still recovering from an Achilles injury, Sutton has an opportunity to become The Guy for Joe Flacco. A somewhat underwhelming rookie campaign (84/702/4) has some skeptical that Sutton can develop into a legit WR1 at the NFL level, but he's worth taking a chance on at his Round 9 asking price as he may easily become the lead target in Denver.

4. **Dante Pettis, SF:** As a rookie, Pettis led San Francisco receivers in fantasy points with a 27/467/5 line despite missing several games with a knee injury. While 27 receptions doesn't really move the needle, Pettis' expected role in 2019 is generating hype. Down the stretch last year, he averaged 6.1 targets per game and is projected at the team's No. 1 receiver with the healthy return of Jimmy Garoppolo under center. His Round 9 ADP in the early going makes for an intriguing middle-rounds WR selection who could end up paying huge dividends if he takes the next step as a pro.

5. **Christian Kirk, ARI:** Late last season, Kirk was touted by fantasy analysts as a waiver-wire target because of his reliable involvement in the Cardinals offense. Even in that stagnant environment, Kirk managed a 43/59/3 line, and he played 79 percent of his team's WR snaps, second only to Larry Fitzgerald. Kirk broke his foot last December, so his rehab should be monitored this summer. But the arrival of Kyler Murray in Arizona is a boon to Kirk's potential outlook, as the two played together for a brief stretch at Texas A&M. Kirk's Round 9 ADP is likely to climb as this narrative expands throughout the preseason, and he could have an explosive campaign.

6. **Chris Godwin, TB:** The departures of DeSean Jackson and Adam Humphries should open up more playing time for the third-year receiver, who played just 44.8 percent of his team's offensive snaps last year. Godwin still saw 95 targets, which he converted into a 59/842/7 line, ranking second on the team in receiving yards and TDs behind Mike Evans. Godwin is an extremely talented player. His new head coach, Bruce Arians, as already stated he thinks Godwin can be a "100-catch guy," and all signs point to him being the team's go-to slot man in 2019. The hype train has left the station, as Godwin's early ADP data shows him going in Round 6, and that value will probably creep up as we see exactly how the Bucs intend to use him in what will be a new scheme under a new staff.

7. **D.K. Metcalf, SEA:** The top WR prospect in the 2019 NFL Draft, the Seahawks traded up to secure the 6-foot-3, 228-pound Ole Miss product. Metcalf destroyed at the NFL Combine, proving his athleticism unmatched in this rookie class. Size and speed make up the ideal combination for a wideout, but there's some speculation that he's still too raw to be a complete WR1 at the NFL level. Metcalf is a key player to watch develop in training camp and preseason, because if he takes advantage of his expected role as Seattle's WR1, he could become an unheard-of bargain as he's currently valued somewhere in Round 10.

MATCHUP PLAYS

1. **Robby Anderson, NYJ:** Anderson has led the Jets in receiving yards, TDs and targets each of the last two seasons and projects as the team's No. 1 option again this year. The speedster is more than capable to handle those duties, but he still has yet to eclipse the 1,000-yard mark in his three seasons in the NFL, but the potential is there with young QB Sam Darnold still developing. The Jets offense should be more productive following some coaching staff changes and additions of talented players like RB Le'Veon Bell. Anderson's outlook is optimistic, but he will likely remain a week-to-week option based on matchups.

2. **Corey Davis, TEN:** Davis saw 112 targets as the Titans' No. 1 receiver last year, but his 65/891/4 line left something to be desired as a guy who was drafted with high expectations. It's not Davis' talent in question; its more about his situation in a run-first Titans offense. He'll have some competition for looks with slot man Adam Humphries joining the team in free agency and potential star rookie A.J. Brown now in the fold. Davis will have some value, but he profiles as more of a fill-in than a weekly starter for most fantasy formats in 2019.

3. **Marvin Jones Jr., DET:** The Lions receiver suffered a knee injury last year, ending his season in Week 10. The emergence of Kenny Golladay as the top target in Detroit signals that Jones will continue to play second fiddle as a receiver in this run-first offense. Jones is always a difficult player to profile for fantasy purposes because his ceiling is sky-high, but his floor can be a scary basement-level low; he failed to eclipse 56 yards in three of his of his first four games last year. He's no more than a bench-depth pick in drafts this summer, considering his knee issues and the fact that he's always been a boom-or-bust fantasy producer.

4. **Dede Westbrook, JAC:** Westbrook led Jaguars receivers in targets last year (101), logging a 66/717/5 line in his second pro season. His production was inconsistent, though, and his only real spike weeks were TD-dependent. Still, with new quarterback Nick Foles in Jacksonville, Westbrook's arrow is pointing up. His Round 11 ADP seems a little rich, given his volatile track record, but with Marquise Lee still recovering from a knee injury that ended his 2018 campaign, Westbrook has a chance to further establish himself as the team's No. 1 option in the early going.

5. **John Brown, BUF:** Another offseason mover, Brown landed in Buffalo and will now have a chance to pair his ridiculous speed with that cannon of an arm holstered by second-year QB Josh Allen. The duo is primed to hook up on a slew of deep balls, the way Brown did with Joe Flacco in Baltimore at the start of last season. Brown's production fell off at the end of the season after the Ravens put Lamar Jackson under center and the offense turned into a ground-and-pound unit. Now, Brown's arrow is pointing up in Buffalo, yet early ADP data shows him as the WR57, virtually a free pick going in the 14th round. He'll be an amazing value selection if things remain that way, but something tells me Brown's ADP is set to climb.

WATCH LIST

1. **Michael Gallup, DAL:** As a rookie last season, Gallup posted a 33/507/2 line and wasn't of much use in fantasy leagues. Now trending upward, the second-year pro had some big games down the stretch and is expected to be Dallas' WR2 opposite Amari Cooper. After Cooper was traded to the Cowboys last season, Gallup's targets per game average bumped up from 3.1 to 5.1. He should see plenty of opportunities and out-return his late-round ADP.

2. **Keke Coutee, HOU:** Entering his second NFL season, Coutee can be considered a sleeper with a Round 12 ADP in the early goings. Coutee dealt with lingering hamstring injuries throughout his rookie campaign and managed to post a meager 28/287/1 line in the six games he played. The slot man in an offense with upside, Coutee is worth consideration if he can get through the preseason without any hammy scares.

3. **Curtis Samuel, CAR:** A versatile offensive weapon, Samuel scored seven total TDs last year to go along with 494 receiving yards and 84 rush yards. Now entering his third season in the NFL, he's been promoted, expected to play the role of WR2 opposite D.J. Moore in Carolina's offense. Samuel is at worst third in line for targets behind RB Christian McCaffrey and Moore. It may not translate into a ton of fantasy value out of the gate, but Samuel is a player worth a monitor or a late dart throw.

4. **Kenny Stills, MIA:** Here's a direct quote from my profile on Stills from last season's edition of the Black Book: "It's about time we stop devaluing Kenny Stills. He simply might be the most reliable WR on the Dolphins roster." He only went on to lead one of the worst offenses in the NFL with six receiving TDs and managed 553 yards on 37 catches along the way. In a new system in Miami with second-year Josh Rosen under center, Stills should improve on his 2018 season, and if that's the case, he's an end-of-draft bargain.

5. **Devin Funchess, IND:** Considering that Chester Rodgers ranked third in targets for Indy (behind T.Y. Hilton and Eric Ebron) last year, it makes sense the team would go out and get a big-bodied WR like Funchess for Andrew Luck to zing the rock toward. Funchess had a down 2018 season with just a 44/549/4 line to follow up his much better 2017 production of 63/840/8. Though TE Jack Doyle's presence still casts doubts, Funchess would obviously be a red-zone weapon and he has some upside considering his Round 11 ADP.

FOR MORE WRITEUPS ON THE ROOKIE WR CLASS,

GO TO THE ROOKIE/DYNASTY CHAPTER

BY SCOTT BOGMAN

Chapter 7

TIGHT ENDS

STANDARD SCORING RPV

TE1

	Player	RPV
1	Travis Kelce	49%
2	George Kittle	31%
3	O.J. Howard	24%
4	Zach Ertz	13%
5	Eric Ebron	7%
6	Hunter Henry	-5%
7	Jared Cook	-12%
8	Evan Engram	-15%
9	David Njoku	-19%
10	Austin Hooper	-24%
11	Chris Herndon IV	-24%
12	Delanie Walker	-25%

TE2

	Player	RPV
1	Trey Burton	20%
2	Vance McDonald	10%
3	Kyle Rudolph	10%
4	T.J. Hockenson	8%
5	Noah Fant	8%
6	Josh Oliver	7%
7	Mike Gesicki	1%
8	Mark Andrews	-1%
9	Jack Doyle	-11%
10	Austin Seferian-Jenkins	-15%
11	Jordan Reed	-16%
12	Greg Olsen	-17%

½ & FULL-POINT PPR SCORING

TE1

	Player	RPV
1	Travis Kelce	50%
2	George Kittle	27%
3	Zach Ertz	23%
4	O.J. Howard	9%
5	Hunter Henry	-2%
6	Eric Ebron	-9%
7	Evan Engram	-10%
8	Jared Cook	-13%
9	David Njoku	-16%
10	Austin Hooper	-18%
11	Trey Burton	-19%
12	Delanie Walker	-21%

TE2

	Player	RPV
1	Chris Herndon IV	13%
2	Vance McDonald	10%
3	T.J. Hockenson	8%
4	Kyle Rudolph	7%
5	Noah Fant	5%
6	Josh Oliver	4%
7	Mike Gesicki	0%
8	Mark Andrews	-5%
9	Jordan Reed	-8%
10	Jack Doyle	-9%
11	Jimmy Graham	-11%
12	Greg Olsen	-14%

RPV ANALYSIS

Joe Pisapia

There's clearly a "have and have not" scenario at TE this year. In PPR, being part of the "have" or elite group is worth the aggressiveness because the drop off is so severe. The middle level can stay competitive. However, they're not without their question marks, either. In the past, one team had Rob Gronkowski, and that was the one team that had a significant RPV advantage. Now there's three of those types and the Antonio Gates class of middle tier has basically disappeared.

In standard, you can live with the TE group that has red-zone appeal. Catch a TD and you're a TE1 that week. But even there, those elite guys are arguably MORE valuable based on their roles in the offense. We can hope that youth emerges and cuts the deficit, but that's not a lock to happen.

POSITION OVERVIEW & PLAYER PROFILES

Derek Brown

The tight end position carries the most drastic and well-defined tier break of any other position in a weekly fantasy lineup.

Draft strategies vary but many times fall into two distinct schools of thought. "Paying up" and selecting an elite option in one of the early rounds or "punting" the position and chasing talented players with a conceivable path to volume upside. Another variant of mining value relative to the average draft position does exist, but that is subject to other factors such as the skill of other fantasy GMs in the league, scoring format, and sometimes locale. Some fantasy gamers tend to reach for the position when the stars align and their favorite or local team rosters one of the elites at this position. The tight end position for 2019 presents a myriad of options for fantasy players of varying palates.

THE ELITE

1. **Travis Kelce, KC:** Being the king is nice. Kelce sits upon the iron throne for tight ends as the TE1 in point-per-reception (PPR) scoring in each of the last three seasons. Kelce's offseason ankle surgery looks to be of minimal concern as early reports have him scheduled to be ready for camp. Heading into his age-30 season, Kelce has been a consistent weekend warrior, having missed only one game during the past five seasons. As crazy as it is to say for a player coming off career highs in targets (150), receptions (103), receiving yards (1336) and receiving touchdowns (10), we may have still not seen Kelce's ceiling. Kelce has seen an increase in targets in each of the last five seasons and remains the team's best weapon inside the red zone. Kelce looks primed for another legendary season in 2019.

2. **Zach Ertz, PHI:** Ertz reached rarified air in 2018, breaking out in a big way with his first 1,000-yard-receiving (1,163) season while also breaking Jason Witten's single-season record for receptions with 116 grabs. During Ertz's three previous seasons he hovered around the 110

target range, but in 2018 he saw a massive bump in usage with 156 targets. Some of that could be attributed to his evolution as a player, but with the Eagles' wide receivers struggling with role (Golden Tate), regression (Nelson Agholor), and the lack of a vertical threat in the offense, other elements were also definitely in play. Regardless of the quarterback under center, many weeks Ertz was the one dependable weapon in the pass game both regarding talent and matchups. In 2018 the Eagles played nine games against teams in the bottom half of the league in defending against the tight end position. Ertz is in line for another stellar season, but with the Eagles offseason influx of a vertical threat (DeSean Jackson), a full season from Alshon Jeffery and talented players in the draft (JJ Arcega-Whiteside), Ertz is in line for some volume regression. Ertz's elite red-zone role (fourth in the NFL in RZ targets in 2018) will keep him firmly entrenched amongst the top tier of tight ends, despite any volume concerns.

3. **George Kittle, SF:** Kittle entered Year 2 in the NFL and bodyslammed every "Kyle Shanahan doesn't feature tight ends" narrative hard upon the mat for a quick three count. Kittle rode the lightning of a perfect storm of events in the San Francisco passing offense to breaking the NFL single-season receiving yardage record for a tight end. The 49ers offense saw Pierre Garcon fall off the age/injury cliff, Jerick McKinnon lost to a torn ACL, and Dante Pettis and Marquise Goodwin both miss significant time with injuries. Kittle proved that he not only can succeed as the number one option in a passing game but as a dangerous downfield threat in doing so. Over the last 10 years only Kittle, Vernon Davis and Rob Gronkowski have logged a season with 75 or more targets, 15 yards per reception and 10 yards per target. Kittle's inline role as a devastating blocker cements his position as a tight end, but make no mistake: Kittle's elite athleticism and playmaking ability cement his standing in the passing offense despite the return of McKinnon and incoming players such as Deebo Samuel.

TOP TALENT

1. **O.J. Howard, TB:** Howard's two years in the NFL have consistently left us wanting more. While Howard did play 14 games in 2017, the fact is he has not been able to stay on the field for a full season yet. Howard succumbed to season-ending injuries in both years with foot and ankle sprains that robbed him of a combined 10 games. Last season, Howard saw his pass-game usage increase with a bump from 2.78 targets per game in games he started to five targets per game in 2018. When on the field, Howard has flashed game-changing talent. Of the 25 tight ends to finish with 45 or more targets, Howard finished with the seventh-highest catch rate (70.8 percent) despite leading all players in yards per target (11.77); you wouldn't think a big-play type would have that. In those eight games, Howard started last year he finished: as a top-10 tight end in 62.5 percent of them and a top-five option in 37.5 percent. The fear for many heading into 2019 is "will Bruce Arians use Howard when he has never featured a tight end heavily previously?". Contrary to popular opinion, when Arians has had talent at the tight end position, he has utilized it. No, the injury-riddled husk of Jermaine Gresham does not count. When Arians was with the Steelers, they never finished higher than 18th in the NFL in pass attempts, but over that same period, Heath Miller averaged 76 targets. Also in 2012 with Indy, Arians funneled 18.5 percent of the target share through Coby Fleener and Dwayne Allen. Arians will prominently feature a player like Howard, who has flashed both elite efficiency and athletic ability.

2. **Evan Engram, NYG:** Engram steps into Year 3 with opportunity again knocking at the door. Gone is Odell Beckham and his target domination, thus paving the way for a new lead dog to rise to

the top of the pack. During his rookie season, Engram was the only act in town, which returned productive but inefficient results. This year, Engram is poised to reap the benefits this year as a more refined player. Engram increased his catch rate from a paltry 55.7 percent in Year 1 to 70.3 percent in 2018. Also despite being third on the team in targets (65), Engram still managed to lead the team in yards after the catch (398). Engram showed both the ability to capitalize on the volume he was presented and create on his own with it. Engram finished the home stretch of the 2018 season with a bang with three consecutive top-five tight end finishes and surpassed 66 yards receiving in each of his final five games. The Giants are holding elections for the new president of targets in 2019, and presently Engram presents a strong case to win the candidacy. Engram will be a solid tight end in 2019 with the upside to ascend to that elite tier if all breaks right and he turns potential into upper echelon production.

3. **Hunter Henry, LAC:** After an uneventful cameo in the playoffs last season, Henry should enter 2019 with a clean bill of health and fully recovered from a torn ACL. Henry as a darling of the hype machine in previous seasons which to his credit has been well deserved. Henry on a per-game production basis over his first two seasons compares very favorably to two top shelf fantasy tight end producers in Zach Ertz and Greg Olsen. All three of these players averaged between 2.8 to 3.1 receptions per game (Henry, 2.8), 32.2 to 36.6 receiving yards per game (Henry, 36.4), and 0.2 to 0.4 touchdowns per game (Henry, 0.4) during their first two years. The volume is there for the taking for Henry with Tyrell Williams and presumably Antonio Gates gone, freeing up 110 targets and 16 red-zone targets from 2018. While ascending talent Mike Williams is in line to garner more looks in the passing game, Henry is deserving of a volume bump as well. In 13 career games of 5 or more targets, Henry has surpassed 60 yards receiving in eight games while scoring seven touchdowns. Henry still possesses the talent and upside to tap into a top-five finish at the position while also maintaining a floor as a top 12 option.

SOLID OPTIONS

1. **Jared Cook, NO:** Cook has tantalized fantasy gamers with standout play in spurts (2016 playoffs with Green Bay). At age 31, Cook finally put together the type of season many have longed for since his early-career flashes with the Titans. Cook is coming off a career year in every sense of the phrase, setting new highwater marks for targets (101), receptions (68), receiving yards (896) and receiving touchdowns (six). The big question is can Cook continue his late-career production surge this season when he's not the only pass-game weapon by default. The Saints were one of the dream landing spots where a player with Cook's skill set could have hoped to land. The first thought of many is to harken back to Jimmy Graham's mammoth seasons in the Big Easy, but let's squash that right now. A 32-year-old Cook is not even in the same stratosphere as a career-prime Graham. Does this mean Cook is going to be a bust this upcoming season? No. Looking at the post-Graham usage of the tight end by the Saints has Cook looking like a reliable option for 2019. From 2015-2018, Coby Fleener and Ben Watson rotated seasons as the primary tight end in New Orleans. Each of them had one healthy season in that four-year span during which each garnered over 70.5 percent of the tight end targets. Watson finished with 110 targets in 2015 and Fleener with 81 in 2016. With a similar volume outlook, Cook will be a steady option as the No. 3 target in the Saints aerial attack.

2. **Vance McDonald, PIT:** McDonald is walking into an enormous opportunity in 2019. Antonio Brown and Jesse James moving on in the offseason opens up 207 targets overall, including 29 in the red zone, on a Steelers team that led the league in pass attempts in 2018. McDonald is coming off a career high in targets (72) despite splitting time with James last year. McDonald will

be an everydown tight end this season with James gone, and if last season's small sample size says anything, he is in for a spike in production. McDonald logged over 70 percent of the snaps in two games last season, and in both weeks, he finished as a top-10 tight end. The Steelers did not invest significant resources in pass-catching options by adding the ever-underwhelming Donte Moncrief in free agency, Diontae Johnson in the third round of the draft and Zach Gentry in the fifth. Despite his impressive college resume, James Washington did not show anything in his rookie season to suggest he is capable or ready to be heavily counted on this year. McDonald has a clear path to slot in as the No. 2 option in this passing offense behind JuJu Smith-Schuster.

3. **Austin Hooper, ATL:** Entering his age-25 season, Hooper has seen his targets, receptions, and receiving yards increase each year in the league. Coming off an 88-target season, Hooper emerged as a consistent outlet for Matt Ryan. Dirk Koetter's return to Atlanta should be seen as a positive for Hooper. During Koetter's last two coaching stops, he has prominently featured the tight end position down the field and around the goal line. Last year in Tampa Bay, O.J. Howard and Cameron Brate combined for 19 red-zone targets, which would have finished tied with George Kittle for fourth among tight ends. Unlike Howard and Brate, Hooper is not splitting his workload with another tight end of consequence on the Falcons roster. The only thing capping Hooper's value and not placing him higher on this list is that at best he slots in for targets behind Julio Jones and Calvin Ridley, but more likely ends up contending with Mohamed Sanu most weeks as the third option for Ryan.

4. **David Njoku, CLE:** Last season Njoku took another step forward from raw, toolsy prospect to productive NFL player. After changes in the coaching personnel during the season with the Browns moving from Todd Haley to Freddie Kitchens, Njoku's season and usage look like a tale of two halves. During the first half of last year Njoku ranked fifth in targets (51), eighth in receptions (31) and 14th in receiving yards (297) among tight ends. Over the second half of last year, however, Njoku ranked 15th in targets (37), 14th in receptions (25) and eighth in receiving yards (342) among tight ends. With the coaching change, Njoku saw his volume dip tremendously as he had five games of seven or more targets through his first eight contests, only to not reach the seven-target mark again until the season's final week. Njoku wasn't receiving the same attention from Baker Mayfield over the second half, but Njoku saw his downfield, field-stretching usage spike. Njoku saw his yards per reception surge from 9.58 through the first eight games to 13.68 after the season's midpoint. Todd Monken arrives in Cleveland after serving as the offensive coordinator for the Buccaneers in 2018. As discussed previously, O.J. Howard was used as downfield weapon under Monken. Look for Njoku's 2019 to more closely mirror his late-season 2018 usage on deep passes, which saw him finish as the 10th-ranked tight end in PPR over that stretch of games. The arrival of Odell Beckham creates some cosmetic concerns regarding Njoku's target share. Baker Mayfield will take the reins more entering his second season. Monken's offense last year finished in the top four in the NFL in passing attempts, passing yards and passing touchdowns. Any concerns with Njoku can be put to bed with the Browns looking to get pass-happier in 2019. Njoku will again be a low-end TE1 with upside should he fall into the end zone a few more times in what will be a vastly improved offense.

RED FLAGS

1. **Greg Olsen, CAR:** Before foot injuries derailed Olsen's 2017 and 2018 seasons, he had been a perennial top-seven tight end in PPR every year since his breakout in 2012. During Olsen's last two injury-shortened seasons, his high-volume role began to wane as his targets slid from the 7.2 per game he averaged from 2013-2016 to 5.42 in 2017 and 5.0 in 2018. Olsen compensated for this decrease in pass-game looks from Cam Newton with an active role near the goal line. During the seven games in 2018 in which Olsen was near full health, he garnered six targets near paydirt. If Olsen can prove the foot injuries are a thing of the past, he could return value as a mid-tier top-12 fantasy tight end even if his elite statistical production is behind him.

2. **Delanie Walker, TEN:** Walker enters this season rehabbing a broken ankle that cost him nearly all of last year. Before 2018, Walker was the epitome of consistency, having finished his previous four seasons with 60 or more receptions and 800 or more receiving yards in each year. The odds are stacked against the 35-year-old to assume his prior level of production. The Titans evolved into a run-centric team in 2018. Even with the assumed health of Marcus Mariota, that outlook does not appear any rosier. The Titans were 31st in the NFL in pass attempts over the entire season (27.3 per game). With Mariota under center, that figure remained relatively unchanged at 27 pass attempts per game. Over the last 20 years, only Shannon Sharpe, Tony Gonzalez and Ben Watson have surpassed 60 receptions and 700 receiving yards after reaching age 35. The Titans also added other weapons in the pass game this offseason in Adam Humphries and A.J. Brown, which makes the picture for Walker even bleaker.

3. **Jimmy Graham, GB:** Graham rebounded from a career-threatening injury to post a top-10 fantasy tight end season (TE6, PPR) and led the position in touchdowns in 2017. Unfortunately, 2018 was not nearly as kind to Graham as he looked every bit the part of the aging veteran. Graham is definitively on the downslope of his career. The last two seasons have seen Graham post the two lowest yards-per-target averages of his career. Of the bottom three catch rates of Graham's career, two of those seasons have come in 2017 (59.4 percent) and 2018 (61.8 percent). Graham must now also contend with Packers third-round pick Jace Sternberger. At the collegiate level, Sternberger's prowess sat in the passing game and not as a run blocker. While Sternberger will not usurp Graham's starting role, any dent he makes in Graham's snaps or targets could knock a declining veteran further down the fantasy ranks in 2019.

4. **Kyle Rudolph, MIN:** Rudolph exploded in 2016 as the apple of Sam Bradford's eye, but over the next two seasons, Rudolph has settled in as a reliable but unspectacular fantasy option. Rudolph has hovered around the 80-target mark in back-to-back seasons. Taking a closer look at Rudolph in 2018 reveals a player trending in the wrong direction for 2019. With Adam Thielen and Stefon Diggs taking the red-zone reins, Rudolph saw his red-zone target share decrease from 31.3 percent (2017) to 21.4 percent (2018). Outside of Rudolph's massive Week 16 box score, the rest of his season was a disappointment. Week 16 versus the Lions accounted for 19.2 percent of his receiving yardage and half of his touchdowns for the season. With the Vikings investing significantly in Irv Smith in the second round of the draft, Rudolph's chances of repeating as a top-12 tight end have grown even slimmer.

5. **Jack Doyle & Eric Ebron, IND:** With Doyle out for much of the 2018 season, Ebron took full advantage of the lack of a secondary passing option. Ebron set career marks across the board while also leading all tight ends in touchdowns. Outside of Doyle's return, the Colts pass catcher corps got a bump with during the offseason with the additions of Parris Campbell and Devin Funchess. Funchess, Ebron and Doyle look to play similar roles for Andrew Luck as the intermediate option across the middle of the field and red zone. Attempting to project how the

Colts will divide up targets amongst these dubious options is difficult. If trying to narrow this down to which tight end from this depth chart to target, the clear answer is Doyle. In the five full games last year in which Doyle and Ebron both played, Doyle out-targeted Ebron overall (29 to 15) as well as in the red zone (six to four). Doyle's snap percentage in those weeks never dipped below 76.1 percent while Ebron's never rose above 40 percent. Considering Doyle's injury and Ebron's output last year, Doyle will fall in drafts. With the target shares for both looking muddy, the best course of action is to draft the player who will make it to the later rounds.

6. **Jordan Reed, WAS:** Reed accomplished a rare feat last season. Reed's 13 games played last year marked the second-highest total of his career. Health issues have been a consistent theme during Reed's entire career. With a laundry list of medical maladies over the years, Reed looked like a player whose athleticism and playmaking ability had been sapped. Reed finished with the lowest average of receptions per game (4.2) and catch rate (64.3 percent) of his career. Reed limps into 2019 with the Redskins adding a bevy of players on the offensive side of the ball. A bounce-back season for Reed does not appear to be in the cards even if he can stay on the field again.

MATCHUP PLAYS

1. **Trey Burton, CHI:** All the "second coming of Travis Kelce" ballyhoo that surrounded Burton heading into last season probably left many disappointed at the end of the year. Burton was a middle-of-the-road option at tight end who never measured up to the effusive love fest from the offseason. Burton only tallied three games in which he was targeted seven or more times. Those three contests accounted for nearly a third of Burton's season-long target total. Nagy deployed Burton with higher frequency against teams like Detroit and Green Bay, who finished the season in the bottom half of the league against the position. While Burton will never be an elite fantasy option, many clamored for with a coach who will heavily feature him when the matchup is right. There will be value to be mined in those weeks.

2. **Tyler Eifert, CIN:** Eifert is a top matchup play when he is on the field. "On the field" is an essential caveat, though. Considering Eifert's injury history, counting on him as anything more than a matchup play is a risky proposition, to put it mildly. Eifert has played more than eight games in a season only twice in his six-year career. Chasing touchdowns is a crucial factor when looking at matchup plays, especially for the tight end position. Eifert has always excelled in filling this area of the box score through his 43 career games. Over the last 20 years amongst tight ends through the first 43 games of their career, Eifert has the fifth-most touchdowns (21). At this stage of his career, Eifert is nothing more than a bye-week fill-in or fantasy stopgap at the position.

WATCH LIST

1. **Dallas Goedert, PHI:** Goedert is an every-down tight end in an offense that is tailored to run through the position. If Zach Ertz were to miss any time, Goedert would immediately slot in as a weekly top-five option at the position regardless of scoring format. Last season, Goedert played 65 percent or more of the snaps in three games. Goedert scored a touchdown and finished as a top-seven tight end in two of those games.

2. **Ian Thomas, CAR:** After some early-season rookie acclimation last year, Thomas showed what he is capable of down the home stretch for the Panthers. In Weeks 14-17 last year, Thomas was a top-eight tight end in three of four games and the sixth-ranked tight end overall during that stretch in PPR scoring. Thomas saw 6.75 targets per game and amassed four red-zone targets. In short, Thomas in terms of production linearly replaced Greg Olsen all the while debunking the "rookie tight end struggles" narrative. Right now, Olsen is set to return in 2019, but if Olsen were to head to the booth (a la Jason Witten) or miss more time because of injury, Thomas will be poised to capitalize again.

3. **Mike Gesicki, MIA:** Gesicki lit the combine on fire last season en route to a second-round draft selection by the Dolphins. The Miami coaching staff mostly burned that pick to turn a potential matchup nightmare into a warm spot on the bench. The Dolphins lost Albert Wilson to injury, buried DeVante Parker on the inactive list and trotted out the ghost of Danny Amendola -- and still saw fit to give Gesicki only 32 targets. To put that into context leaves Gesicki ranked 40th in targets among tight ends, tied with Geoff Swaim, who only played nine games last season. Gesicki's new offensive coordinator (Chad O'Shea) might know a thing or two about how to deploy a tight end coming from New England. Also, small side note: O'Shea's first coaching job ever was as a collegiate tight ends coach.

4. **T.J. Hockenson, DET / Noah Fant, DEN:** Athletic, explosive tight end from Iowa gets drafted in the first round and lands on a team with a massive need for the position. Stop me when you've heard this one before. Hockenson and Fant landed in different situations, but both carry the high draft position to garner early opportunity and snaps. Both would be outliers if they were fantasy producers out of the gate because of their rookie status. Over the last five seasons, only four tight ends have finished their rookie season with 500 yards receiving or more (Evan Engram, George Kittle, Chris Herndon IV, Mark Andrews). Of those four tight ends, only Engram (TE5 in PPR scoring) finished higher than the 16th-ranked tight end in PPR scoring. Hockenson and Fant both enter depth charts that are concentrated for targets, and with aging receivers like Marvin Jones Jr. and Emmanuel Sanders, respectively, the room is there for either to ascend. Considering all of these factors, they are players to monitor but not draft.

UP & COMING

1. **Chris Herndon IV, NYJ:** Last year as the season wore on, Herndon carved out a role in the Jets offense. Herndon had six or more targets and 50 or more yards receiving in three of the Jets' final six games. Herndon's 2019 carries a wide range of outcomes considering the Jets' offseason moves and depth chart. Herndon showed impressive playmaking ability in his rookie season that could allow him to ascend if Jamison Crowder, Quincy Enunwa and Robby Anderson continue their injury-prone ways. Herndon could just as easily find himself buried on the target ladder behind Le'Veon Bell, Anderson, Crowder and Enunwa, just to name a few. Herndon could go primarily overlooked in drafts this year but has the talent profile and rookie-season foundation to excel should everything break right.

2. **Mark Andrews, BAL:** Andrews quietly posted an impressive rookie season. Among all rookie tight ends with 10 or more targets in 2018, Andrews finished first in receiving yards, second in yards per target and second in receiving touchdowns. The Ravens jettisoned John Brown and Michael Crabtree during the offseason. The only notable addition to the pass-catching corps was Marquise Brown during the NFL Draft. Andrews' spot in the target hierarchy will be one to monitor. Once Hayden Hurst returned from a foot fracture, the Ravens deployed Nick Boyle, Andrews and Hurst weekly to varying degrees. Boyle's acumen as a run blocker gave him the

weekly edge in snaps played, which could repeat with the Ravens looking to remain a run-centric team. The Ravens could easily continue the tight end merry-go-round or commit more to a player in Andrews who succeeded when given opportunity. Given his first-year production, Andrews could start on a path to finish the year as the Ravens' leading receive, making him a player to target at the end of drafts.

Chapter 8

KICKERS

Derek Brown

The kicker position has never been shown much love by fantasy gamers -- for a good reason. Kicker is a position of high variance and "replaceability", both from a weekly and yearlong view.

Only two kickers in 2018 had more than one week as the top-scoring kicker in fantasy, with Wil Lutz leading the way with four weeks and Ka'imi Fairbairn racking up two weeks. Over the past five seasons, only one kicker has repeated as the top-scoring kicker in fantasy (Stephen Gostkowski, 2014-2015). Looking at yearly finishes, the difference between the top-scoring kicker to the 12th-ranked kicker over the last five years is a mere 3.16 points. Kickers should be streamed weekly.

Personally, I never draft kickers and instead take a preseason or training camp flier on a player that has the possibility of being one injury away from fantasy relevance. In season, I drop kickers weekly, which depending on your league rules can free up an extra bench spot. This temporary extra bench spot can be used to pick up an additional waiver-wire name for whom you might not have the room otherwise on your roster. After waivers run and the week churns along toward Sunday, that extra player can be used in a trade to upgrade a position, deployed as a bye-week fill-in, or simply dropped Sunday before kickoff. The ability to find a kicker that fits one or both of the criteria discussed next is relatively easy, even on Sunday morning.

Two critical factors deserve attention when looking for a weekly kicker: Target a team that (1) enters the red zone often and (2) struggles to score touchdowns once in the red zone. These two factors held the highest correlation with kicker scoring in fantasy: 58.3 percent of the top 12 kickers in 2018 played for a team that finished among the top 12 in red-zone attempts per game and among the bottom half of the NFL in red-zone touchdown-scoring percentage. Offenses that met both criteria in 2018 were the Rams, Buccaneers, Texans, Panthers, Ravens, Eagles and Giants. With consideration to both criteria mentioned previously, I have tiered my top 24 kickers for 2019, weighing offenses that will have the offensive firepower to move the ball consistently but could struggle to make it into the end zone.

TIER 1
1. Greg Zuerlein, LAR
2. Justin Tucker, BAL
3. Wil Lutz, NO
4. Harrison Butker, KC
5. Adam Vinatieri, IND

TIER 2
6. Cairo Santos, TB
7. Graham Gano, CAR
8. Jake Elliott, PHI
9. Stephen Gostkowski, NE
10. Mason Crosby, GB
11. Aldrick Rosas, NYG
12. Jason Myers, SEA

TIER 3
13. Matt Prater, DET
14. Chris Boswell, PIT
15. Brett Maher, DAL
16. Giorgio Tavecchio, ATL
17. Robbie Gould, SF
18. Michael Badgley, LAC
19. Dan Bailey, MIN

TIER 4
20. Ryan Succop, TEN
21. Chandler Catanzaro, NYJ
22. Brandon McManus, DEN
23. Steven Hauschka, BUF
24. Daniel Carlson, OAK

Chapter 9

TEAM DEFENSE RANKINGS

Gary Davenport

Even in today's era of spread offenses and rules skewed heavily toward the offensive side of the ball, defenses still have some value in today's NFL. Just ask the Chiefs: Their inability to get a stop in overtime of last year's AFC Championship game cost them a trip to the Super Bowl.

That KC "defense" was truly awful.

It's a similar situation in fantasy football. Team defense is hardly the most important spot in the game; it's the least impactful position this side of kickers. But getting a big score from a team defense in a given week can still mean the difference between a win and a loss in your fantasy football league.

The best bet to get that weekly edge defensively is by "streaming." Working under the assumption that add/drops are unlimited, the smart play is to find a defense with a couple of juicy matchups early in the season that's available relatively late on draft day.

Even after an offseason of attrition, the Baltimore Ravens might fit that bill. They face the Miami Dolphins on the road in Week 1 before hosting the Arizona Cardinals in Week 2.

When these favorable matchups dry up, simply cut them or any other team loose and acquire another defense off the waiver wire. Wash, rinse, repeat.

It even works if transactions cost money (be it FAAB or cold, hard cash). You just have to be a bit more judicious in how often you turn and burn.

Maybe that makes sense to you. Maybe it doesn't, and you want an "elite" defense like the Bears you can just start every week.

Whatever the case, here's a look at the top 32 team defenses in fantasy football in 2018.

You don't want No. 33 -- largely because it doesn't exist. Kind of like Kansas City's defense.

1. **Chicago Bears:** In 2018, the Bears were third in total defense, third in sacks, first in takeaways and first in fantasy points -- by a fairly sizable margin. If I didn't know better, I'd think Khalil Mack was good at this whole football thing or something.
2. **Los Angeles Rams:** Only the Bears and Chiefs (no, really -- the Chiefs were second in fantasy points among defenses last year) outscored the Rams in 2018. Ndamukong Suh may be gone, but the Rams are still loaded with defensive talent.
3. **Jacksonville Jaguars:** The 2018 season was a nightmare for the Jaguars, who jettisoned some veterans to free up the money needed to sign Nick Foles. But Jacksonville is loaded for bear in the secondary and added Josh Allen to an already-stacked defensive line.

4. **Los Angeles Chargers:** The Chargers added a pair of rookies to an already talented defense in safety Nasir Adderley and defensive tackle Jerry Tillery. The Bolts also have arguably the best 1-2 punch at DE in the NFL in Joey Bosa and Melvin Ingram.

5. **Minnesota Vikings:** Speaking of disappointing teams, the Vikings started 2018 a Super Bowl favorite and ended it missing the playoffs. But the Vikings were a top-10 fantasy defense in 2018 and return all their impact players this season.

6. **Houston Texans:** The Texans took a hit in the secondary with the loss of safety Tyrann Mathieu and cornerback Kareem Jackson, but the Texans still have J.J. Watt and ranked inside the top 5 a year ago in both takeaways and fantasy points among defenses.

7. **Philadelphia Eagles:** Philly struggled to put up fantasy points last year, but the Eagles aren't short on talent and can probably be had much later than this on draft day. Signing inside linebacker Zach Brown in the first week of May was one of free agency's bigger steals.

8. **Cleveland Browns:** The Browns added edge-rusher Olivier Vernon in a trade with the New York Giants and got a steal in Round 2 of the NFL Draft with LSU cornerback Greedy Williams. Only the Bears had more takeaways in 2018 than the Browns.

9. **Denver Broncos:** It happened with little fanfare last year, but the Broncos were sixth among team defenses in NFL.com default fantasy scoring. Youngster Bradley Chubb and veteran Von Miller form a formidable duo of pass rushers.

10. **Dallas Cowboys:** Like the aforementioned Eagles, the Cowboys weren't really fantasy-relevant in 2018. But Dallas has young talent at all three defensive levels and gets four games against the offensive dumpster fires that are the Giants and Redskins.

11. **Pittsburgh Steelers:** The Steelers were 10th in the NFL in fantasy points among defenses in 2018 -- largely because of their league-leading 52 sacks. Pittsburgh plugged its biggest hole on that side of the ball with the addition of first-round inside linebacker Devin Bush.

12. **Baltimore Ravens:** Baltimore lost its best inside linebacker (C.J. Mosley) and two best edge-rushers (Terrell Suggs and Za'Darius Smith) in free agency and finished outside the top 12 in 2018. But man oh man those first two matchups look good.

13. **New England Patriots:** The Patriots were quietly a top-12 fantasy defense in 2018, and while the loss of top edge-rusher Trey Flowers stings, no team is better at absorbing personnel losses than Darth Hoodie and the Beantown Bombers.

14. **New Orleans Saints:** The Saints weren't a great fantasy defense a year ago, but they weren't terrible, either. New Orleans tied for fifth in the NFL with 49 sacks and ranked inside the top half of the league in takeaways. Count them as a solid matchup play.

15. **Seattle Seahawks:** Seattle finished the 2018 campaign 11th in sacks, 10th in takeaways and ninth in fantasy points among defenses. But the loss of defensive end Frank Clark looms as a real problem unless rookie L.J. Collier is a quick study up front.

16. **Indianapolis Colts:** The Colts bolstered their pass rush (in theory) with the addition of Justin Houston and possess the reigning Defensive Rookie of the Year in linebacker Darius Leonard. There could be some fantasy "sleeper" appeal with this unit in 2019.

17. **Buffalo Bills:** Buffalo ranked inside the top 10 last year in takeaways, but a 26th-place finish in sacks dropped them outside the top 20 in fantasy points. The addition of rookie defensive tackle Ed Oliver should help Buffalo improve in that latter regard.

18. **Carolina Panthers:** For years the Panthers were one of the league's best fantasy defenses. But last year, Carolina wasn't great at getting after the quarterback or taking the ball away, and it's hard to find sources of potential improvement.

19. **Atlanta Falcons:** The Falcons weren't a good defensive football team in 2018, finishing 28th in the league in total defense and 24th in fantasy points. But that was largely due to injuries to stalwarts like linebacker Deion Jones and safety Keanu Neal.

20. **San Francisco 49ers:** With the addition of Dee Ford in free agency and Nick Bosa with the No. 2 overall pick in the draft, the 49ers now have five first-round picks on the defensive line. The question is whether they'll play up to their draft slots.

21. **Kansas City Chiefs:** The Chiefs tied for the NFL lead in sacks last year and ranked inside the top 10 in takeaways. However, a new defensive scheme and a ton of personnel turnover set the Chiefs up for significant regression in both categories this year. Don't overpay for 2018 production.

22. **Washington Redskins:** The Redskins were tied for 10th in the NFL in takeaways last year, eighth in sacks and 12th in fantasy points. However, when the offense came off the rails later in the season, the defense's fantasy production cooled off substantially.

23. **New York Jets:** The Jets were a top-10 fantasy defense last year and added the likes of C.J. Mosley and rookie Quinnen Williams in the offseason. But there's a new defensive coordinator in New York this year, and the pass rush is a major question mark.

24. **Green Bay Packers:** DC Mike Pettine got a major influx of talent with free-agent veterans Za'Darius Smith and Preston Smith along with rookie Rashan Gary. But sacks weren't the problem a year ago: That was the team's measly 15 takeaways.

25. **Tennessee Titans:** Tennessee wasn't a bad defensive team in 2018, ranking eighth in total defense. But the Titans ranked outside the top 20 in sacks, takeaways and fantasy points. This unit just doesn't make enough big plays to be fantasy-relevant.

26. **Arizona Cardinals:** After one miserable year under Steve Wilks, the Cardinals are flipping back to a 3-4 base defense in 2019. A year ago, the team was excellent at chasing down quarterbacks but awful at forcing takeaways. The team's offense could put them in quite a few bad spots.

27. **Detroit Lions:** Like many of the teams ranked outside the top 20 on this list, the Lions were OK at notching sacks last year but had a terrible time forcing turnovers. There isn't much reason to suspect a big turnaround in 2019.

28. **Miami Dolphins:** The Dolphins were a top-five fantasy defense in 2018, but Miami has hemorrhaged veteran talent all offseason long as it began a ground-up rebuild. Last year's five defensive and return touchdowns also isn't a sustainable number. Gonna be a *long* year in South Beach.

29. **Tampa Bay Buccaneers:** The Buccaneers were not a good defensive team in 2018, ranking outside the top 20 in just about every category fantasy owners could possibly care about. The arrival of rookie linebacker Devin White and a new DC in Todd Bowles isn't going to magically fix that.

30. **Cincinnati Bengals:** The Bengals were the NFL's worst defense last year, allowing over 413 yards a game while ranking 28th in sacks and 21st in takeaways. If any of those numbers sound good to you, you should probably take a break for a few hours and sober up.

31. **New York Giants:** The Giants used two of their three first-round picks on defense, but there isn't a level on this unit that doesn't face serious question marks. You can do better than the Giants on fantasy draft day -- but you'd be hard-pressed to do worse.

32. **Oakland Raiders:** I said you'd be hard-pressed to do worse than the Giants, but I never said it was impossible. The league had six players last year who had more sacks individually than the 13 the Raiders tallied as a team. Ouch.

Chapter 10

WHY YOUR FANTASY LEAGUE NEEDS IDP
(And how to convince your league mates)

Gary Davenport

The National Football League in 2019 may be dominated by gaudy offensive statistics, pass-happy offenses and rules that forbid looking sternly at wide receivers (unless you play for the Los Angeles Rams), but defense still plays a big part in determining the NFL's champion.

Ask the 2018 Chiefs how important having a defense can be: The fact they didn't cost them dearly in the AFC Championship game. Or the 2017 Eagles, who won the highest-scoring Super Bowl in history when Brandon Graham strip-sacked Tom Brady.

However, in fantasy football, defense is an afterthought. Sure, there are a few "elite" team defenses that will go from the middle rounds on, but more fantasy owners than not pay about as much attention to team defenses as they do to kickers.

Relegating an entire side of the ball to kicker status is just *mean.*

However, it's not that hard to give the defense its due in fantasy football. By incorporating Individual Defensive Players into your fantasy league, you can add additional levels of excitement, fun and strategy to the game -- and avoid the ghost of Chuck Bednarik coming to your house while you sleep to stomp the crap out of you.

Don't laugh. You won't think it's funny when it happens.

WHY PLAY IDP?

The easy answer? It makes your league better.

Would the Rams have made it to the Super Bowl a year ago had Aaron Donald not been the force he was on the defensive line? Nope. And the story of that Super Bowl was the job that the Patriots did defensively on that potent young offense.

By allowing linemen like Donald, linebackers like Carolina's Luke Kuechly and defensive backs like Jamal Adams of the Jets to have their say as individuals rather than part of a (mostly irrelevant) group, you're giving those players their due, just as you would any hyped skills player on offense.

Defenders have names, positions, roles and talent same as JuJu Smith-Schuster and Todd Gurley. Lumping them into nameless, faceless, mostly valueless groups in fantasy football does a disservice to both the players and the game.

By adding Individual Defensive Players to your league, you'll be bringing that much more football into fantasy football. Bringing defense -- *real* defense -- into the game we all love. It adds more strategy. It adds more excitement. It adds more fun.

The last I checked, that's why we do this: to have fun.

OBJECTIONS

Say that after that little sales pitch from me you are *sold* -- champing at the bit to get your leaguemates to agree to add IDPs.

I know. I'm just that damned persuasive.

I guarantee to you that when you propose the addition of IDPs, at least one team owner will act like you just asked them to eat broccoli covered in monkey feces. They will object *strenuously*, claiming IDPs will ruin the league. And it's almost always one of a few standby gripes I've heard so many times throughout the years that I long ago lost count.

Here are those objections -- and how to counter them.

"IDP is too confusing."

Poppycock I say! Is PPR too confusing because you have to add a whole extra point for every catch? Here's IDP in a nutshell: Defensive linemen, linebackers and defensive backs tally fantasy points just like offensive players, only instead of getting those points for rushing yards and touchdowns they are awarded for things like tackles, sacks and interceptions.

Rocket surgery, it ain't. I'm supposedly an expert in the field, and my better half will gladly tell you I'm half a moron.

"IDP makes the draft too long."

What in the actual hell? Fantasy draft day is the absolute single best day of the year for many fantasy owners -- the Christmas of the game. Folks look forward to it for months. And now you're complaining that it's going to be too long? Do children complain that Christmas is a whole 24 hours? No, they do not, because children know what's what.

Besides, you don't have to go nuts off the get with IDPs. I'll get to that in a second.

"IDP will put me at a competitive disadvantage."

This is the preferred cop-out of folks who have never tried IDP and are scared that owners who have will wipe the floor with them.

When I first started writing about fantasy football, I chose to focus on IDPs for two reasons. The first was simple: I love the format. The second is that at the time, there weren't that many scribes who did focus on IDP. I figured I could make a name for myself more quickly.

It worked, although I like to think my rugged good looks, wit and charm had something to do with it.

The thing is, that's not the case anymore. There are all sorts of knowledgeable IDP experts out there who can help turn novices into hardened vets in no time. Whether it's draft strategy, rankings, sleepers, you name it, it's out there, whether it's my work at Fantasy Sharks, RotoWorld and The Athletic or elsewhere. And plenty of it is free.

If you're willing to do the work, of course. If you aren't, the only thing putting you at a competitive disadvantage is you.

HOW TO INTRODUCE IDP TO YOUR LEAGUE

OK, so you've climbed the mountain, made the sale: Your fantasy league is willing to give IDP a try -- or at least take a long look at doing so. Now it's nuts-and-bolts time.

First, you need a scoring system.

Stat Category	System A	System B
Tackles	1.5	2
Assists	.75 (or .5)	1
Forced/Recovered Fumbles	2	3
Interceptions	4	6
Sacks	4	6
Passes Defensed	1	1
Safeties	4	6
Defensive TDs	6	8

System A is a fairly standard scoring setup that you'll see in a large percentage of IDP leagues -- a "starter set" of course. IDPs will make a dent, but the top guys still won't be in the same league as the Odell Beckhams and Travis Kelces of the world.

System B is weighted a bit more toward the defense. It will get guys like Cleveland Browns defensive end Myles Garrett closer to the top of the fantasy heap and the top of draft boards.

Whatever works for you.

Now that you have the scoring sorted out, you need lineup requirements.

If you're willing to dive in with both feet and add a full defensive lineup of 11 players that includes separating out cornerbacks from safeties and defensive tackles from defensive ends, then God bless and good luck. The majority of first-time IDP players will get the vapors from that thought though.

There are other options available, though:

LIGHT IDP: One defensive lineman, one linebacker, one defensive back … and maybe a "flex"

The upside to this is it's easy. Folks won't be as likely to freak out, and the draft doesn't get that much longer. The downside is that in this format IDPs have no more relative value than team defenses in most standard fantasy leagues. They are late-round afterthoughts and nothing more.

MEDIUM IDP: Two DLs, two LBs, two DBs and a "flex" or two

This, or something pretty similar, is the setup you'll find in more IDP leagues than not. It's not overwhelming for novices, and there will still be a fair amount of defensive talent on the waiver wire most weeks. But there are enough IDPs that they make a real difference in matchups. Get your defensive ducks in a row, and you can gain a real edge.

HEAVY IDP: Two DEs, one DT, three LBs, two S's, one CB, two "flexes" … and a partridge in a pear tree

This is the deep end of the pool. Bedlam. Sweet, sweet chaos. Depending on scoring settings, the top IDPs in this format can be every bit as valuable as the top offensive players. The draft may be long, and starting 20 players (or more) every week may seem daunting. But once you've played this format a year or two, everything else seems tame by comparison.

You can always climb the ladder. Start with a lighter format and add IDPs gradually over the span of a few years. That's a good way to help assuage the same jitters that cause so many people to reject IDPs to begin with.

There you have it: why to add Individual Defensive Players to your fantasy football league, how to do it, and how to deal with the naysayers who equate IDP leagues to monkey-poop-covered broccoli.

I was going to go with "beat them with a foam swimming pool noodle until they relent," but people keep telling me foam violence is wrong.

You now have a step-by-step guide for how to turbocharge your fantasy football league with the addition of Individual Defensive Players.

If this doesn't work, there's just one other potential course of action: Find a better league … and better friends.

Just kidding. I'm sure they're delightful people.

For a bunch of chickens.

2019 IDP RANKINGS

Yes, the NFL now is an offensive game. Teams are scoring points and gaining yards like never before. The rules are weighted heavily toward the offense -- when the officials enforce them.

Pass interference? What's that?

But defense still plays an important role in today's NFL. You try telling J.J. Watt of the Texans, Khalil Mack of the Bears or Aaron Donald of the Rams that what they do doesn't matter. Go ahead.

I'll visit you in the hospital.

However, defense is an afterthought in fantasy football. In the overwhelming majority of leagues, team defenses are only slightly more valuable than kickers. They're not worth a second thought -- a throwaway pick at the end of the draft.

This from the dude who ranked the team defenses for this very publication.

I'm a mystery.

However, if you play in an Individual Defensive Player (IDP) league, it's a different story. Depending on the league's scoring, top defensive players like Donald and Colts linebacker Darius Leonard can have just as much fantasy value as the top running backs and wide receivers.

Once you try IDP and see the added strategy and excitement it adds to fantasy football leagues, you'll never go back.

Try it. You'll like it. Love it, even. Trust me.

Before we unveil the top 50 IDPs in 2019, some quick notes.

First, and I cannot over-emphasize this: KNOW YOUR SCORING. Scoring variances can have a huge impact on the relative value of players in IDP leagues. If your league is tackle-heavy (a scoring ratio of 3:1 or less between sacks/interceptions and tackles) then "tackle vacuum" linebackers rule the day. But if your league is big-play-heavy (4:1 or more) then pass-rushers and ball-hawking corners get a boost.

The scoring used to generate these rankings falls somewhere in between, so adjust as needed to fit your individual format.

Second, while it's tempting to acquire an elite defensive back like Jamal Adams of the Jets, keep this in mind about the position: Defensive backs are as plentiful as they are unpredictable. Adams was a stud in 2018, but he could easily tail off this year. You can wait on draft day in the secondary and still be fine.

The defensive front is the flip side of that coin. There are maybe 20 reliable weekly starters on the defensive line in a given season. This year's a bit deeper than recent ones, but it's still entirely possible that in 12-team leagues that start two (or more), someone's going to be left out.

Don't be shy about attacking the defensive line early. The depth's better at linebacker and on the back end.

With those caveats out of the way, here's a look at the:

Top 50 Individual Defensive Players for 2019

1) **Darius Leonard, OLB, IND:** Leonard was the No. 1 IDP overall last year by a wide margin, and while it's a tall order to expect a repeat, I can't rank anyone ahead of him.

2) **Bobby Wagner, ILB, SEA:** Wagner's had fewer than 110 total tackles once and less than 100 total tackles nonece. That's a word, for reals. Look it up. Inside my head.

3) **Luke Kuechly, ILB, CAR:** If he's healthy, there isn't a better linebacker in the NFL than Kuechly. His 130 total stops last year were his most since 2014.

4) **Aaron Donald, DE, LAR:** Given that Donald's the two-time defending DPOY and had approximately all the sacks ever in 2018, it almost feels like this is a low-ball ranking.

5) **J.J. Watt, DE, HOU:** Watt only had 61 total tackles and 16 sacks last year after two injury-marred campaigns. I swear, some people are just flat-out lazy.

6) **Blake Martinez, ILB, GBP:** Martinez led the NFC with 144 total tackles last year, and he's in position to once again be among the NFL leaders in that category.

7) **Leighton Vander Esch, OLB, DAL:** Vander Esch was another of last year's rookie linebackers who just went nuts, posting 140 total tackles and topping 100 solos for the season.

8) **Joey Bosa, DE, LAC:** Not only is Bosa one of the NFL's best young defensive ends, but he was also at the Battle of Winterfell. I'm not kidding even a little.

9) **Roquan Smith, ILB, CHI:** Despite no offseason to speak of thanks to a contract dispute, Smith had over 120 total tackles and five sacks as a rookie. It appears he's pretty good at the football.

10) **Deion Jones, ILB, ATL:** Between all the rookies who blew up last year and Jones' injury-marred season, he has the potential to be a massive value pick in IDP leagues in 2019.

11) **Danielle Hunter, DE, MIN:** In four seasons, Hunter has blossomed into a legitimate superstar. He piled up 72 stops and 14.5 sacks during Minnesota's disappointing 2018 season.

12) **Jamal Adams, S, NYJ:** After a shaky rookie season, Adams had his lightbulb year in 2018: 115 total tackles, 3.5 sacks and four takeaways. He's an elite talent coming into his own.

13) **Tremaine Edmunds, ILB, BUF:** Consider this a public service announcement: The best linebacker for the Buffalo Bills is going to rack up stats. It's as certain as death and heartburn after Burger King.

14) **Myles Garrett, DE, CLE:** Garrett's a DPOY-caliber talent, and Olivier Vernon's going to pull some attention off him in 2019. He's the DL to target after you grab an elite linebacker.

15) **Landon Collins, S, WAS:** Collins may be in a new home, but he didn't get all that cash from Stale Peanuts Snyder to sit on his hands. The LB in front of him might be an issue though.

16) **Lavonte David, ILB, TBB:** New Buccaneers DC Todd Bowles has long been a coach who attacks offenses with his inside linebackers. David could be set for a monster year -- if he stays healthy.

17) **Cory Littleton, ILB, LAR:** Is Littleton the most talented linebacker in the NFL? Nope. But he's solid, and if the opportunity's there, solid can stomp the crud out of talent in IDP leagues.

18) **Cameron Jordan, DE, NOS:** Jordan was long considered a low-ceiling, high-floor "steady Eddie" type in IDP leagues. Well, Eddie's piled up 25 sacks over the last two seasons. Adjust the ceiling accordingly.

19) **C.J. Mosley, ILB, NYJ:** His 2018 wasn't great, and batterymate Avery Williamson isn't cat food. But Mosley's a really good inside linebacker in his prime in a plus IDP situation. Top-10 isn't out of the question.

20) **Derwin James, S, LAC:** James was as advertised in 2018, topping 100 tackles as a rookie. The only concern is Adrian Phillips eating into his box snaps, and that's a minor one.

21) **Calais Campbell, DE, JAX:** Campbell's long been a favorite of IDP owners. 60-plus tackles and double-digit sacks the last two years launched him to a whole new level.

22) **Demarcus Lawrence, DE, DAL:** The ceiling's as high with Lawrence as any 4-3 DE in the NFL. The worry is that a lack of talent around him will mean double teams all day every day.

23) **Joe Schobert, ILB, CLE:** Don't let the trade rumors around the draft scare you off of Schobert. The Browns wanted to move him because they know he'll get paid in free agency. He's, um, good.

24) **DeForest Buckner, DT, SFO:** Buckner rolled up 12 sacks last year and is headed toward a monster payday. He's also the No. 1 defensive tackle in IDP -- and he's going to get better.

25) **Keanu Neal, S, ATL:** Like Deion Jones, Neal has the potential to be a huge value for IDP owners who are willing to look past his 2018 season that was over almost before it started.

26) **John Johnson, S, LAR:** Johnson was a top-five fantasy defensive back in most scoring systems last year and finds himself in a similar IDP situation in 2019.

27) **Jaylon Smith, ILB, DAL:** Smith appeared to finally have fully recovered from his horrific knee injury during the 2018 season -- and the result was a breakout performance.

28) **Budda Baker, S, ARZ:** Despite an up-and-down year in 2018, Baker still finished as an IDP DB1 in 12-team leagues. He's well-positioned to better that production this season.

29) **Chris Jones, DT, KCC:** Jones exploded for 15.5 sacks as a 3-4 end in 2018, but with the Chiefs moving to a four-man front Jones will man the three-technique spot this season.

30) **Kwon Alexander, ILB, SFO:** Alexander hasn't been able to duplicate his 108-solo 2016 campaign the last two years and is coming off an ACL tear. But still … 108 solos is a LOT.

31) **Khalil Mack, OLB, CHI:** If Mack has DL eligibility in your IDP league his value gets a boost, but even as a linebacker, he's a force to be reckoned with. Just an amazing talent in his prime.

32) **Frank Clark, DE, KCC:** The key to Clark backing up last year's big numbers in his new home is simple: Chris Jones (or whoever) keeping opponents from double-teaming Clark all game long.

33) **Devin Bush, ILB, PIT:** In dynasty IDP leagues, I prefer Devin White's talent a bit more, but Bush won't have to compete with Lavonte David for stops in Pittsburgh, so he gets the nod in redrafts.

34) **Kiko Alonso, OLB, MIA:** Alonso's the bane of many Dolphins fans existences, but the cold hard fact is a tackle four yards down the field counts the same as a stuff at the line of scrimmage.

35) **Jordan Poyer, S, BUF:** There are certain constants in life. Death. Taxes. The Jets being awful. And safeties in Buffalo piling up fantasy points year after year after year. Last year's DB6.

36) **Shawn Williams, S, CIN:** Williams came from nowhere to have a huge season in 2018 in large part because the Cincinnati LB corps was terrible. The Cincinnati LB corps is still terrible.

37) **Christian Kirksey, OLB, CLE:** Kirksey had a miserable 2018 season, missing nine games and posting just 43 stops, but when he's healthy, he's fully capable of top-10-IDP numbers.

38) **Melvin Ingram, DE, LAC:** Ingram had a down 2018 season, but he also had a lot of misses on QB pressures. Expect the eighth-year veteran to convert more of those into sacks in 2019.

39) **Justin Reid, S, HOU:** Reid's an underrated young talent who was a top-20 fantasy option on the back end last year. He's going to improve on those numbers in 2019 with Tyrann Mathieu gone.

40) **Akiem Hicks, DE, CHI:** Hicks gets overlooked playing in the shadow of Khalil Mack, but he's a solid IDP DL2 who will get you solid tackle production and throw in 7-9 sacks. A poor man's Calais Campbell. That's a compliment.

41) **Jayon Brown, ILB, TEN:** Brown was a top-15 fantasy linebacker in his second NFL season and played the most snaps (855) of any LB on the Titans roster. Could have top-10 upside.

42) **Trey Flowers, DE, DET**: Keep an eye on the $90 million man's positional eligibility with some IDP providers. A switch to LB would decimate his value, but it's rather unlikely.

43) **Devin White, ILB, TBB:** White was a top-five draft pick for a reason, but the presence of Lavonte David may cap his fantasy upside just a tick, especially in the early going.

44) **Myles Jack, ILB, JAX:** With the bombshell that Telvin Smith plans to sit out the entire 2019 season, Jack's set up to make a ton of tackles. If only it were that easy, folks.

45) **Zach Cunningham, ILB, HOU:** Cunningham topped 100 tackles for the first time in his career a year ago (in 14 games) and could be on the verge of a breakout third season.

46) **Carlos Dunlap, DE, CIN:** If you hit the linebacker position early, Dunlap's a great defensive lineman to target. He won't win you your IDP league, but he's a steady source of fantasy points.

47) **Demario Davis, ILB. NOS:** I'd be a lot more inclined to say that Davis can't back up last year's five sacks had the 30-year-old not now hit that benchmark in each of the last two seasons.

48) **Harrison Smith, S, MIN:** Smith tailed off quite a bit down the stretch last season (as did the Vikings), but he still finished the year as a top-12 fantasy defensive back ... again.

49) **Jordan Hicks, ILB, ARZ:** If Hicks can stay healthy for 16 games, he could substantially outperform this ranking. But staying healthy's long been an issue for the four-year veteran.

50) **Jarrad Davis, ILB, DET:** Davis hasn't produced up to his potential to this point in his career -- or come especially close. But the situation remains highly favorable, and he's young.

Chapter 11

ROOKIES & DYNASTY ANALYSIS

Scott Bogman

QUARTERBACKS

Kyler Murray (Oklahoma), Cardinals - Round 1, Pick 1

The positives: Murray is dropped into a perfect scheme that he ran in college. The Cardinals have surrounded him with weapons on offense, adding draft picks Andy Isabella, Hakeem Butler and KeeSean Johnson to 2018 second-round pick Christian Kirk, Pro Bowl RB David Johnson and future Hall of Famer Larry Fitzgerald. The bad news: The Cardinals offensive line is suspect. They have added a few FAs in J.R. Sweezy and Marcus Gilbert, but it's patchwork at best. Murray is small. His height doesn't concern me, but his weight (listed just over 200 pounds) isn't prototypical of an NFL QB with a bad OL. He'll have to learn when to take a sack and step out of bounds quickly to make it through the season. He has the arm to make any throw on the field and wheels to run for days, and he's been compared to Michael Vick by a lot of people.

2019 Value: High-ceiling/low-floor QB, worth a risk as a backup in a 1QB league for the upside. In 2QB leagues, he can be the second QB, but I would make sure to get my QB3 quickly after I draft Murray.

Dynasty/Keeper Value: High ceiling, low floor here, too. Murray had over 4,000 yards passing and 1,000 on the ground last year in college, so the ceiling is enormous! If head coach Kliff Kingsbury is a failed experiment in Arizona, it will most likely be because Murray didn't work out. Murray can always fall back on a baseball career as he was a first-round pick there, too.

Daniel Jones (Duke), Giants - Round 1, Pick 6

I'm one of the few people who didn't despise this pick by the Giants. It's not what I would have done, but I actually like Jones over Dwayne Haskins. The plan is to have Jones sit for this season as general manager Dave Gettleman has said that Eli Manning "has proved that he has plenty left in the tank." Jones is a protégé of David Cutcliffe, the same man who taught the Manning brothers, and has the same look as the Mannings on the field, making pre-snap reads and adjustments. The knock on Jones is the low completion rate (60.5%, the second-lowest among drafted QBs), but he had one of the highest drop totals from his WRs at Duke. I'm excited to see what he does with NFL talent around him.

2019 Value: Most first-round QBs play the season they were drafted at some point. Last year all five QBs taken in the first round ended the year as the starting QB of their teams. The plan is to go with Eli for as long as that is possible, so I wouldn't expect anything from Jones until the back end of the season. He's a handcuff in deep leagues.

Dynasty/Keeper Value: While I'm not the biggest fan of any of the QBs in this class, I do think that Jones can be a successful NFL QB. Hopefully he gets to sit and learn for this entire season and then becomes the starter in 2020. He's a project, and if you draft him this year, it should be with expectation that he can be your QB2 next season.

Dwayne Haskins (Ohio State), Redskins - Round 1, Pick 15
This is the guy Redskins owner Daniel Snyder wanted, and they didn't have to trade up to get him. Haskins should be in a camp battle with Case Keenum for the Week 1 starting job. Because Haskins has only one season of experience in college, I would expect Keenum to win the gig to begin the season. Haskins had an incredible 70% completion rate in college, and if he can bring that to the NFL, he should find sustained success. We will find out quickly if he was a product of the great players around him at Ohio State, though, as the Redskins at best have average starting wideouts in Josh Doctson, Paul Richardson and Trey Quinn, along with oft-injured TE Jordan Reed.
2019 Value: Haskins' lack of a guaranteed a starting spot makes it difficult to count on him in a redraft league. Even if he gets the nod, he's at best a QB3 for this season.
Dynasty/Keeper Value: Haskins could have useful value in dynasty leagues, but I'm not going to bank on it. The Redskins don't have great weapons for him to utilize, and with a backfield of Derrius Guice and Adrian Peterson, the early part of his career will be turning around to hand off the ball a lot.

Drew Lock (Missouri), Broncos - Round 2, Pick 42
Lock has already been told that he will strictly be the backup to Joe Flacco. Lock has a cannon of an arm, so sitting for at least a year and learning from a player a lot like himself should be great for him. I can't imagine him starting in Year 1, unless it's at the end of the year and the Broncos have either clinched a playoff spot or are eliminated from contention. Lock is a little more of a project coming out of an Air Raid-style offense. Lock has all the tools to be successful, but the learning curve is bigger in the NFL.
2019 Value: Close to none. The Broncos have already said Lock is the straight backup. Of course, opinions tend to change once we start seeing these guys in training camp and preseason, but that is the plan as of now.
Dynasty/Keeper Value: He'll get a chance and some leash for sure as long as Elway is in charge. The longer Lock gets to sit, the better his chances are to succeed. Draft him in a dynasty league as a long-term project.

Will Grier (West Virginia), Panthers - Round 3, Pick 100
The Panthers prioritized getting a quality backup QB to Cam Newton, and that is exactly what they have in Grier. Newton is tough, but he has missed a handful of games over the last few seasons. Cam takes a beating by pulling the ball down and running; he's had at least 90 rush attempts every year of his career. This seems a lot like the Bill Belichick plan of drafting a QB: He'll have a few starts, and if he looks good, the Panthers can flip him to a team that needs a QB. Once again, this is a QB coming from an Air Raid/Spread system in West Virginia. He has to transition toward taking a lot of snaps from under center, and that can take a while for a QB. Since the 2012 draft that landed Russell Wilson, Kirk Cousins, Nick Foles and Case Keenum, the only QB drafted in the third round or later to land a starting job is Dak Prescott.
2019 Value: None, unless Newton gets hurt AND he beats out Taylor Heinicke for the backup job
Dynasty/Keeper Value: Unless something changes, Newton is the starter for the foreseeable future in Carolina. Grier can earn time by playing well when/if Newton misses time and maybe be traded to another team -- or take over if something serious happens to Newton.

Ryan Finley (NC State), Bengals - Round 4, Pick 104
New Cincinnati head coach Zac Taylor's first draft showed that he prioritized offense by using seven of his first 10 picks on such players. Andy Dalton has been around awhile and found some success -- but not enough to keep the job for much longer if the Bengals can't make the playoffs or win a playoff game. ESPN's Todd McShay says Finley makes better reads than anyone else in the 2019 class and thinks Finley

can start as soon as next season. I'm not sure I see that. I think we'll either see Taylor stick with Dalton or use a high first-round pick on one of the QBs coming out next season in the draft. Finley has a better shot than other third-day QBs because he isn't blocked by an entrenched starter, but his path isn't exactly clear, either.

2019 Value: Dalton would have to REALLY struggle or get hurt for Finley to end up playing. He still needs to beat out Jeff Driskel in the preseason to get the immediate backup job.

Dynasty/Keeper Value: It's better than most QBs drafted in the fourth round; he is not behind a starter with a long contract, and he is Taylor's pet project.

Jarrett Stidham (Auburn), Patriots - Round 4, Pick 133

Stidham is the latest in the long list of QBs we have seen the Patriots take, develop for a few seasons and then hopefully trade off. We have seen it with Matt Cassel, Jimmy Garoppolo and Jacoby Brissett. Stidham fits this mold perfectly, but eventually one of these guys has to step in and take over for Brady. Stidham probably isn't that guy, but he has a much better shot than last year's late-round QB pick Danny Etling. Stidham has great physical tools, but his decision making has to get better. Hopefully sitting behind and learning from the best QB of all time will get him prepped for some actual playing time, whether it's in New England or somewhere else.

2019 Value: None. He'll be firmly third on the depth chart behind Brady and Brian "The Destroyer" Hoyer.

Dynasty/Keeper Value: Meh. It's nice that he went to New England, but I wouldn't be drafting him in too many rookie drafts unless you have space for a longshot QB.

Easton Stick (North Dakota State), Chargers - Round 5, Pick 166

Philip Rivers reportedly isn't too keen on the idea of having his eventual replacement on the roster. I think drafting Stick in the fifth round is a nice way for the Chargers to develop someone they like while not having a clear replacement for Rivers on the roster. Stick won't even be the backup as the Chargers signed Tyrod Taylor for that job in the offseason. Stick has some impressive film; he took over for Carson Wentz at North Dakota State and led the Bisons to back-to-back national titles in 2017 and '18. He didn't have a great week at the Senior Bowl, and presumably that dropped his draft stock, but he also played in the East-West shrine game, *and* his season didn't end until Jan. 9, when they won the FCS championship. Stick can make all the throws, and he can tuck it and run.

2019 Value: None. While I really like Stick, he's still a project. He has to beat out Cardale Jones to stick on the roster.

Dynasty/Keeper Value: He's one of my personal favorites, but QB success stories in Round 5 or later are few and far between. He's a DEEP-league option in a rookie draft, but most will want to take a flier on an RB/WR/TE, and I am 100% behind that.

Clayton Thorson (Northwestern), Eagles - Round 5, Pick 167

Thorson came one pick after Easton Stick, and I couldn't feel any more differently about these two. Thorson was a good starter for Northwestern, but I don't think his game will translate in the NFL. He makes his money on short, easy passes and doesn't push it downfield enough for my taste. The Eagles need a decent backup now that Nick Foles is gone, but I don't think they got one with Thorson.

2019 Value: He might be able to beat out Nate Sudfeld for the backup job, but that isn't a tall task. I guess that gives him a clearer path to playing time than Stick or Stidham.

Dynasty/Keeper Value: Pure flier. Arm strength is usually something you have or you don't, and Thorson hasn't really shown much of it. I won't be spending any of my rookie picks on him.

Gardner Minshew (Washington State), Jaguars - Round 6, Pick 178
This is a tough spot for Minshew. It's not as if the Jaguars are flush with talent at QB; they wouldn't have given Nick Foles a four-year, $88 million deal. However, the Jaguars have a project QB they drafted last year in Tanner Lee, and Cody Kessler is the clear backup, having started 12 games in the NFL already. Minshew put up monster numbers at WSU, but he's a QB coming from an Air Raid system that has an uphill climb to make the roster.
2019 Value: None. Minshew has to concentrate on making the practice squad first and working his way up to getting a helmet.
Dynasty/Keeper Value: Minshew was a fun player to watch at the college level and I have no doubt he will put everything he has into making an NFL roster but expecting him to win a starting job is asking a lot.

Trace McSorley (Penn State), Ravens - Round 6, Pick 197
I wouldn't like McSorley going to many other situations outside of this one in Baltimore. McSorley never really had a shot at becoming an NFL-caliber QB -- some teams thought he would move to safety or wide receiver -- but he will be used in the Taysom Hill role with the Ravens. He'll get some situational snaps -- probably near the goal line -- and will play special teams while Robert Griffin III backs up Lamar Jackson.
2019 Value: I can't imagine there's a ton here, but if he is used in goal-line packages, he could boast some TD upside. The problem is that he will have to qualify at any position outside of QB to register any value.
Dynasty/Keeper Value: It's doubtful that McSorley gets much more than a handful of snaps a game but Lamar puts his body on the line A LOT and RGIII is made of glass so maybe he can work his way into a backup QB role but it's pretty doubtful.

UDFAs

Brett Rypien (Boise State), Broncos
Rypien had a ton of starting experience but will have to compete with Kevin Hogan for the third-string job. Minshew is probably the only QB in a worse spot than Rypien.
Tyree Jackson (Buffalo), Bills
Jackson had an amazing SPARQ score during the pre-draft process. The Bills will give him a shot to stick at QB, but I think he'll end up with a career similar to Logan Thomas'. He'll probably be a TE in a few years.
Jake Browning (Washington), Vikings
Browning had a ton of experience and broke all kinds of records at Washington, but he had shoulder problems, and teams are worried about his arm strength. His ceiling is most likely a career backup.
Nick Fitzgerald (Mississippi State), Buccaneers
I am genuinely intrigued by what Bruce Arians wants to do with Fitzgerald. It's clear to most who have watched him play that he will most likely move positions or play the Taysom Hill role. Arians drafted Logan Thomas and tried to make him a QB before he was moved to TE in Buffalo.

RUNNING BACKS

Josh Jacobs (Alabama), Raiders - Round 1, Pick 24

The most important thing we need to know about this pick is that Jon Gruden used the word "workhorse" to describe what he wanted out of Jacobs. Jacobs is a great pass catcher and can pass block (although he didn't get many chances to do it), so he can play all three downs. Jacobs just didn't have that role at 'Bama; he only had more than 20 touches in one game in his college career, and his 140 touches from last season marked his highest total. With Isaiah Crowell tearing his Achilles, the Raiders brought back Doug Martin, but he was ineffective last season. Jacobs might get fewer touches than we expect this season, but the Raiders seem intent with throwing him into the fire early.

2019 Value: I would love to take Jacobs as an RB3, but being the shiny new toy, he will most likely go in the RB2 range. Hope for Nick Chubb and expect Marlon Mack.

Dynasty/Keeper Value: Jacobs is a MUCH better pick in long-term leagues; he might be eased into action this year because of his lack of touches in college. If he proves he can stand up to the feature back workload, the Raiders will start feeding him the ball more often.

Miles Sanders (Penn State), Eagles - Round 2, Pick 53

I love the player but hate the landing spot. The Eagles traded for Jordan Howard, and I would expect him to get the majority of the carries early in the season. He's had at least 250 carries all three seasons he has played in the NFL. Doug Pederson has never had a back carry the ball more than 180 times for the Eagles in his three seasons as head coach. I think if Sanders were at a different school and hadn't sat behind Saquon Barkley before replacing him, we would have heard a lot more of his name in the pre-draft process. A versatile weapon, Sanders should show that he's the best back in Philly at some point this season and start earning more touches.

2019 Value: It's hard to guess his value for this season. While the Eagles spent a high pick on him, they have a wealth of experience on the roster. They traded for the bruising Howard; Corey Clement is still on the depth chart; and Wendell Smallwood had over 100 touches last season. I expect Sanders to earn the majority of the touches by the end of the season, hopefully sooner rather than later.

Dynasty/Keeper Value: While 2019 seems to be the stepping-stone year for Sanders, all of Howard, Clement and Smallwood are all gone after this year. Maybe one re-signs, but I expect Sanders will be the clear-cut leader in touches out of the backfield for Philly before the year is through.

Darrell Henderson (Memphis), Rams - Round 3, Pick 70

This one is hard to read. Todd Gurley isn't even 25 years old as I'm typing this, and he hasn't had a year with fewer than 250 touches, and the last three seasons, he's gone over 300. There isn't a lot of wiggle room with those types of numbers. We have heard Gurley has an arthritic knee, so taking some work off his plate makes sense, but the Rams also matched the Lions' offer to restricted free agent Malcolm Brown. Henderson is explosive and has been compared to Jamaal Charles because he doesn't need many touches to make a big impact. Hopefully that's the case. With Gurley and Brown on the roster, I'm not sure where the touches are going to come from out of the gate. I do love the fit of Henderson in Sean McVay's offense, though; he could be great if given an opportunity.

2019 Value: Henderson won't need many opportunities to make an impact, but he could be hit-or-miss from week to week. I'll definitely be taking fliers on him at the end of drafts.

Dynasty/Keeper Value: If you have Gurley, you should prioritize getting Henderson on your dynasty teams. Everyone could be making a bigger deal out of this than it actually is, but it's better to be safe than sorry, and having Henderson as a handcuff makes a lot of sense. This seemingly isn't the greatest of situations for Henderson, but I refuse to believe McVay would take Henderson to only give him a handful of snaps per game.

David Montgomery (Iowa State), Bears - Round 3, Pick 73

Montgomery was my No. 2 back coming into the draft, and he is going to sit at the same spot after being drafted by the Bears. This season might be better than I had initially thought, as well, because head coach Matt Nagy has already called Montgomery a three-down back and compared him to Kareem Hunt. Tarik Cohen will always have a role -- he is versatile and doesn't need a lot of touches to make a big impact in a game -- but Mike Davis was signed as well. I expect the touches to favor Montgomery from the jump now and Montgomery to get gradually more involved as the season moves on. Montgomery makes tacklers miss, can catch out of the backfield and was the unquestioned leader for the Cyclones.

2019 Value: Will probably get better as the year goes on, but we have to like what Nagy is already saying about him. He'll be in the RB2/3 class.

Dynasty/Keeper Value: As with almost every rookie, the long-term outlook is better. Montgomery should earn his touches this year and be a true three-down back next year and moving forward.

Devin Singletary (Florida Atlantic), Bills - Round 3, Pick 74

This one surprised me. The Bills already have LeSean McCoy, Frank Gore and T.J. Yeldon on the roster. The good news is that any of those backs can be cut without costing too much or eating up dead space on the cap. Singletary isn't my favorite back from this class, but I do like this situation for him. This year might be more about learning behind whoever the starter might be, but next year McCoy and Gore will be gone. They are both UFAs in 2020, and his only competition will be Yeldon, if he can hang around. Singletary has a nose for the end zone: He scored 54 TDs in his final two seasons at FAU. He can catch out of the backfield, too, although he wasn't asked to do it last year with only six receptions.

2019 Value: This is hard to know because we don't know who is going to make the roster, but I would expect Singletary to at least get a handful of touches to start the season and hopefully move up to a bigger role as the year moves forward. He's a stash in deeper leagues and probably a pickup in most leagues.

Dynasty/Keeper Value: Singletary should get at least 2020 to prove he can carry the rock for the Bills as a starter. I wouldn't guarantee much beyond that, but if he proves he can play in the NFL, he can last as a starter for a while.

Damien Harris (Alabama), Patriots - Round 3, Pick 87

It's hard to imagine not being happy about a player being drafted on Day 2 to one of the best offenses in the league, but here we are. Harris is the quintessential 'hard-nosed' RB, so from whom is he going to steal touches? Harris being drafted to New England probably ruins Rex Burkhead's value, at best, and he might end up eating into Michel's touches. Harris seems like a bruiser, but he caught 22 passes out of the backfield for 'Bama last year as a rotational back, so he can take touches from White, as well. Not only is this not a great spot for him, but he can also mess up other players.

2019 Value: Harris can be anyone from Mike Gillislee in this offense to the lead dog. Belichick keeps his cards close to the vest, so I don't expect us to get any type of information before the season, and even if we did, the game plan changes like the wind for New England.

Dynasty/Keeper Value: This really depends on how Harris looks and what his role is this season with the Pats. I would venture a guess that his 2019 role will probably be similar to what his role is in 2020. Sony Michel and James White are both still under contract.

Alexander Mattison (Boise State), Vikings - Round 3, Pick 102

I was surprised Mattison went over some of the backs I like much more in this draft, but as the saying goes, 'it only takes one team to fall in love.' I'm guessing Mattison was added to be Dalvin Cook's immediate backup. Mattison is a true three-down back; he had 329 touches in 13 games last season. A three-down back is what the Vikings needed behind Cook as he has only played in 15 games in the last two seasons. Mattison can pick up the torch and handle multiple carries when/if Cook goes down, or he can handle multiple carries per game immediately if they want to take pressure off Cook on a game-to-game basis. Mattison isn't going to impress anyone with his athleticism, but he will bowl over a tired defense in the fourth quarter.

2019 Value: I'm thinking Mattison will get close to 10 touches per game to start for the Vikings. Taking Mattison in the third round signals to me that they want someone to come in and help out Cook by taking some of the carries from him. He will also be the go-to guy should Cook go down again. He is the purest of handcuffs.

Dynasty/Keeper Value: If Cook goes down again it might be a wrap with him and the Vikings. If that is the way they go Mattison would be in line for a ton of carries next season. The only problem I see with that is Mattison is more of a bridge guy than a guy that should come in and get the ball 25 times a game. It will probably be a 50/50 shot for Mattison to get sustained carries should the Vikings decide to move on from Cook. Most likely the Vikings would draft someone else early next season.

Bryce Love (Stanford), Redskins - Round 4, Pick 112

I wasn't exactly excited to see Love go to Washington. I wasn't as upset as Derrius Guice, of course, but I'm not sure this is the greatest fit, either. Adrian Peterson can be cut next season without really hurting the cap. Chris Thompson is a free agent, too, so it looks like Love will just jump in and take that Thompson role, but that isn't the case. Love is just as, if not more, injury-prone as Thompson – having torn his ACL in December -- and while he can catch the ball, it wasn't something Stanford asked him to do often. Love has a ton of athleticism and can definitely be an explosive player, so maybe he is in Washington to be a change-of-pace guy, but I wouldn't expect much more than that, especially if he takes long to recover.

2019 Value: Love will almost assuredly start the season on the PUP after tearing his ACL in December. Love is more of a 2020 investment than anything this year with Peterson and Thompson still on the team to go with Guice.

Dynasty/Keeper Value: Love is never going to be what we have seen from his college teammate Christian McCaffrey. Love can be a nice complementary back, though: Think more of a Dion Lewis type.

Justice Hill (Oklahoma State), Ravens - Round 4, Pick 113

I really like this fit for Baltimore. Hill is an explosive runner, shown by his super high SPARQ score in the pre-draft process. Draft analysts Daniel Jeremiah and Bucky Brooks were talking about how the Ravens are going to beat teams with speed and are making a track team. Hill fits that mold, for sure. Lamar Jackson's presence should give Hill some wide-open holes to run through, and he can catch the ball on some dumpoff passes too.

2019 Value: Despite his potential in the offense, the depth chart is a problem. The Ravens signed Mark Ingram, who is going to get the bulk of the carries. Jackson averaged 17 carries per game as a starter, and Gus Edwards worked himself into playing time. I like Hill long-term in Baltimore, but getting more than a handful of touches per game this season is asking a lot. He should be the Ingram handcuff for this year.

Dynasty/Keeper Value: Ingram will be turning 30 this season, and Edwards will be an RFA in 2020, so it seems like Hill will have an opportunity to start getting way more carries starting next season. Hill is a stash if you can afford it and probably more of a pickup should something go wrong with Ingram. The fact he's tailor-made for this scheme doesn't hide the fact he'll face an uphill battle to earn touches.

Benny Snell (Kentucky), Steelers - Round 4, Pick 122

Snell is a pure north-south runner who's going to 'outwill' his opponents. Teams that played against Kentucky knew Snell was going to get the ball 20-plus times, and he still had seven 100-yard games last year. I'm not 100% sure how Snell is going to fit in Pittsburgh, but my initial guess is that he'll be the closer when the Steelers are up in the fourth quarter to come in and run downhill against stacked fronts, while also giving James Conner the occasional series off. Snell only caught 29 passes over three years at Kentucky, so it's safe to assume Jaylen Samuels will still be used on third downs when Conner isn't available.

2019 Value: Snell will be hit-or-miss most games. Conner should stay in close games longer. If the Steelers are losing, Samuels will come in more often on passing downs to help them play catch-up. Snell should shine if the Steelers are in control during the final quarter. I don't want to depend on guessing when those Snell-centric weeks will happen.

Dynasty/Keeper Value: This could be interesting. If Conner gets hurt again this season, the Steelers could mix in Snell a bit more frequently to keep Conner fresh. If the mix works this year, Snell will only be a situational back moving forward. High ceiling and low floor....

Tony Pollard (Memphis), Cowboys - Round 4, Pick 128

This isn't the worst landing spot for Pollard. Although he isn't going to take carries away from Ezekiel Elliott at all, the Cowboys have said he'll get about 30 plays a game. I don't know that the 30 plays will come to fruition, but that is what they wanted from Tavon Austin, who didn't even log 30 snaps at any point last season; he only played in seven contest with a high of 23 snaps. Pollard can return kickoffs and punts, line up in the backfield and serve as a wideout. Pollard isn't a giant back, but he's bigger than Austin and might also be the direct backup to Zeke when he needs a series off.

2019 Value: Probably not too much. The Cowboys seem to have a plan, so he won't be worthless, but Zeke is the best weapon they have, and taking him off the field is not a smart move. Pollard is probably the closest thing to a handcuff the Cowboys have; the other backs are Mike Weber, Darius Jackson and Jordan Chunn.

Dynasty/Keeper Value: Pollard has to prove he is a legit weapon this year to get more involved down the line. It's rough for him that his rookie season is his make-or-break year, but that's the deal.

Ryquell Armstead (Temple), Jaguars - Round 5, Pick 140

Armstead is probably more of a two-down back in the NFL. Armstead on film seems like a grinder, but he timed out well in the 40-yard dash and had some explosive plays for Temple. Armstead has lined up out wide a few times, but it was really only as a decoy: He only caught eight passes last season. Only Devin Singletary and Ty Johnson had fewer catches of the drafted RBs.

2019 Value: Fifth-round picks aren't locks to make the roster, but with only Alfred Blue and Benny Cunningham in Armstead's way, I assume he'll beat out at least one for the role of backing up Leonard Fournette.

Dynasty/Keeper Value: If I'm thinking about drafting Fournette or already roster him in a long-term league, Armstead is his handcuff. The veteran Blue might be the guy with more carries this season, but he is only signed to a one-year deal.

Qadree Ollison (Pittsburgh), Falcons - Round 5, Pick 152

Ollison is a solid north-south runner who has the potential to fit well in Atlanta. The Falcons adding offensive line help was more about keeping franchise QB Matt Ryan upright but can help the run game as well. Ollison is more than likely only a two-down back; he doesn't have much experience running routes and only had 50 catches over four seasons at Pittsburgh. Ollison will more than likely need to make an impression early to stick around, and he may get that chance. Tevin Coleman is off to San Francisco, and Devonta Freeman is coming off a year in which he only played two games.

2019 Value: There is some competition for a roster spot in the form of Brian Hill, who had a decent performance late last season against Carolina, and veteran journeyman Jeremy Langford. If he is to secure a spot on the roster from week to week, Ollison will probably need to contribute in kick coverage on special teams.

Dynasty/Keeper Value: He would have to really impress to hold value long-term. It's not impossible, but if the Falcons decide to move on from Freeman, either Ito Smith or a high-round draft pick next season would be the likely leader for snaps.

Jordan Scarlett (Florida), Panthers - Round 5, Pick 154

Scarlett probably hasn't yet scratched the surface of his potential. He carries incredible athleticism but needs to improve his vision and receiving ability. Scarlett has also had some off-field issues in the past that probably made him slip down the board even more than his skill shortcomings. Scarlett can be a steal if he gets coached up and earns an opportunity.

2019 Value: Ron Rivera has already said he wants to get Christian McCaffrey more plays off his season so that they don't run him into the ground, meaning Scarlett may have an opportunity for touches. Cameron Artis-Payne has had four years to make an impact and hasn't done so. UDFA Elijah Holyfield and Elijah Hood are depth options, so Scarlett has a real shot to make the roster and get carries this season.

Dynasty/Keeper Value: Like anyone picked on Day 3, Scarlett will have to prove a lot in Year 1 to last, but I give him a better shot than a lot of players. His athleticism can't be taught.

Trayveon Williams (Texas A&M), Bengals - Round 6, Pick 182

I'm not 100% sure why the Bengals not only spent this pick on an RB but also a later one on another good RB. Williams had a ton of explosive plays for A&M last season and is a great pass protector. The two reasons he slipped to this point in the draft: (1) he lacks great vision, and (2) he is small for an NFL running back at 5-foot-8, 206 pounds. Williams has great burst past the line of scrimmage and can catch the ball out of the backfield, but he doesn't have a ton of moves, so if he's caught he will go down quickly.

2019 Value: He likely won't take anything away from Giovani Bernard and definitely isn't going to eat into Joe Mixon's snaps at all. The good news for Williams is that he's only competing with Quinton Flowers and Darrin Hall for snaps this year.

Dynasty/Keeper Value: The Bengals also drafted Rodney Anderson, who is an injury waiting to happen but highly skilled. Bernard is an UFA after this season, and Mixon only has 2020 left on his rookie contract after this season, so Williams can hold significant value in the future. Still, he has to impress this season to be guaranteed anything in the future.

Ty Johnson (Maryland), Lions - Round 6, Pick 186

I watched Johnson torch my Texas Longhorns, so I don't have a ton of negatives to say about him as a player. The explosive back averaged 7.6 yards per carry, but he was rotational in college and didn't contribute in the receiving game much with only 17 catches over four years. He might have his best football in front of him.

2019 Value: I really like Johnson as a prospect, but I don't know why the Lions took him. They already have Kerryon Johnson, they signed CJ Anderson, Theo Riddick is the pass catcher and Zach Zenner has stuck around for the past four seasons. Johnson will have to return kicks and contribute as a special teamer to stick on the roster. Danny Amendola will likely return punts unless the Lions want to take him out of that role.

Dynasty/Keeper Value: Johnson is in a similar situation to Alex Collins' time with the Ravens. There might not be a spot for him in Detroit, as they are already stacked at RB, but if another team has injuries, he might get a shot.

Dexter Williams (Notre Dame), Packers - Round 6, Pick 194

Jake Ciely and I can't agree on Williams. The explosive big man has good vision and can catch the ball out of the backfield. He particularly has explosive plays up the gut when he bursts through the correct hole. The reason I'm not high on him is that he goes down with *any* contact. It's like he is running on ice skates or something; it's really incredible how fast he goes down. I'm not saying he can't be coached up and be successful in the NFL, but I wouldn't bet on it.

2019 Value: Surprisingly (to me), he might actually have some value for this season. The Packers can't seem to pick a back to whom they want to give a ton of carries. Aaron Jones is the better than Jamaal Williams, but he has been suspended and missed games with injuries. Williams has averaged a plodding 3.7 yards per carry.

Dynasty/Keeper Value: Williams could hold some value in the future, but he *has* to get better at staying on his feet after initial contact and prove himself in the passing game. He has to take advantage of this opportunity with Green Bay almost immediately.

Travis Homer (Miami), Seahawks - Round 6, Pick 204

Homer is going to be able to contribute in kick and punt coverage immediately. Beyond that, he will have to wait for an injury to make an impact in the running game. He has great lateral quickness to run around the corner and make defenders miss, but he lacks patience in letting his blocks set up and will occasionally attempt to run over tacklers. He could have a little use as a pass protector on third downs; he's great at picking up blitzers.

2019 Value: Homer has close to no value other than he'll stick on the roster because he is already great in kick and punt coverage.

Dynasty/Keeper Value: Meh. Homer's long-term outlook is as a special-teams ace; the Seahawks spent a first-rounder on Rashaad Penny last year before Chris Carson outplayed him; and J.D. McKissic already is a great pass-catching option.

Rodney Anderson (Oklahoma), Bengals - Round 6, Pick 211

Daniel Jeremiah said during his draft coverage on NFL Network that if he were healthy, Anderson would be the first RB off the board in this draft, and I completely agree with him. The film on Anderson is incredible: He honestly looks like Marshall Faulk. The only real weakness in his game at all is his effort in pass protecting. Anderson has incredible vision, balance and speed combined with the ability to run every route out of the backfield, and he lines up as a WR on some snaps. The reason he wound up a sixth-round pick is that he only played 17 games over three seasons because of injuries. Anderson broke his leg, fractured a vertebrae and tore his ACL all in just his college career. He is an unbelievable risk-reward player for the Bengals and for fantasy.

2019 Value: This all depends on where Anderson is in the rehab process coming off the torn ACL. He wasn't able to participate in pre-draft drills outside of the bench press because of his knee. There is of course the question of whether he will have the same explosion and lateral quickness, so he has a lot of hoops through which to jump. Even if Anderson is healthy, Joe Mixon and Giovani Bernard are pretty set at their rolesm so Anderson will have to impress at practice to get on the field, of which he is clearly capable, but everything has to be right.

Dynasty/Keeper Value: As I mentioned with Trayveon Williams' writeup, Bernard is an UFA next year, and Mixon only has one year left, so if (and it's a big "if") Anderson can stay healthy, he has a real chance to make a big impact with Cincy, especially if he's healthy at the end of this season and going into 2020.

Darwin Thompson (Utah State), Chiefs - Round 6, Pick 214

We all look at this landing spot and salivate. We know what an Andy Reid offense with Patrick Mahomes can do for an RB if given the opportunity. Thompson is explosive and can motor past the LOS for big chunk gains, and he's great at catching the ball on screens and short routes. Thompson did only have one year of experience at Utah State, and while he was successful, he is going to have to prove he can do all of the little things before Reid will let him see the field.

2019 Value: The fit is nice, but Damien Williams averaged 5.1 yards per carry and looked great as the starter after Kareem Hunt was cut. The Chiefs also signed veteran Carlos Hyde, to whom they could give a long leash as well, so Thompson will have to impress in limited opportunities to earn more time.

Dynasty/Keeper Value: Williams was extended after a great performance down the stretch last year, but the deal only lasts through the 2020 season, and Hyde is a FA after this season. So if Thompson impresses, the path to playing time is pretty clear for 2020 and beyond.

Mike Weber (Ohio State), Cowboys - Round 7, Pick 218

Weber's strength is that he isn't really bad at anything. He follows blocks well, can catch the ball out of the backfield and can shake a tackler. He didn't run a ton of routes out of the backfield and didn't have to play in pass protection often, though, so he probably won't be asked to do too much of that off the bat. He is being brought in to compete for touches whenever Ezekiel Elliott needs a rest, and I wouldn't expect much more than that.

2019 Value: I think he's better than current Zeke backups in Darius Jackson and Jordan Chunn, but he will have to earn his spot having been a seventh-round pick. My guess would be a few touches behind Zeke per game whenever he needs a breather, but the Cowboys have already said they want to get fellow draft pick Tony Pollard involved to the tune of 30 snaps per game, so there might not a lot of meat left on the bone if that is the case.

Dynasty/Keeper Value: Not a ton; Weber is in the same type of situation Ryquell Armstead faces in Jacksonville. We know who the clear-cut leader for carries is, and Weber will have to make an impact with few looks to either gain interest in free agency or get looks should Zeke go down.

Kerrith Whyte (Florida Atlantic), Bears - Round 7, Pick 222

To be blunt, Whyte has a long uphill battle for a roster spot. The Bears have David Montgomery, Mike Davis and Tarik Cohen to split carries. Whyte returned kicks at FAU, but the Bears signed Cordarrelle Patterson in the offseason, so I would think that he'd get that job and Cohen will return punts. Being in a Matt Nagy system is the upside here, of course, as we have to assume that he has a plan for Whyte. Nagy has already complimented Whyte for his raw speed and said he will need to play special teams.

2019 Value: Not much; Whyte fits perfectly for what the Bears do -- he can line up out wide and return kicks as well as being a good RB -- but everywhere we look on the roster, he's blocked. An injury or two could make him a nice late-season addition.

Dynasty/Keeper Value: I would think Nagy has a plan for him, but I wouldn't count on anything after this year. Seventh-round picks are cheap, and if Whyte doesn't impact this season, Nagy will fall in love with another prospect next year.

Myles Gaskin (Washington), Dolphins - Round 7, Pick 234

Gaskin is one of my favorite backs in this class. The fact he was the last one drafted was extremely surprising. The big knock on him is his size: He's 5-foot-9 and just barely 200 pounds, meaning not many teams will trust him with a ton of carries -- despite the fact he had over 1,000 touches at Washington. Gaskin has great vision, balance and burst past the line. He will get run over in pass protection on occasion, but the effort is there.

2019 Value: The Dolphins have a ton of guys I really feel were underrated coming out of college on the roster. I would assume that new OC Chad O'Shea will give everyone a fair shake, so Gaskin might actually have a shot to get some carries this season. If Gaskin does get some run this year, it will probably mean Kenyan Drake and Kalen Ballage either got hurt or were inefficient, so if we get to that point, this whole situation might be annoying.

Dynasty/Keeper Value: Gaskin can make an impact for the Dolphins as early as this season, but seventh-round picks are cheap and expendable, so he better earn trust in special teams early to stick, and then maybe he can wrestle the job away from whomever might be the starter.

UDFAs

Devine Ozigbo (Nebraska), Saints

Ozigbo is probably a lock for a roster spot: He's better than Dwayne Washington and probably should have been drafted. Ozigbo follows blocks well, is tough to bring down and has lined up as a WR, which all seem to fit perfectly for the Saints. He wasn't great in blitz pickup, which will make him firmly third-string behind Alvin Kamara and Latavius Murray as depth (not rotational), unless he learns to do it.

Karan Higdon (Michigan), Texans

The good news is that there isn't much keeping Higdon from a roster spot in Houston. We have heard D'Onta Foreman looks healthy, but he didn't at the end of last season. Higdon will win with effort. He has a nice motor and can grind his way against stacked boxes like he had at Michigan. I just don't think he's much more than depth or Just A Guy, but if Lamar Miller were to get hurt and Foreman were to prove ineffective (or get hurt again), Higdon could win more snaps.

Alex Barnes (Kansas State), Titans

Barnes is a lot like Derrick Henry in terms of size and running style. As far as skill goes, he's kind of a poor man's Henry. The thumper can run through tacklers, but he tends to run a bit upright and get off-balance on occasion, which makes him easier to bring down. Barnes can catch the ball out of the backfield, as well, though he'll never be confused for Dion Lewis. Barnes should have no issue making the roster, but touches will be hard to earn behind Henry and Lewis.

Elijah Holyfield (Georgia), Panthers

I'm a bit of a Holyfield truther. He went undrafted, most likely because of a poor 40 time and performance at the combine. I was impressed with what I saw on film. It's tough to earn time at Georgia surrounded by five-star players all over the place, and Holyfield was able to do that. He is a two-down type who wasn't asked to catch the ball out of the backfield, so if he's going to do that, he'll have to learn at the NFL level. He'll have to beat out one or two of Cameron Artis-Payne, Barner, Elijah Hood and Jordan Scarlett to get a roster spot.

Bruce Anderson (North Dakota State), Buccaneers

Anderson is less of a RB and more of a weapon. He has good speed and runs great routes as a WR … *and* he can do everything as a special teamer, returning and covering kicks/punts. Anderson will struggle to make this team as just a RB with Peyton Barber, Ronald Jones II, Shaun Wilson and Dare Ogunbowale on the roster, but he can contribute in so many other ways, and Bruce Arians loves those guys. He'll probably have to battle with Andre Ellington for a roster spot.

WIDE RECEIVERS

Marquise Brown (Oklahoma), Ravens - Round 1, Pick 25
Brown's best trait is his unbelievable speed. The dude is fast on fast on fast. It makes his route breaks awesome. It makes getting the ball to him in space dangerous. He should be utilized on reverses and trick plays, too. If he does get bodied up, he's not great at making the contested catch, and a lot of people are worried about him getting hurt. He is coming off a Lisfranc injury from college and weighed in at 166 pounds at the Combine, so his size could be a concern for his long-term health.
2019 Value: We are going to see if Lamar Jackson can make adjustments in his second year and throw the ball with more accuracy. I expect Brown to be open on plenty of routes and be one of the top -- if not *the* top -- options in the Ravens receiving game. He probably won't be used in special teams at all, so it's all about how the Ravens decide to use him. If they end up running as much as most suspect, fantasy players will struggle to trust Brown's production from week to week.
Dynasty/Keeper Value: This is going to be tied to how long the Ravens decide to stick with Jackson. If he works out for them, they are going to be a run-first team for the foreseeable future, and Brown will be a WR3 at best for fantasy leagues. If Lamar breaks down or doesn't perform up to standards, they will probably move to a more traditional QB, and Brown could be more of a PPR threat in that scenario.

N'Keal Harry (Arizona State), Patriots - Round 1, Pick 32
I love this landing spot for Harry. Getting the best QB of all time has to be a dream come true for a first-round pick. Harry's hands stand out, and he turns 50/50 balls into 75/25 balls, so he can be an immediate red-zone threat. He will need to work on the little things -- like route-running polish and fighting off a block -- to make sure he's on the field every down for New England. Even if that stuff isn't 100% ready, he should be on the field and ready to catch a lot of passes from the jump.
2019 Value: New England has 143 receptions from 2018 gone between Rob Gronkowski, Josh Gordon, Chris Hogan and Cordarrelle Patterson. It's between Harry, Benjamin Watson, Austin Seferian-Jenkins, Demaryius Thomas (who might not play at all in 2019 coming off the Achilles tear) and Phillip Dorsett to get the majority of that, which I'd bet will go to Harry. He should come in and start immediately next to Julian Edelman.
Dynasty/Keeper Value: I expect a big rookie year from Harry and think it'll only get better from there. Especially as long as Brady is there, Harry should improve every year moving forward. He's an easy top-three pick for me in any rookie draft this season.

Deebo Samuel (South Carolina), 49ers - Round 2, Pick 36
I am so excited to see Samuel not only get 1-on-1 coverage but play with a QB who can get him the ball consistently. Jake Bentley had good stretches at South Carolina, but he doesn't seem to be NFL-caliber like Jimmy Garoppolo. Deebo's strength is that he's pretty good at just about everything. His runs outstanding routes; will line up out wide in the slot; run a reverse; pass on a trick play; and can return kicks and punts. He had missed all of 2017 with a broken leg but showed no ill effects last season. He will have an occasional drop, though.
2019 Value: This has a large range of outcomes. The 49ers don't have a dominant WR, but TE George Kittle will get the most targets. It all depends on how much time Samuel earns in the preseason. I think he should at least be the No. 3 WR option off the bat and earn more snaps over Marquise Goodwin or Dante Pettis as the season progresses. He also has the ability to return kicks and punts, but the 49ers have a bunch of those types in Richie James and Pettis did the majority last season. This season, Samuel is probably a waiver-wire add who could pay off come fantasy playoff time.

Dynasty/Keeper Value: With Kyle Shanahan at the helm, this offense is going to improve, and Deebo will climb with it. He should be the No. 1 option at WR for San Francisco by next season (unless they draft or sign someone) and has the ceiling of a nice No. 2 PPR wideout.

A.J. Brown (Ole Miss), Titans - Round 2, Pick 51

Brown is probably a better fantasy option that he is a real-life asset in most cases, but I'm not the biggest fan of him landing in Tennessee. He runs almost exclusively out of the slot, and I expect that to be the same with the Titans. Brown runs crisp routes -- that's probably the best part of his game. He doesn't have great moves to make tacklers miss, but he follows and will set up his teammates for great blocks to maximize that YAC. He was the leader in targets for a team that had D.K. Metcalf, DaMarkus Lodge and Dawson Knox, so he could be a nice security blanket for Marcus Mariota.

2019 Value: Meh, I'm not as excited as I should be about Brown. He's a catch magnet, but the most receptions a WR has had in a season with Mariota throwing the ball is 65. I'm not sure if Brown is going to be able to get Mariota to his ceiling, but if anyone can, he can. He should play off of Delanie Walker and Corey Davis perfectly, so there's a lot of upside. But I just don't trust Mariota.

Dynasty/Keeper Value: The good news for Brown is that if Mariota doesn't perform this season, the Titans will let him walk in free agency, and if he does perform, that's no longer an issue to worry about. Brown has a ceiling a lot like Deebo Samuel of a fantasy WR2, but plenty has to go right.

Mecole Hardman (Georgia), Chiefs - Round 2, Pick 56

The hype train is completely off the rails for Hardman. He's as quick as a hiccup and explosive with the ball in his hands. He's also a successful kick and punt returner and will most likely be asked to do that for KC. Hardman also had 60 catches over two seasons at Georgia. Hardman was recruited as an athlete out of high school, where he was an option QB. He's going to need to learn the nuances of playing WR before he becomes an All-Pro.

2019 Value: The need is obviously there for the Chiefs, but I don't see Hardman coming in and getting 130 targets. He will probably start the year firmly behind Sammy Watkins and Demarcus Robinson on the roster. With some explosive plays, he will earn more playing time by the end of the season and should be the No. 2 WR for the Chiefs, either because Watkins is hurt or he has passed Robinson in production. He'll probably be dropped by frustrated owners who overdrafted him and then added by people during the race to the playoffs.

Dynasty/Keeper Value: Hardman has tremendous upside. He could be close to what the Chiefs are going to lose in Hill. I just think it's going to take some time to get there. It could mirror Hill's career: He could take off in Year 2 after a decent rookie season. He could be the next Hill or the next early-round bust. Still, having Reid and Mahomes helps!

J.J. Arcega-Whiteside (Stanford), Eagles - Round 2, Pick 57

JJAW is a 'box out' WR who should be an immediate threat in the red zone. He is great at contested catches: He gets his big frame in front of a defender or high-points a ball with his insane arm length. He won't blow by any defenders, but he should be able to make most catches, and he's tough to bring down. The one negative on JJAW is that he's slow through his routes, so he will on occasion telegraph where he's going and let the corner jump his route.

2019 Value: The Eagles tried to trade Nelson Agholor before the draft, but his back-loaded contract has him making over $9 million this season. JJAW should be used in red-zone and goal-line packages immediately, but with Zach Ertz, Dallas Goedert, Alshon Jeffrey, DeSean Jackson and Jordan Howard, he may not have a ton of opportunities to produce this year.

Dynasty/Keeper Value: This is going to get better and better with every year, in my opinion. The only big pass catcher that comes off the books before 2021 is Agholor after this season, so as DJax is playing out his contract and Jeffery is getting long in the tooth. JJAW should be establishing himself. Probably not a fantastic option in keeper leagues, but dynasty leagues should like him when planning far ahead.

Parris Campbell (Ohio State), Colts - Round 2, Pick 59

I wish A.J. Brown would have landed with the Colts instead, but Campbell going to Indy is the next-best thing. Campbell was one of only three WRs in this class with 90 catches, and he goes to a perfect situation with Andrew Luck as his QB and the slot role seemingly open for some new blood. With T.Y. Hilton getting double teams and Eric Ebron and Jack Doyle occupying the LBs, Campbell should see a lot of easy crossing routes, just like he had at Ohio State. He needs to develop more of a route tree; he wasn't asked to do too much outside of run deep and cross at Ohio State, and he will need to learn to get off a jam at the line because he just doesn't have much experience with that.

2019 Value: With all due respect to Chester Rogers, who stepped up when needed for the Colts last season, Campbell can take over as the slot WR for the Colts in Week 1. I'm probably a little too excited about him, but the potential of him getting matched up 1-on-1 with LBs and safeties gets me all steamed up! He could be a PPR darling from the jump playing in Indy.

Dynasty/Keeper Value: This just seems to get better. Build a rapport with Luck and get better and better every year. The only thing that could hold him back (outside of injuries, which could happen to anyone) is if he just turns into a one-trick pony and gets figured out by defenses. I just can't imagine that happening, though. Here's another from this class who could become a fantasy WR2.

Andy Isabella (Massachusetts), Cardinals - Round 2, Pick 61

Isabella gets everything he can in every situation and might have one of the best motors I've ever seen on any player. He uses his incredible speed to break off routes and torch defenders. The best thing about Isabella landing in Arizona is that an Air Raid system should mask his deficiencies; he will most likely run out of the slot with Christian Kirk while Larry Fitzgerald and fellow pick Hakeem Butler will be on the outside. He won't get jammed at the line, won't be asked to make too many contested catches and might not be asked to block too often.

2019 Value: Ugh, this is difficult to know. He has a brand-new QB and HC, and we don't even know if either is going to pan out at this level. Isabella led this class of WRs with 102 catches last season, so we know he can be productive, but knowing what his role will and how the offense and QB will perform is a lot to ask. This season, he should be a 'just in case this all works' flier at the end of the draft.

Dynasty/Keeper Value: Multiply the 2019 uncertainty by five here. We know the Cardinals are willing to scrap a HC after one year, so if 2019 is an embarrassment, Isabella could wind up with a new playbook and/or QB as early as next season. If Kyler Murray and Kliff Kingsbury create a rousing success, Isabella could be a Wes Welker-like contributor. Brace for a high ceiling but perhaps a low floor. I wish we could find a more definitive answer, but we can't yet.

D.K. Metcalf (Ole Miss), Seahawks - Round 2, Pick 64

I was really surprised by the fall that Metcalf had during the draft. I think it had more to do with the neck injury that ended his 2018 season rather than his bad agility drills at the combine. Either way, the important thing to know is that Metcalf ends up in a great spot where he can take over for retiring Doug Baldwin and play opposite budding star WR Tyler Lockett. Metcalf got a lot of grief those agility drills, but I didn't see that stiffness when he was playing. Metcalf can burn past or run through/over defenders, and when he times his jumps right, he isn't going to get beat at high-pointing the ball. He did have some problems getting off a block, which was surprising for his size, and he didn't time those jumps perfectly all the time, which led to more contested drops than a man of his size should have. He will have to get a more advanced route tree at the NFL level; with the wealth of talent at Ole Miss, he wasn't asked too much outside of fly patterns.

2019 Value: Great fit. Baldwin goes out and Metcalf should be able to step right over David Moore for a starting spot opposite Lockett. Metcalf won't be a huge producer every game -- he averaged fewer than four catches per game last season -- but he did have almost 22 yards per catch. If he paced out the same way for the Seahawks, he would get about 50 catches for over 1,000 yards and double-digit TDs. Take about 25% off, and 30-40 catches for 700-ish yards and six or seven TDs sounds about right.

Dynasty/Keeper Value: Metcalf has as high -- if not the highest -- ceiling of anyone in this class. If he can get a more polished route tree and learn how to use his body to box out DBs, he can be an absolute monster. On the other hand, if he stays a one-trick pony, he is going to max out at 50 catches, which might not be bad considering his explosiveness but would be leaving a lot of meat on the bone.

Diontae Johnson (Toledo), Steelers - Round 3, Pick 66

Johnson is probably the most polarizing WR in this class as I saw him with grades as high as the second round and as low as UDFA/practice squad. I really liked watching his film because he reminded me a bit of Antonio Brown. Lo and behold, the Steelers take him in the third! He was pretty polished from what I saw: He can get off a jam at the line or beat a CB that gives him space. He had great body control and sticky hands. He probably isn't going to win many contested catches, he won't fight off many tacklers, and he might have ball security problems at the next level. His body control is what really reminded me of AB when watching him. He gets his feet down in bounds and can really adjust to an overthrown or underthrown ball.

2019 Value: I'm not expecting much in Year 1. Hopefully this is the year where James Washington proves himself for the Steelers and Johnson will come into the game and make some good catches, but let's not forget the Steelers signed Donte Moncrief, who is expected to be the No. 2 behind JuJu Smith-Schuster this season. He will have to beat out Washington and Eli Rogers (or an injury) to see significant snaps his rookie year, and I wouldn't count on that.

Dynasty/Keeper Value: Johnson could have his big break as soon as 2020. If Moncrief doesn't produce this season, he'll be an easy cut, especially if Johnson or Washington do produce. Washington also isn't a huge hit against the cap if he falters this season. Even if they both put up numbers this year, Johnson is too talented to take a back seat, and he'll up seeing more snaps than at least one of them in 2020.

Jalen Hurd (Baylor), 49ers - Round 3, Pick 67

Hurd played RB for three seasons at Tennessee before transferring to Baylor for his final season and flipping to WR. The most impressive thing to me was how good his hands were right off the bat. He is too big to play RB anyway at 6-foot-4, so the switch makes a lot of sense for his NFL career. Obviously, he's going to need to learn the little things: polishing his route running, getting off a block, and adjusting to poorly thrown balls and contested catches. I'm 100% positive Kyle Shanahan has a plan for him. He'll probably play a bit of RB and run reverses, and Shanahan has already hinted at Hurd possibly playing some TE.

2019 Value: The hard thing about 'Swiss Army knife' players is that their fantasy value is at best inconsistent and at worst muted because the few plays for which they're in may not work. I won't be taking Hurd in any redraft league this year unless he gets TE eligibility -- and it would still have to be a fairly deep league.

Dynasty/Keeper Value: This is tough to discern without knowing for which position he is ticketed. He'll be a nice pickup in deep leagues, especially if he gets TE eligibility and the 49ers give him a decent amount of snaps lining up at multiple positions every game. He could always wind up as a homeless player who has to contribute on special teams like Cordarrelle Patterson, but that's worst-case scenario.

Terry McLaurin (Ohio State), Redskins - Round 3, Pick 76

I would actually compare McLaurin a lot to Deebo Samuel in this class in that he doesn't have too many weaknesses. He's fast (4.35 40 at the Combine) and a pretty good route runner who can do all the little things, and he walks into a situation starving for talent at receiver. All of that *plus* he will probably get his college QB throwing him the ball for the majority of the season. The only knock I had for McLaurin is that his body catches a bit too much, but that was pretty much it.

2019 Value: He holds a huge opportunity in Washington. Paul Richardson was hurt last year, but he's never gone over 44 catches anyway. Calling Josh Doctson a failure might be too nice. RB Chris Thompson played five fewer games than Doctson and had three fewer catches. Jordan Reed is still talented but misses games every year. McLaurin is more of a home-run hitter, so he'll be pushed down in PPR formats, but he can hold some value this season with the lack of talent there.

Dynasty/Keeper Value: I like McLaurin, and I like the fact he already has had time with QB Dwayne Haskins, but I'm not the biggest Haskins fan, so I'm not going to put too much value on McLaurin for the future. I think a borderline fantasy WR3/4 is what I would expect from him if everything is working.

Miles Boykin (Notre Dame), Ravens - Round 3, Pick 93

Boykin landed in a great spot for his actual value. He probably would have been overdrafted for fantasy if he had wound up in a situation with a great QB. Boykin is the type of prospect I hate. He had an AMAZING SPARQ score -- we're talking in the 99th percentile of all WRs that have ever had a score -- so he has a mountain of athleticism. The problem is that his film doesn't match up with that score. He had flashes, and his highlight reel is awesome, but on a play-to-play basis, he hasn't hit his ceiling yet. He has a shot to get coached up and really learn the position in Baltimore, though.

2019 Value: I would say close to none, but there isn't a ton of talent on the roster to start with. Keep expectations low: He is most likely a project that should pay off in a few years, but a few injuries or poor performances could thrust him into early action. He's a waiver-wire add at best.

Dynasty/Keeper Value: Boykin is a lottery ticket. If you take him in a dynasty league, you have to be ready to wait until Year 3 for him to really break out if he can get better at the little things while retaining that incredible athleticism. Think Adam Thielen upside with a Devin Funchess floor.

Hakeem Butler (Iowa State), Cardinals - Round 4, Pick 103

Landing in Arizona is great for any WR. I do think that a Kliff Kingsbury offense will mask Andy Isabella's weaknesses better than it will Butler's, but the Cardinals have a ton of targets to go around, so everyone should eat. Butler is going to own press coverage, so the CBs better be laying off him; he's not the best at contested catches for his size (6-foot-5), and he isn't going to beat many defenders deep. But if he gets the ball in his hands, bringing him down is going to be a chore.

2019 Value: With Arizona's crowded receiving picture, Butler needs to build a quick rapport with Kyler Murray to get fed. He should be a decent red-zone target, but with Larry Fitzgerald and David Johnson on this team as well, he's at best third fiddle. He's worth a flier at the end of deeper redrafts, but for most leagues, he should be a waivers add.

Dynasty/Keeper Value: Rinse and repeat of what I said with Isabella. Butler can play in any offense, and Isabella might be more restricted, but Kingsbury being successful is the best thing for any WR in Arizona.

Gary Jennings (West Virginia), Seahawks - Round 4, Pick 120

Jennings was probably a bit of a reach in the fourth. He is a good slot WR who will get tons of YAC and turn it upfield quickly. He had too many drops because he body-catches a bit too much. With Doug

Baldwin retiring and Amara Darboh being a bust so far, he shouldn't have much trouble making the roster.

2019 Value: Jennings will be waiting for an injury to see snaps, so he should be a waiver add if anything at all.

Dynasty/Keeper Value: There are worse WRs in this class, but there are also a few drafted after him that I would take first. If your rookie draft goes deeper than five rounds, he's a pick for sure, but he's borderline if it's any shorter than that.

Riley Ridley (Georgia), Bears - Round 4, Pick 126

I really like Ridley as a prospect. I guarantee you if he had wound up in Kansas City, he would be getting the hype that Mecole Hardman is (also undeservedly). Ridley doesn't have the athleticism that his former teammate at Georgia, but he has way more polished routes, and he plays way faster than his combine times. He can develop into a good WR, but being buried on the Bears aerial hierarchy shovels some dirt on that assumption.

2019 Value: Allen Robinson, Taylor Gabriel and Anthony Miller will all be ahead of him on the depth chart, with Cordarrelle Patterson possibly as well. Should Ridley see the field, the Bears also have Trey Burton, Adam Shaheen, David Montgomery and Tarik Cohen as receiving options. So Ridley's single-year value is … pretty much nothing.

Dynasty/Keeper Value: The sliver of hope for Ridley comes with Gabriel possibly getting cut next season. Gabriel hasn't been wildly successful in his NFL career, but he did have his best year in 2018 in his first campaign with the Bears. Ridley has to slide down rookie draft boards because of the landing spot.

Hunter Renfrow (Clemson), Raiders - Round 5, Pick 149

Mike Mayock came into this draft not only looking for talent but high IQ/leadership from his picks. Renfrow has those locked up. He was able to stay on the field at Clemson surrounded by a ton of five-star athletes because he had the trust of the coaches to run the right route and play with intensity on every snap. He isn't the most physically gifted option, but he made his teammates better, and that's what the Raiders are looking for.

2019 Value: The Raiders added Antonio Brown and Tyrell Williams, who should easily be the No. 1 and 2 receiving options, but the No. 3 WR spot should be up in the air, and that is what we would like to see Renfow come away with. If he does, he can be a nice underneath option for Derek Carr, who lost confidence in his deep ball last season -- possibly because of the lack of talent at WR.

Dynasty/Keeper Value: Renfrow probably only has the ceiling of a WR3 on his own team, so expecting him to do a ton on a year-to-year basis is asking a lot. He's the last WR on your bench, at best.

Darius Slayton (Auburn), Giants - Round 5, Pick 171

Out of all the picks GM Dave Gettleman made, this one probably surprised me the most. Slayton is a good player, but I thought there were better WRs on the board. Slayton is a deep threat; he averaged 20.3 yards per catch over three seasons at Auburn, so he could contribute early if he's only asked to run deep routes.

2019 Value: The nice thing for Slayton is that the guys in front of him all flamed out in their first chances. Cody Latimer, Corey Coleman and Bennie Fowler can all be beat if Slayton has a standout preseason. Even if he does surpass those guys, Golden Tate, Saquon Barkley, Sterling Shepard and Evan Engram are going to absorb 90% of the targets.

Dynasty/Keeper Value: Maybe getting to a system that doesn't run the ball a million times and throws the ball will be nice for Slayton, but I'm not sure he'll develop into much more than a deep threat. If I'm wrong about Daniel Jones, there's no way Slayton makes an impact.

KeeSean Johnson (Fresno State), Buccaneers - Round 6, Pick 174
Kliff Kingsbury drafted the two WRs with the most production in this class. Andy Isabella is the only WR over 100 catches, and Johnson was second with 95. The good news is that the Cardinals are going to need plenty of WR depth, but they have some guys ready to challenge Johnson for a roster spot.
2019 Value: Kevin White, Chad Williams and Pharoh Cooper are all guys that I liked coming out of college more than Johnson, so he is going to have to contribute on special teams and outplay at least 2 of those guys to get a roster spot.
Dynasty/Keeper Value: Arizona is a nice landing spot if he makes the roster and Kingsbury sticks, but he's going to have to be just a waiver add for me in almost all formats.

Travis Fulgham (Old Dominion), Lions - Round 6, Pick 184
Fulgham is going to be a special teamer for the Lions IF he makes the 53. He was productive at Old Dominion, and should an opportunity rise, he could seize some work. He crisp routes and had a nose for the end zone.
2019 Value: The Lions are already five-deep at WR. It would take more than one injury for a significant chance at production to find Fulgham.
Dynasty/Keeper Value: Not much -- a waiver wire add in almost all formats

Juwann Winfree (Colorado), Broncos - Round 6, Pick 187
This is a flier pick for the Broncos. Winfree wasn't on too many radars because he has been hampered by injuries in his collegiate career. His numbers from Maryland and Colorado aren't bad, but they also don't jump out.
2019 Value: The Broncos are at least four-deep at WR already with Emmanuel Sanders, Courtland Sutton, DaeSean Hamilton and Tim Patrick. Winfree will have to battle River Cracraft and small-school UDFAs Kelvin McKnight and Trinity Benson to make the roster.
Dynasty/Keeper Value: None right now

Marcus Green (Louisiana-Monroe), Falcons - Round 6, Pick 203
Green is a candidate for kickoff- and punt-return duties. Green had some productive seasons at ULM, but his special-teams focus all but erases any fantasy appeal.
2019 Value: Kick Returner
Dynasty/Keeper Value: None

Kelvin Harmon (North Carolina State), Redskins - Round 6, Pick 206
This is the last WR drafted that holds value for this year. It's clear now as a late sixth-round pick that Harmon made a mistake leaving NC State early, but landing with the Redskins can help. He probably already has a roster spot locked up. He is a natural catcher with great athleticism but lacks top-end speed and suddenness. He has had 1,000 yards the last two seasons and was talked about as potentially being the first WR off the board during the CFB season last year.
2019 Value: Sixth-round picks are at best a coin flip to make the roster usually, but with Harmon's production and the need at WR for the Redskins, I think he's a lock. I wouldn't be surprised to see him earn a role quickly, but he shouldn't be drafted in any leagues until he proves himself.
Dynasty/Keeper Value: I'm a fan of Harmon, so I wouldn't mind taking him over a lot of the WRs who went ahead of him in a rookie draft. The stigma of being a post-200 pick doesn't do him any favors, but I think the bad reception to his Combine numbers was overblown, and he'll be productive enough to call a late-round steal in a few years.

The Rest

Scott Miller (Bowling Green), Buccaneers - Round 6, Pick 208

Miller had some great production at Bowling Green, and I would be excited about him if he hadn't landed in a spot that has WR covered already. The top three spots are locked for TB with Mike Evans, Chris Godwin and Breshad Perriman. I also like the UDFAs Justin Johnson and DaMarkus Lodge more than I like Miller. It'll be an uphill battle for him the make the roster.

John Ursua (Hawaii), Seahawks - Round 7, Pick 236

The Seahawks are going to have a fun competition at WR this season. Ursua will have to prove useful on special teams; he has returned punts before, but I don't think he's played in coverage units. He was productive at Hawaii and can be a slot option, but he has a lot of people to beat out for a roster spot.

Terry Godwin (Georgia), Panthers - Round 7, Pick 237

Godwin was highly recruited coming out of high school but never lived up to the hype at Georgia. The Panthers are already five-deep at WR with D.J. Moore, Torrey Smith, Chris Hogan, Curtis Samuel and Jarius Wright, so Godwin will have to impress in the preseason and be a ST contributor to make the roster.

Dillon Mitchell (Oregon), Vikings - Round 7, Pick 239

Mitchell has upside because he's great at creating after the catch. His attitude is what pushed him all the way to the end of the draft, though, before which NFL decision makers said that 'he has to take the game seriously.' The skill is there; we'll find out in camp and the preseason if the 'want to' is.

Bisi Johnson (Colorado State), Vikings - Round 7, Pick 247

Johnson is the complete opposite of Mitchell. The high-effort player has refined his game to make up for a lack of athleticism. They could both make the roster, but I'd bet on Bisi first.

David Sills (West Virginia), Bills - UDFA

Sills going undrafted really shows the depth of the talent in this draft. Sills is a converted QB (forgive me if you've heard that a million times on every WVU broadcast), so he is still learning refining his game at the position. He can already box out defenders, especially in the red zone, as he's had 33 TDs over the last two seasons. Landing in Buffalo should give him a chance to make an NFL roster.

Anthony Ratliff-Williams (North Carolina), Titans - UDFA

Another converted QB playing WR who went undrafted this season, ARW had some impressive tape for a guy with only two seasons of starting at WR. He was surprisingly instinctive at WR: He bodied up defenders well and can already make a contested catch. He's probably more game-quick than test-quick, and he lined up all over the place, out wide, slot, RB, reverse, trick-play passes and kick/punt returns. He may not make the team in Tennessee but hopefully can latch on somewhere.

Preston Williams (Colorado State), Dolphins - UDFA

Williams was undrafted because of a domestic incident that happened while at school. He was passed over for the Combine because of it, and with there being so many talented WRs in this draft, he fell off many teams' boards. When he finally got a shot last year at Colorado State, he was productive with a 96-1,345-14 line. While the Dolphins don't have a big-time playmaking WR, they have Brice Butler and Isaiah Ford, who have experience, in front of Williams. Going to be tough for him to make the roster….

Jakobi Meyers (NC State), Patriots - UDFA

Meyers was productive at NC State, but he really only has one NFL-caliber tool: his hands. He tied for the slowest WR 40 time at the Combine, ran exclusively out of the slot and isn't explosive after the catch. New England has been able to pick WRs of the scrap heap and turn them into treasure, so there's a little hope here.

Jaylen Smith (Louisville), Ravens - UDFA

The only reason Smith was added to the Ravens roster is because he was Lamar Jackson's favorite target at Louisville. It's a nice story, but don't expect him to make the squad.

Antoine Wesley (Texas Tech), Ravens - UDFA

Wesley had an incredible season at Texas Tech with an 88-1410-9 line. I really liked him coming into the draft: He's one of the best in this class at coming down with contested catches. What concerns me: Not only was he not drafted by his college head coach Kliff Kingsbury, but the Cardinals didn't even get him after the draft. That's a bigger red flag to me than his slow speed.

Stanley Morgan (Nebraska), Bengals - UDFA

I guess I should stop being surprised that some of these guys ended up as UDFAs, but Morgan really jumps out at me as a head scratcher. He had an arrest in 2017 for marijuana, so I'm going to chalk it up to that. Cincy adds a dude with great route-running polish who has the occasional concentration drop. His high motor could make him a great special teamer to start his career.

Penny Hart (Georgia State), Colts - UDFA

The word "sleeper" was kicked around a lot for Hart in the pre-draft process, and it looks like everyone slept on him. He's well-rounded, ran out of every spot as a WR, returned kicks and punts, and was productive, especially in his sophomore season. He's small and didn't participate in the Combine, so he fell of radars. The Colts are stacked at WR, so he might need to land somewhere else to make a roster.

Emanuel Hall (Missouri), Bears - UDFA

Hall and Mecole Hardman were pretty similar to me. I think there's more upside for Hardman. But Hall is more established as Drew Lock's go-to guy at Missouri, and his record was much better when Hall was healthy. Hall has never played in every game in a season, and during three of his four years, he only played in eight. Riley Ridley is going to have a tough time making the roster as a fourth-round pick, so Hall has next to no shot.

Anthony Johnson (Buffalo), Buccaneers - UDFA

This is one of those UDFAs I like better than Scott Miller for Tampa Bay. Johnson can be a better pro than college player if given the chance. He is a big-bodied WR who can make most contested catches. He suffered from bad QB play at Buffalo, and even after he was getting doubled after his great junior year, he still ended up with double-digit TDs for Buffalo. He's hasn't played much special teams, so he'll probably need to impress head coach Bruce Arians to make the roster.

DaMarkus Lodge (Ole Miss), Buccaneers - UDFA

I know Lodge was draft guru Dane Bruglar's favorite of the bunch coming out of Ole Miss. He isn't going to blow anyone away with incredible athleticism, but Lodge has great body control and will catch just about anything thrown his way. It's the same deal with him as it is with Anthony Johnson: He hasn't done much in ST, so he needs big performances in the preseason.

TIGHT ENDS

T.J. Hockenson (Iowa), Lions - Round 1, Pick 8

He was the most complete TE coming into the Draft since O.J. Howard. Hock had a great season seemingly out of nowhere last year. He's a tremendous blocker, ran all the routes on the line and split out wide. He makes contested catches and can make a tackler miss or run him over. He didn't really have many weaknesses -- maybe experience? He came out as a rSO and only played two seasons at Iowa. He's the closest thing to Gronk we've had since he came into the league.

2019 Value: I have some reservations about going all-in on a TE in Year 1. There aren't too many TEs that come into the league and light it on fire. Matthew Stafford didn't get the ball to Eric Ebron, and as soon as he moved on, he had a career year in Indianapolis. Someone is going to draft him as a fantasy TE1. That's not something I would do.

Dynasty/Keeper Value: Much better here, of course, as talented TEs with time to develop are enticing. Hockenson should just scratch the surface this year and really turn it on next year. He has the ceiling of a top-five fantasy TE in the next three years.

Noah Fant (Iowa), Broncos - Round 1, Pick 20

Fant is my favorite fantasy player in this class. I wouldn't rank him the highest, of course, because TEs take a while to develop. Fant reminds me A LOT of Jimmy Graham. He's not as great a blocker as Hockenson is, but he is still pretty damn good. Fant will be such a good weapon in the receiving game that he probably won't be asked to block too often. He's going to be a nightmare matchup for a long time.

2019 Value: I think he'll be the most productive TE of this class, but once again, I don't think I can put a rookie at TE1 just yet. If you have deep benches or one of those crazy leagues that has two TEs as starters, I would take him as a bench player just in case he impresses from the jump.

Dynasty/Keeper Value: HUGE! Fant is going to be an absolute stud for a long time. Like I mentioned before, he seems a lot like Graham -- except he comes into the league more polished with better blocking skills. It'll be hard to pass Travis Kelce, Zach Ertz and George Kittle, but he has the ceiling to be in that group.

Irv Smith Jr. (Alabama), Vikings - Round 2, Pick 50

Smith would be getting a lot more run if he weren't in a class with the two monsters from Iowa. Smith's run blocking will get him on the field early, but he is also a great pass catcher. Smith has enough speed to torch LBs, and he runs crisp routes. Alabama had so much talent to spread defenses thin that he didn't really have too many contested catches, so I have no idea how he'll handle that. He body-catches a bit too much, as well, but that's fixable.

2019 Value: Drafting Smith probably means that this is the swan song for Kyle Rudolph in Minnesota, who will probably let Smith sit and learn behind Rudolph for his rookie year as well. I wouldn't expect a high snap count for Smith in 2019 unless there's an injury to Rudolph.

Dynasty/Keeper Value: 2020 will be his year to shine. Rudolph will be gone, and Smith will be experienced enough to take over the full-time gig. I would expect to get similar production from Smith that we had from Rudolph. He probably won't be a top-five TE ever, but he will be good enough to eventually be a TE1 with Kirk Cousins throwing him the ball.

Drew Sample (Washington), Bengals - Round 2, Pick 52

This was a surprising pick. The Bengals have needed a Tyler Eifert replacement for a while, so getting a TE in this draft was a priority, but taking Sample in the second round seemed like a bit of a stretch. Sample already is a superb run blocker, so that part of his game is going to help Joe Mixon and the RBs from Day 1. For our fantasy teams, he will be a bit of a project as he only caught 46 passes total over four college seasons, leading with 25 last season.

2019 Value: Not much; he will be used as a blocker in the run game way more than as a receiver. There is some upside for him in the receiving game, but I wouldn't count on it coming to fruition this season.

Dynasty/Keeper Value: The good thing about Sample is that with him being a second-round pick, the Bengals are likelier to give him as long as possible to contribute in the receiving game. I won't be taking him in any of my dynasty leagues even with him getting a long leash. I don't have the patience to wait that long.

Josh Oliver (San Jose State), Jaguars - Round 3, Pick 69

Oliver is way more of a receiving option than a blocker. Oliver had plenty of snaps where he lined up inline and was throwing blocks for RBs; he also lined up at H-Back and threw blocks. Blocking just isn't his forte. Oliver shined when he was able to split out wide and catch a pass. He had a 56-709-4 line his senior year at San Jose State and was more productive than his previous three seasons.

2019 Value: Oliver will come into Jacksonville and most likely instantly be the best receiving option they have at TE. However, his suboptimal blocking skills will most likely keep him off the field on most snaps. He has a shot to develop and maybe earn more of a role later in the season, but he should be left to the waiver wire.

Dynasty/Keeper Value: Oliver is much more valuable in a dynasty league. He should be able to develop and build a rapport with Nick Foles and become an actual weapon in the offense. The Jaguars potentially adding better WR targets (or them becoming better with Foles) should open things up for him moving forward as well.

Jace Sternberger (Texas A&M), Packers - Round 3, Pick 75

Begrudgingly, I have to admit that really enjoyed watching the film on Sternberger. His motor is incredible, and he will outwill a lot of the guys across from him especially late in the game. Sternberger really shined after leaving Kansas and transferring to the Aggies after one season at JUCO. Sternberger runs crisp routes, can body up a defender and was an incredible red-zone threat with 10 TDs in his only season with the Aggies. He will have to get better at blocking to see an increased snap count. The effort was there for his blocking, but the skill is lacking.

2019 Value: Not much; even though Sternberger can come in and be an immediate threat in the receiving game, he has to get by Jimmy Graham and Marcedes Lewis on the depth chart. I don't expect him to see much of the field barring an injury or Lewis being cut before the season starts.

Dynasty/Keeper Value: I'm excited to draft Sternberger in dynasty rookie drafts. He will be able to learn behind one of the bests in Graham and can be a red-zone threat as soon as he starts seeing regular snaps. Patience is a must with any TE, but Sternberger should be contributing in 2020.

The Rest

Kahale Warring (San Diego State), Texans - Round 3, Pick 86

Warring is a nice option for the Texans, but I just have no idea what they are doing with the position, and it seems like they don't either. The Texans released Ryan Griffin after he was arrested, and they drafted two TEs in 2018: Jordan Akins in the third and Jordan Thomas in the sixth. I assume Warring is going to make the roster, but I have no idea how much time he's going to see as a rookie, and I wouldn't be surprised if the Texans keep going to the TE well next year until they figure it out.

Dawson Knox (Ole Miss), Bills - Round 3, Pick 96

Knox is a project actually worth taking. He has tons of physical upside and is already a legit threat on a vertical route. He converted to TE from QB at Ole Miss and has only had 18 total games at the position, so he is going to need some time to be molded. He has 39 catches in his college career with none of them resulting in a TD which is a weird anomaly, but having D.K. Metcalf, A.J. Brown and DaMarkus Lodge on your team leaves you low on the totem pole. If you have a deep enough roster to add him and wait, he's worth a shot for sure, but in redraft and keeper leagues, he can be ignored.

Trevon Wesco (West Virginia), Jets - Round 4, Pick 121

Wesco is more of a pick that is going to help Le'Veon Bell with run blocking and Sam Darnold with pass protection. Chris Herndon IV is still going to be the main pass-catching TE. Wesco only ended up with 26 catches last season as the starter at WVU, so expecting aerial work for him is a bit much.

Foster Moreau (LSU), Raiders - Round 4, Pick 137

The Raiders are looking for a TE since Jared Cook bolted for New Orleans. Even with that need, Moreau is more likely a depth TE. He is going to be brought in as an extra blocker and probably won't get much more than that this season. He probably won't make an impact down the line as a pass catcher either. Leave him on the wire.

Zach Gentry (Michigan), Steelers - Round 5, Pick 141

Gentry comes in as a Jesse James replacement. He did well last season as a pass catcher for Michigan last season, posting a 32-514-2 line. Standing at just a shade over 6-foot-8, he could be an immediate red-zone threat with Ben Roethlisberger throwing the ball. Gentry will have to earn his spot over Xavier Grimble to make any kind of impact this season. I think the same type of production James left is what we can expect as upside for Gentry, with maybe some more TD chances.

Kaden Smith (Stanford), 49ers - Round 6, Pick 176

The good news is that Smith is great as a pass catcher. The bad news is he might not be able to do enough of anything else get and stay on the field. I would really not be into Smith if he hadn't ended up on the 49ers with Kyle Shanahan as his HC. Even still, there isn't a lot of upside, he doesn't block well and he's slow enough to make almost every catch contested. If he doesn't get better at the little things, he'll have a quick NFL career. There's also this fella named George Kittle ahead of him, and he's decent....

Isaac Nauta (Georgia), Lions - Round 7, Pick 223

I like Nauta as a player, but this situation is definitely not the best. The Lions drafted T.J. Hockenson eighth overall, signed Jesse James in the offseason and still carry Michael Roberts, who already had a little success last season. Nauta will either have to be great on special teams or to make the squad. He dropped because of a terrible Combine and will most likely either be a practice squad guy for the Lions or latch on with another organization that has some TE injuries in the preseason.

Tommy Sweeney (Boston College), Bills - Round 7, Pick 228

Sweeney is pretty much the complete opposite of new teammate Dawson Knox. He was extremely productive for BC and was one of the few good options they had. He should be able to contribute right away as a pass catcher, and while he's not the best blocker, he can still get the job done. He does have way less upside than Knox, but if there are injuries for the Bills, he can contribute immediately. Still only a waiver-wire add, though....

Alize Mack (Notre Dame), Saints - Round 7, Pick 238

I love Mack landing in New Orleans. He has had such bad QB play at Notre Dame that it would be great to see him paired up with future HOFer Drew Brees. The Saints have no fear of reaching down the depth chart and having a relative unknown contribute -- like Keith Kirkwood and Dan Arnold from last season. Mack does have his work cut out for him to make the roster, though, with Jared Cook, Josh Hill and Arnold all ahead of him. His best skill is making contested catches, so maybe he will be used in goal-line formations should he make the team. He's not rosterable for fantasy but has a shot to make an impact.

Caleb Wilson (UCLA), Cardinals - Round 7, Pick 254

Wilson is a perfect fit in Arizona. The only skill he really has is getting to the soft spot in a zone and catching the ball. Should he make the roster in Arizona, he could be a nice weapon for the Cardinals. Ricky Seals-Jones and Charles Clay aren't going to relinquish playing time anytime soon, and Maxx Williams may break camp and join the fray, so Wilson will have to wait for an injury. Still, this is the likeliest scenario for him to become anything relevant for fantasy leagues.

TOP 25 PROSPECTS FOR 2020

QUARTERBACKS

Justin Herbert - Oregon, Sr.
Herbert probably made a mistake by staying in school for his senior season, but he wanted to play a season with his brother Patrick, who is an incoming freshman. He will need to have a great season and improve on his completion rate (59.4%) to hold onto first-round value for next season.

Tua Tagovailoa - Alabama, Jr.
We can start the 'Tank for Tua' chants right now. Tua is a legit first-overall prospect; last season he completed 69% (Nice!) of his passes and had a 43:6 TD:INT. The only reason he was second in the Heisman voting is because he was bad in the SEC Championship game. He has incredible weapons around him and will of course have to be just as good this season, but he's about as much of a lock for a first-round QB as we have.

Jake Fromm - Georgia, Jr.
Fromm was good enough to push fellow top QB prospect Jacob Eason off the roster to Washington. The 'QB1' Netflix star took the Bulldogs to the National Championship Game his Freshman year, but they lost to the Tua-led Crimson Tide. He improved his numbers in his sophomore season jumping his completion rate from 62.2 percent to 67.4 and threw for more yards, more TDs and fewer INTs in one fewer game. He lost 63% of his catches to the NFL from last season in Riley Ridley, Mecole Hardman, Isaac Nauta, and Terry Godwin, so he'll have to adjust there. If he decides to come out, he would probably be the No. 2 QB off the board behind Tua.

Jacob Eason - Washington, Jr.
Before Eason was pushed off the roster at Georgia by Fromm, he was considered a pro prospect, and a lot of scouts have him on the early-season lists. I'm not really sold on him. His completion rate wasn't great in his one season starting at Georgia (55.1%), and he has yet to be named the starter at Washington at this point. He's a guy to keep an eye on. He can vault himself way up boards -- or be undrafted at the end of this season.

<u>Others to watch</u>
Brian Lewerke - Michigan State, Sr.
Riley Neal - Vanderbilt, Sr.
Feleipe Franks - Florida, Jr.
Ian Book - Notre Dame, Jr.
Jordan Love - Utah State, Jr.
Hunter Johnson - Northwestern, 3-So.

RUNNING BACKS

Zack Moss - Utah, Sr.
The entire Utes offense has been QB Tyler Huntley and Moss, who only played nine games last season due to a late-season knee injury. Moss has increased his YPC for three straight seasons, and according to Pro Football Focus, he had the most missed tackles of any RB in the Pac-12 last season. He is the only Senior I have on this list because the list of juniors is outstanding. If he doesn't have any more injury issues, he should be a Day 2 or early Day 3 pick next season.

Travis Etienne - Clemson, Jr.

Etienne makes it look easy for Clemson. The All-American was the ACC Player of the Year last season and averaged 7.8 yards per touch. He had 26 TDs and will be a Heisman favorite this season along with Clemson QB Trevor Lawrence. If we were drafting right now, he would be the first RB off the board for me.

Jonathan Taylor - Wisconsin, Jr.

Stop me if you have heard a Wisconsin RB going in the draft before. Like Etienne, Taylor was an All-American last season. He went over 2,000 yards, and even against stacked boxes he averaged 6.9 YPC. He will have to become more of a pass catcher (only 16 receptions in two seasons) to move up draft boards, but former Badger Melvin Gordon only had three going into his junior year and had 19 that season. I will say that I've seen Taylor put the ball on the ground more than a few times, so he's going to have to clean that up too, but he will be going early should he decide to leave after this year.

Eno Benjamin - Arizona State, Jr.

When I was watching N'Keal Harry's film, I got lost on occasion when Benjamin would carry the ball. He's already a pretty complete back going into his junior season. He had 335 touches last season, which might go up with QB Manny Wilkins and Harry leaving. If the production stays close to the same with the defenses shifting the focus to him, he will come off the board early next year.

AJ Dillon - Boston College, Jr.

Few freshman RBs are going to come in and get 300 carries off the bat, but Dillon did just that for the Eagles. He quickly became the focal point of the offense at BC and will be tasked with that again in 2019. An ankle injury cost Dillon the final two games of the regular season, and his bowl game was canceled due to lightning, so he should be rested up and ready to go this season. The combine will probably play into what kind of buzz he gets should he decide to leave for the draft next year.

D'Andre Swift - Georgia, Jr.

I would argue Swift is Fromm's favorite target because he was the checkdown guy on almost every play, and he wound up with a 32-297-3 receiving line last season to go along with a 163-1049-10 rushing output. He was beat out by Elijah Holyfield at the end of the season for carries, and Georgia is always going to have a wealth of talent. 2019 is going to be a big season for Swift's draft stock.

J.K. Dobbins - Ohio State, Jr.

When Mike Weber was banged up in 2017, Dobbins proved that he was the best RB at Ohio State, since taking the job and not looking back. He should see even more carries this season. Weber went on to the Cowboys, and new starting QB Justin Fields is going to be learning on the job. ESPN draft expert Todd McShay already has Dobbins in the first round of his first 2020 mock. Eyes are on him.

Cam Akers - Florida State, Jr.

Akers had an enormous amount of buzz around him coming into FSU his freshman year. He has been a huge letdown so far in his college career; the Seminoles have gone through two coaches and haven't had any success with choosing a QB. Hopefully getting some new faces along the OL and a new QB in Alex Hornibrook will show us what Akers can actually do with some help around him.

Najee Harris - Alabama, Jr.

We don't have a ton of film on Harris, but he had more experience than Josh Jacobs, who was the first RB off the 2019 NFL Draft board. Harris is a five-star recruit who's going to get the most carries out of an always rotational backfield at 'Bama. It will be no surprise to see Harris skyrocket up boards with a great 2019-2020 season.

Others to watch

Patrick Taylor Jr. - Memphis, Sr.
Joshua Kelley - UCLA, Sr.
Scottie Phillips - Ole Miss, Sr.
Brian Robinson Jr. - Alabama, Jr.

Michael Warren II - Cincinnati, Jr.
JaTarvious Whitlow - Auburn, Jr.
CJ Verdell - Oregon, Jr.
Salvon Ahmed - Washington, Jr.
Kennedy Brooks - Oklahoma, Jr.

WIDE RECEIVERS

Collin Johnson - Texas, Sr.

I was happy to see my man Collin stay at Texas for his senior season. It's tough to say whether he hurt or helped his draft stock: This class has more top-end talent but doesn't seem as deep as 2019. Johnson is big-bodied (6-foot-6) and highly athletic; he should be off the board in the first two days. He's been Sam Ehlinger's No. 1 target and will be again this coming season.

Tyler Johnson - Minnesota, Sr.

Johnson has steadily improved three seasons in a row and will be hard-pressed to get to the 78-1169-12 line he had in 2018. If he puts up these types of numbers again with a rotational QB spot like he had last season, NFL front offices will take notice.

K.J. Hill - Ohio State, Sr.

Hill might have done better for himself by coming out in this year's draft, but he stuck around for his senior season with the Buckeyes and is hoping to cash in. He'll be by far the No. 1 returning option with 70 receptions in 2018 to 26 for RB J.K. Dobbins and WR Austin Mack. Hopefully, run-first QB Justin Fields will pick Hill as his favorite target early.

Jerry Jeudy - Alabama, Jr.

Jeudy has already been compared to Odell Beckham and is probably the only WR on Heisman lists right now. Jeudy was not only a first-team All-American last year, but he won the Biletnikoff award for the nation's best receiver. Hs 68-1315-14 line was crazy for a 'Bama team that is traditionally run-first. Jeudy would have been the first WR off the board if he were eligible for the 2019 Draft and is in line to be the first non-QB skill position player off the board in 2020.

Laviska Shenault Jr. - Colorado, Jr.

Like Jeudy, Shenault has been compared to another NFL great: Julio Jones. Seemingly out of nowhere, Shenault went from a 7-168 line in 2017 to 86-1011-6 with 17 rushes for 115 yards and 5 more scores this past season. He only played in nine games due to turf toe that also kept him out of the 2019 spring game. If he's healthy and looked anything like he did in 2018, he's a lock for the first round in 2020.

Tee Higgins - Clemson, Jr.

More five-star talent at Clemson…. Higgins is a big-bodied WR who turns 50/50 balls into 80/20 balls at 6-foot-4, and he's the second option behind Travis Etienne. He might even slip to third as Justyn Ross (another top recruit) is emerging as a stud as well. Higgins is having a great collegiate career and is probably going to be a better pro when he becomes a QB's focal point.

Henry Ruggs III - Alabama, Jr.

Everyone was a runner-up next to Jeudy last season, and while I don't know that Ruggs is as talented as the other WRs on this list, he is going to be the second option in the receiving pecking order, and scouts will have eyes on him. He will probably have to be strong at the Combine, especially if the top-end talent all decide to declare, but he could be helped by staying at 'Bama after Jeudy leaves. His 46-741-11 line might seem like a yawner next to Jeudy's, but only five returning WRs in the nation had more TDs than Ruggs.

CeeDee Lamb - Oklahoma, Jr.

Lamb led the Sooners in TDs last season with 11, and that came with first-rounder Marquise Brown on this team. While Jalen Hurts is not Kyler Murray, Lamb should be far and away the No. 1 target for him this season. Lamb is a lot bigger than Brown and will be seeing a lot of short targets he can turn upfield. His value is teetering right now, but a great 2019 performance can land him firmly as a Day 2 pick.

Tylan Wallace - Oklahoma State, Jr.

Wallace had a *monster* 2019 season, putting up a 86-1491-12 season, and he will have to prove that he can do it again with a new QB this season. I watched Wallace carve up my Longhorns last season to the tune of 10-222-2, and he did it finding the soft spot in the zone and breaking off clean routes in man. I don't think he can be a Day 1 pick in 2020, but if he decides to declare, Day 2 is within reach for sure.

Jalen Reagor - TCU, Jr.

I got the chance to see Reagor in person, but it was at the Cheez-It Bowl that infamously had nine interceptions, and he didn't even get a reception. Even in that game, I was able to see that he was the best player on the field, and he is going to be a much better pro than college player. Reagor has great speed and the ability to return kicks and punts. I fear he won't even get to his 72-1061-9 line he had last season with run-first QB Alex Delton coming in via transfer. Hopefully he'll have a great Combine that vaults him up boards.

Others to watch

Rico Bussey Jr. - North Texas, Sr.

Kalija Lipscomb - Vanderbilt, Sr.

Van Jefferson - Florida, Sr.

Tyrie Cleveland - Florida, Sr.

Lawrence Cager - Georgia, Sr.

Anthony Gandy-Golden - Liberty, Sr.

Aaron Fuller - Washington, Sr.

Donovan Peoples-Jones - Michigan, Jr.

Tarik Black - Michigan, Jr.

Corey Sutton - Appalachian State, Jr.

Tamorrion Terry - Florida State, Jr.

JD Spielman - Nebraska, Jr.

TJ Vasher - Texas Tech, Jr.

TIGHT ENDS

Albert Okwuegbunam - Missouri, Jr.
As it stands right now, there's no Noah Fant, T.J. Hockenson or O.J. Howard types in this class of TEs. Albert O is a nice receiving TE option, but he's going to have to stay healthy this season as he's only played in nine games the past two seasons. He also lost QB Drew Lock to the NFL, and Kelly Bryant is coming in. Bryant isn't bad, but he's going to run way more than Lock. If Albert O doesn't declare, this class is going to be fairly ugly.

Grant Calcaterra - Oklahoma, Jr.
Calcaterra only has 36 catches over the past two seasons. He does have nine TDs, though, for a crazy 25% rate on his catches. He's kind of a 'tweener' at TE, meaning he didn't line up much inline (I don't remember seeing him do it once), but he did a lot of blocking downfield for RBs and Kyler Murray. He could be a nice option for Jalen Hurts, who's used to throwing to TEs like O.J. Howard and Irv Smith Jr.

Others to watch
Jared Pinkney - Vanderbilt, Sr.
Harrison Bryant - Florida Atlantic, Sr.
Jared Rice - Fresno State, Sr.
Brycen Hopkins - Purdue, Sr.
Hunter Bryant - Washington, Jr.
Colby Parkinson - Stanford, Jr.

Chapter 12

DFS FOOTBALL

Chris Meaney

For me, DFS is all about finding value. I don't know what you do with your Sunday mornings, but I like to go bargain shopping for opportunity and volume.

When I hosted The FanDuel Show on FNTSY Sports Network, I used to have Joe Pisapia on, and we would create value lineups where we would only spend 75% of our budget. The goal wasn't to spend the least amount of money as possible, but to provide the viewers with a value play at each position, so they could afford studs in good spots.

I remember my first big call ... a guest spot on the Fantasy Footballers podcast. It was the most ridiculous suggestion ever and after I finished my segment, I wondered if I really did suffer a concussion at hockey earlier that week. As you likely know by now, the tight end position in fantasy football is pitiful. You either spend up for Travis Kelce, Zach Ertz or George Kittle, or you look for value and spend down (punt) at the position.

I still remember Mike Wright asking if we should even bother with the tight end position because at that time, it was either you spent up for Rob Gronkowski or you took a shot with a much lesser name. I said "Well, the Oakland Raiders allowed 14 catches, 194 yards and four touchdowns to Crockett Gillmore and Tyler Eifert in their first two games. Gary Barnidge has six targets through two games, maybe there's something there." We all laughed. Awkwardly. I thought my fantasy football career was done. Barnidge entered career game No. 72 that week, and he only had 48 catches on his NFL resume. The Browns' tight end caught six of his 10 targets for 105 yards and found the end zone that day. Now I co-host the Fantasy Footballers DFS For the Rest of Us podcast.

Oddly enough, Barnidge went on to score four more touchdowns over his next three games. He crushed his previous career highs with 79 catches, 125 targets, 1,043 yards and nine touchdowns. It turns out it wasn't just about the Oakland Raiders, who allowed the most touchdowns to tight ends in 2015, but it was about seeking out value through opportunity. Barnidge wasn't just called on for blocking that season as the Browns were limited with passing options and played from behind often.

Later that year, I talked to Matt Forte =- former Chicago Bears running back and big fantasy football player -- about their game plan vs Oakland. I told him that in the daily fantasy community, word was out that the Raiders couldn't cover the tight end and many were on Martellus Bennett having a big game. He chuckled and said "yeah, we knew ... it's a copycat league." Bennett had a season-high 13 targets, 11 catches, 83 yards and a touchdown against Oakland.

Of course, the players are aware of what matchups they can exploit, but you need to be as well. It's important to follow team trends, news, lines and totals throughout the year. You need to be on top of each team's tendencies. Which teams struggle to stop the run, which struggle against backs who catch, which get beat over the top or over the middle and which play at the fastest or slowest pace. Be on top of personnel changes.

Before we get into strategy and how to attack each position, let's talk about the types of contests that are available to you. There are two separate types of games in daily fantasy sports: cash games and tournaments. I'll go over each game type and the differences between the two, including which strategies to take when building your lineups.

CASH GAMES

Cash-game contests are the way to go if you're a brand-new DFS player. You don't need to ignore tournaments, but this is a great way to start, and you don't need to spend much if you don't want. I know lots of buddies who play multiple 25 cent contests. You don't need to score as much, either, as these contests are much smaller. The majority of cash games consist of contests such as head-to-head, double-ups, triple-ups and 50/50s. In a head-to-head contest, you only have to beat one other person. In a 50/50 contest, you must take down half of your competition to double your entry.

These contests are the easiest for earning a profit and maintain a bankroll throughout the season. That's if you play with little risk and roster the safest lineup as possible, because the playing field is much smaller in these types of contests. That's the goal here. You're not so much looking for upside. For example, a quarterback who likes to run and a running back who plays on a run-heavy team provide a sturdy foundation. They are considered safe cash-game players as they provide little risk. Drafting a lineup of players who have a solid floor is the way to go.

If you're a brand-new player, don't go looking for head-to-head matchups. Create them and let people join them. This way, you are not joining one of many possible leagues set up by experts. Also, look for beginner leagues as DraftKings has done a nice job over the past couple years catering to those who are just starting out.

GUARANTEED PRIZE POOL (GPP) TOURNAMENTS

You can roster some of the same players in tournaments as you do in cash games, but you'll have to take somewhat of a different approach with the rest of your lineup if you want to have success. These contests are typically harder to win as you're competing against a larger group of people. The tougher the competition, the more satisfying it is when you win, though. Some of the prize pools in tournaments can be life-changing.

When putting together your lineup, you still want to jump on value when possible, but overall, you're looking for upside plays. Imagine each player hitting their maximum potential, or at least close to it. In cash contests, you're looking for a solid floor, but in tournaments you're looking for the highest ceiling. Your entire lineup doesn't need to be filled of only boom-or-bust players, but think big when you're drafting. Unlike the cash contests, you'll need to finish near the top 17-20% to earn a profit.

It's important to try taking a different approach with your lineups in tournaments by avoiding some of the obvious plays, which many in the industry call "chalk plays." If a player is in a good spot with a cheap price tag, it's certainly OK to roster that player, but you should know he'll probably have a high ownership number. You don't want to avoid all the high-ownership players, but it's key to separate your roster from others in case that "for-sure play" bombs. Projecting ownerships can go a long way, and it sometimes means taking a contrarian approach with your roster. That could be as simple as taking a QB or WR in a bad matchup.

Be careful of which tournaments you enter. I typically don't like to go in tournaments where people can play hundreds of lineups. I like to enter a contests where the max is set at 3-5 per person. It eliminates a lot of randomness, which by the way is not a bad strategy if you play multiple lineups. Satellites are always worth your time if you're a big tournament spender as the reward can involve a trip along with a big payout or an entry to a bigger contest.

QUARTERBACKS

Quarterbacks typically rack up the most fantasy points, but that doesn't mean you need to spend up at the position every week. There's a ton of variation, and the gap between QB1 and QB10 sometimes isn't that big at all. If you can get your QB to score three times the amount of his price tag, you're off to a good start. If Carson Wentz is $6,700, for instance, he would have to score 20.1 points to return a profit you want.

I typically shy away from the high-priced quarterbacks as I reserve my money for wideouts and backs. It doesn't mean I won't break the bank as it all depends on the matchups that week. Don't ignore an expensive quarterback if they are playing in a high-total game, but make sure that game is going to be competitive. There's some risk in rostering a QB on a team who may win by 20-plus points. Sometimes targeting players on bad teams is a strategy to take. The Falcons struggled on defense in 2018, which resulted in 608 passing attempts from Matt Ryan -- 80 more than he had in 2017 and the most he's had since 2015. Good QBs on bad defensive squads check the box.

Stacking a wide receiver and a quarterback is not a must, but it's a strategy that works in cash and tournaments. You should mostly always want to match your QB with one of his favorite targets due to the correlation between the points their receivers will rack up. There's certainly risk this strategy could flop; that's why it's one to take in tournaments. For the most part, if your WR has a good day, your QB will too.

Stacking a running back with a quarterback is becoming more of a thing as it used to be considered a contrarian play, until Jared Goff and Todd Gurley combined for six scores in 2017. Stacking increases your variance and, although it's not the best strategy to take, I've seen millions get won from rosters only represented by one team. The first millionaire maker winner I saw had a team full of Pittsburgh Steelers.

RUNNING BACKS

I couple things I like to look at when selecting my running backs are touches, carries, snaps and team implied totals. If the New England Patriots are favored by 17.5 at home, I'll more likely lean towards Sony Michel than I will Tom Brady or Julian Edelman. My feeling here, is that the Pats will be up big and lean on Michel to run out the clock. Of course, the Patriots may be a bad example because they like to rotate running backs, but Michel's 42 red-zone rushing attempts were the sixth-most last season, and he only played 13 games as a rookie. If I feel New England will be involved in a bit of a shootout, I may lean James White.

Early last season, you couldn't roster Derrick Henry. In the first few weeks, Henry only saw the field when his team was up, and they were always playing from behind, so the game script favored Dion Lewis. Henry went from a failed contrarian tournament play ... to a complete fade ... to a tournament-winning player, while finishing as one of the strongest cash-game plays of the season.

If you're a FanDuel player, a back who isn't involved in the passing game isn't that big of a downgrade as it is on DraftKings, where you get a full point for a catch. It's much harder to roster a running back who won't see the field if his team gets down in the game. Garbage time is real, and three or four catches on a final drive goes along way. Red-zone rushing attempts are always an important stat to follow, and even more so if you're playing on FanDuel as you can take a risk on a back who doesn't catch a lot of balls because you only get half a point per reception.

WIDE RECEIVERS & TIGHT ENDS

Targets are the name of the game when it comes to selecting wide receivers. Target shares, red-zone targets and the average depth of target (aDOT) are things you should focus in on. You want to select wideouts who not only play for teams who like to throw the ball but like to throw it in the red zone.

Wideouts who receive short targets benefit more on DraftKings where you get the full point for a catch. The deeper the target is, the greater the scoring ceiling. In tournaments, you should focus on wide receivers with a high-scoring potential.

As mentioned above, the strategy for picking a tight end is simple, although it can be frustrating. There's nothing worse than spending up and getting a dud performance. Focus on tight ends who are part of the game plan, especially when their team gets inside the red zone.

DEFENSE/SPECIAL TEAMS

It's not always about attacking low-scoring total games as I typically like to roster a DST that has the ability to create turnovers. Of course, the fewer points your DST allows, the more fantasy points you'll get, but takeaways will set you apart.

That means attacking a team who will likely have their way on offense, which will force the opposing team to step back and throw more than they may have liked. A strong offense will allow the defense to dial up pressure which will relate to turnovers. Keep in mind you get a point for a sack and two points for fumbles recovered as well as interceptions.

SCORING

DraftKings uses PPR scoring and rewards a three-point bonus for 100 yards rushing, 100 yards receiver and 300 yards passing, while FanDuel uses half-point scoring.

STRATEGY & TIPS

As you know, I like to find value, and the best way to do that is to project targets and touches. Sometimes it happens when injury occurs, a matchup is sweet or someone's promoted up the depth chart. It's not always about picking players on the best teams, though you want to maximize your ceiling.

The first thing I do each Tuesday morning when the schedule flips -- before even looking at the price of players -- is look at the NFL schedule. I'm looking for opening lines and team implied totals. Las Vegas' odds should have a huge influence on your thinking and construction of lineups. They don't build big buildings in Vegas for nothing. They have a pretty good idea of what's going on from week to week. It doesn't mean you have to agree with them, but looking at totals and team implied totals will help you paint a picture of how you think each game will go.

Sometimes seeing the price of a player will influence how you feel about him, so I rank everyone before I look at the price tags. Predicting a script is half the battle. If the Bills-Ravens total is at 36.5, and you believe it'll be a low-scoring game like Vegas has predicted, then there really isn't much of a point in rostering many from this contest. Maybe the backs or the DSTs from this game and that's all.

Maybe the biggest tip of all surrounds around patience. Though you are spending money, don't let a bad week shake you up. There's so much variance in fantasy sports, and losing streaks happen. You just have to accept them and be willing to move on. Recency bias is a thing, so don't get caught up in it.

As mentioned earlier, don't get trapped into spending all of your money. It's OK to leave a few hundred off the board. Be aware of ownership projections, but don't ignore someone you like because you think they'll be chalky. The fantasy community is more in touch than ever and can easily pump up a player who moves up a depth chart. Don't ignore public perception, but as my ol' buddy Joe says, "If it's right, it's right."

There are a couple different ways you can look at ownerships. You can either side with the chalk or against it. Don't be afraid to be contrarian. You don't have to do this all the time, but if you like a QB atop the board, but you're afraid of spending all that money ... it's likely others are, too. On the flip side, don't be afraid to fade some of the talent atop the board. Have a unique lineup in tournaments, but most of all, have fun! If you have any questions along the way, you can always reach me on Twitter @chrismeaney.

Chapter 13

2019 ALL-OVERRATED/UNDERRATED TEAMS

OVERRATED

Quarterback

Joe: Russell Wilson, SEA

Although Wilson has star power, don't confuse that with fantasy power. He had just one 300-yard game last year and 10 weeks of fewer than 20 fantasy points. That's not going to be worthy of his name-recognition-based ADP.

Jake: Baker Mayfield, CLE

Let's be clear. I was on the Mayfield train last year and am for 2019, but it's now speeding out of control. When people start debating Mayfield versus Deshaun Watson, the excitement and hype have gone too far. Mayfield should have one of the best breakout seasons of all time with Odell Beckham now in town, but let's not anoint him as the second- or third-best quarterback in fantasy just yet.

Matt: Patrick Mahomes, KC

Last season, Mahomes solidified himself as a fantasy football superstar. His 50 TD passes and 5,097 pass yards earned him the NFL MVP, and he finished the year as fantasy's QB1 by a wide margin. All this after going undrafted or selected as a bench option in the majority of leagues. His unparalleled athletic talent under center separates him from the pack; that's not in question. But as a result, he's flying off draft boards as early as the second round, and his ADP could creep higher as the summer wears on. Not to take anything away from Mahomes (he's one of my personal favorites to watch week in and week out), but why would you reach into the second round to draft him, when he's living proof that you can get a league-winning fantasy QB in the later rounds? His 50-TD mark has been tied or eclipsed by only two other quarterbacks in NFL history (Tom Brady in 2007, Peyton Manning in 2013). For him to repeat would be completely unprecedented. Now, there's an entire season of film on the young star for the opposition to pick apart. Save your QB pick for later.

Nate: Russell Wilson, SEA

I had Wilson ranked as my 6th QB prior to the 2018 season and was heavily criticized he wasn't in my top 3. He finished 2018 as the #9 QB. Sometimes, you have to evaluate the environment over the talent of a player. Jimmy Graham and Paul Richardson accounted for 47% of Wilson's TDs in 2017 and they were gone. The duo also combined for 61% of his RZ TDs, 48% of his RZ targets, and 51% of his RZ completions. Now, Wilson is the highest-paid QB in the NFL (at the time this was written), but the Seahawks haven't done much to improve their offense. Tyler Lockett may end up being the WR1 on this team as Doug Baldwin now appears retired. I just don't see enough in this offense to draft Wilson at his current ADP.

Gary: Russell Wilson, SEA

From an NFL perspective, Wilson's absolutely deserving of contract he just signed that made him the league's highest-paid player. But that fat contract, past performance and name recognition also combine to inflate Wilson's fantasy value. Last season, the 30-year-old barely cracked the top 10 fantasy quarterbacks, and with Doug Baldwin apparently retired, Wilson has lost his most dependable option in the passing game. If the Seahawks are going to have success in 2019, it's going to be by playing ball-control offense and grinding out victories, not by Wilson airing it out. There may be a few big games, but not enough to justify his ADP.

Bogman: Philip Rivers, LAC

My answer would really be all QBs. I tend not to take QBs until late anyway, but while Rivers is moving down draft boards, I'm not sure he's even a QB1 in a 16-man league anymore. He was boom-or-bust last year with 7 games with fewer than 20 points last season and only 3 games of over 25. Rivers should be your backup if you take a risk on a young QB like Lamar Jackson or Kyler Murray.

Derek: Jared Goff, LAR

The word "system quarterback" gets thrown around a lot, but after Goff's system was tampered with by Cooper Kupp's torn ACL, he proceeded to sink like the Titanic. After Kupp's injury, Goff was QB17 over the remainder of the season. Kupp sustained his injury during November (Week 10) last season. Considering the timeline for recovery for ACLs, Kupp being 100 percent and not being limited in snaps or effectiveness for much of the season can't be ruled out. The version of Goff without a fully functional Cooper Kupp has not been pretty. Add Todd Gurley's injury concerns and a group of unproven running backs behind him, and Goff suddenly becomes a less surefire top-12 quarterback and more of a borderline streamer.

Chris: Patrick Mahomes, KC

This is not a knock on Mahomes; he's simply amazing. He's coming off an MVP season in which he racked up 5,097 yards and finished as QB1 in fantasy. Mahomes became just the third player to throw 50 TDs in a season, joining two of the best to ever do it in Tom Brady and Peyton Manning. Pretty remarkable considering it was his first season as a starter. All that said, you'd be silly not to expect some regression out of the Chiefs' QB in 2019. Mahomes will struggle to repeat last year's showing, and there's no reason to reach in the early rounds for him. If you've been a frequent reader, you know to wait it out a bit at the QB position. My feeling is Hill will miss a good chunk of the season, and Sammy Watkins has had his fair share of injuries. This KC team may be one Travis Kelce injury away from a 4-12 season.

Running Back

Joe: Leonard Fournette, JAC

He has a long injury history dating back to his college days. He has off-field issues and was in the doghouse with his organization last year. The Jaguars offense will not be remade all of a sudden into a juggernaut with Nick Foles leading the charge. Too many negatives for his consensus ADP.

Jake: Devonta Freeman, ATL

Freeman should not be anywhere near fringe-RB1 talk with the way he runs … and the injury history. The talent is RB1-quality, and his career workload wouldn't even be much of a concern if he didn't insist on running headfirst into every defender. Freeman has a better chance to miss half the season than finish in the top 15.

Matt: Marlon Mack, IND

Mack finished 2018 as fantasy's RB19 with 161.1 standard points through the 12 games he played. The Colts didn't make any headlining additions to their running back room this offseason (they signed Spencer Ware, didn't draft any backs), so there's a drumbeat building that the team believes Mack can be its feature back, hence his RB16-ish ADP in early mocks. But if you take a closer look at his 2018 production, he scored about 50% of his total points in just three games and only hauled in 17 passes in 12 games. That doesn't scream three-down back to me, and sophomore Nyheim Hines will likely remain in the mix; he put himself on the radar as a talented pass-catching weapon out of the backfield as a rookie. Mack also comes with serious durability issues. He's been hampered by (or out with) ankle, foot, hamstring and hip issues throughout his short NFL career. I understand the hype about the Colts offense heading into 2019, but Mack brings some baggage and is a back I'll be avoiding in drafts all summer.

Nate: Nick Chubb, CLE

Don't get me wrong, Chubb is a top-end talent at the position, but he has too many variables heading into 2019. The Browns signed Kareem Hunt and traded for Odell Beckham. Both of these moves can negatively impact the second-year running back. OBJ will not only demand volume but will likely take away scoring opportunities from the run game. Hunt is suspended the first 8 games but returns at the peak of the fantasy season -- just in time to make you uncomfortable as a Chubb owner. Hunt isn't coming back from injury. He just had a season in which he rushed for 824 yards and 7 TDs. He added another 378 receiving yards and another 7 TDs through the air ... in just 11 GAMES. It would be irresponsible for the Browns to not utilize that talent along with Chubb in the second half of the season. Hunt, more so than OBJ, is why I'm a bit weary on Chubb's 2019 value.

Gary: Todd Gurley, LAR

Could Gurley finish the 2019 season as a fantasy RB1 -- or even a top-5 producer at the position? Sure. The 24-year-old could also wind up a season-killing, first-round bust. Gurley's knee has gone from potentially problematic to damned concerning -- so much so that the Rams both matched the offer sheet for Malcolm Brown and drafted Darrell Henderson. The best-case in 2019 is that Gurley stays healthy because the Rams limit his touches (and opportunities to produce). The worst case is that he can't stay on the field at all. There's just far too much risk for my blood. You can't win a fantasy league in Round 1. But you can absolutely lose it.

Bogman: Chris Carson, SEA

It's not that I dislike Carson; he was very impressive last season grabbing the starting job and keeping it all year. My issue is the elephant in the room, with first-round pick Rashaad Penny. Pete Carroll already said that he wants to maintain a '1-2 punch' at RB as well. This could easily turn into a straight split situation or Penny winning the job outright. I just don't know what to expect from this situation, and I don't want to burn my pick at RB2 on a guy with someone breathing down his neck to take his carries.

Derek: Chris Carson, SEA

This is not so much of a knock on Carson, but it's complete distrust in Pete Carroll. After the Seahawks invested a first-round pick in Rashaad Penny, the forgone conclusion was that he would be given the keys to the Seattle backfield. Kudos to Carson for playing well last season en route to RB15 in PPR. Carroll reversing Carson's fortunes by splitting the touches or Penny ascending in his second year can't be ruled out, which makes Carson, currently ranked among the top 20-24 running backs, overrated. At that price point, I will have zero exposure to Carson this year.

Chris: Leonard Fournette, JAC

Fournette has been limited to 21 games in his two years in the league, and he only played eight last season. He's endured far too many injuries dating back to his LSU days and has caused far too many off-field issues. Trust me, he's not worth the headache.

Wide Receiver

Joe: Sterling Shepard/Golden Tate, NYG

Both Sterling Shepard and Golden Tate appear to be strong ADP values. However, you have to look to the future, where Daniel Jones could be taking over mid-season at QB and that could potentially kill their value as early as Week 6. Tate especially is a trap. He has a consistent track record as a Lion, but last year struggled in Philly and is potentially looking at the downside of his career. Don't confuse talent with value. These guys have talent, but their potential value is far more uncertain than many realize.

Jake: Brandin Cooks, LAR

Yes, the Rams run more 3-wide than anyone, and all 3 receivers will be in the WR2 conversation. However, Cooper Kupp is Jared Goff's main man, and Cooks' inconsistency was already present both before and after Kupp's injury. As Kupp continues to grow, Cooks will slide back a bit in use, and even a mild dip will make his inconsistency even worse.

Matt: Stefon Diggs, MIN

Diggs is coming off a career year, with 102 catches for 1,021 yards and nine TDs and early ADPs show him as a top-15 fantasy receiver, and he's a total stud skill-set wise. I'm not buying him at that price, though, for a few reasons. His production has been notoriously inconsistent week-to-week. Over half of his TDs in 2018 came Week 11 or later -- and 3 were scored in Weeks 15-17 after most fantasy playoffs had been determined, rendering useless to the majority of his owners. He actually went on a streak of seven games in the middle of the season when he only found the end zone once. Diggs simply is a boom-or-bust fantasy receiver who also comes with durability issues: He hasn't played a full 16-game slate ever in his four years in the NFL. He missed time in 2016 and 2017 with a groin injury, in addition to knee and hip injuries, and something about him just feels fragile. Add to it that Adam Thielen demands volume on the other side of the field (153 targets last year), and while Diggs saw 149 targets himself for a near 50/50 split, I just can't buy in when there are receivers like Kenny Golladay, Cooper Kupp and A.J. Green I'd rather have ahead of Diggs.

Nate: Robert Woods, LAR

There are 3 quality WRs on the Rams' offense. Brandin Cooks has over 1,000 receiving yards in each of his last 4 seasons. Robert Woods just had a career high in receiving yards (1,219), targets (130), receptions (86), and receiving TDs (6). Prior to 2018, Woods had career highs of 781 receiving yards (2017), 104 targets (2014), 65 receptions (2014) and 5 TDs (2014/2017). He's been in the league since 2013. Woods being drafted ahead of Cooks is criminal and a classic example of recency bias. Let's not forget Cooper Kupp will be healthy and back into the mix in 2019. Expect a decent regression from Woods this season.

Gary: JuJu Smith-Schuster, PIT

Smith-Schuster had an outstanding season in 2018, piling up 111 catches or over 1,400 yards and finishing the year as the No. 8 wide receiver in PPR scoring systems. With Antonio Brown in Oakland now, plenty of folks are predicting Smith-Schuster will at least back that season up -- and maybe exceed it. With Brown gone, Smith-Schuster's the unquestioned No. 1 wideout in the Steel City, and while that means more targets, it also means a lot more defensive attention. Smith-Schuster's going to have a fine third NFL season. But he's not going to live up to the increased expectations surrounding him.

Bogman: Alshon Jeffery, PHI

I love Jeffery, but the situation in Philly just keeps getting more convoluted. Zach Ertz is going to get his, Dallas Goedert was impressive in his rookie season, they traded for DeSean Jackson and drafted JJ Arcega-Whiteside. Not only is there competition, but Carson Wentz isn't inspiring much confidence that he can stay healthy. I would love to get Jeffery as a WR3, but it seems like he is firmly going off the board as a WR2. He hasn't had 1,000-yard season since 2014, and he has been everywhere from 10 to 2 TDs in the past 4 seasons. The only Eagle who has my confidence to produce for fantasy is Zach Ertz.

Derek: Corey Davis, TEN

Since Davis was drafted, hope and faith have been rampant regarding his eventual ascension as the target hog, No. 1 wide receiver for the Titans. This year the Titans added another versatile high-end college producer to their wide receiver room in A.J. Brown. In what projects to be a low-volume passing offense, to begin with, the additions of not only Brown but Adam Humphries to catch passes do not bode well for Davis. The best-case scenario was for Davis to be given a majority piece of a small pie. Right now it looks as though the Titans are passing out extra spoons to everyone else invited to the party.

Chris: Corey Davis, TEN

Davis had all the opportunity in the world to produce WR1 numbers in 2018, and he failed to do so. He was the only weapon in Tennessee and reeled in just 65 of his 112 targets for 891 yards. Some of that was on him, and some of that was on Marcus Mariota and Blaine Gabbert under center. Davis only found the end zone four times last season, and he had fewer than five catches in 10 games. The Titans added A.J. Brown at the draft and signed Adam Humphries. Delanie Walker, who missed last season, returns, and the Titans finally figured out to run the ball with Derrick Henry -- two developments that make Davis an easy pass on draft day.

Tight End

Joe: Greg Olsen, CAR/Hunter Henry, LAC

The hard truth is that Olsen is breaking down, and I fear name recognition alone will carry his value in 2019 in a questionable bottom tier of tight ends. Even a good preseason can't get me to buy back in on Olsen. Henry will be a fantasy community darling in 2019 drafts, but I want to remind everyone that he was underwhelming in 2017, so being too aggressive on him is a dangerous move.

Jake: Jared Cook, NO

Cook has made a career out of inconsistency and fooling owners into getting their hopes up for more and more. Now, Cook heads to the Saints, which of course looks amazing on paper. Of course, we need to remember that Drew Brees spreads the ball around too much and has also taken a significant step back in the passing game, as the Saints have focused on balancing the offense. Let someone else draft Cook too early.

Matt: Austin Hooper, ATL

Stop treating Hooper like some savior at the tight end position for your fantasy squad. Last season, the games in which Hooper scored touchdowns (four) were the only ones when he finished with double-digit fantasy points (standard scoring). Every other week was a bust. And this is a guy who's going among the top 10 at the position. Why pay up for inconsistency when you can simply stream it (or better)?

Nate: Eric Ebron, IND

Ebron was the beneficiary of 13 touchdown receptions in 2018. He was 1 of only 2 players to have double-digit touchdown receptions and under 800 receiving yards -- a tall order to repeat in 2019. Ebron saw increased looks from Andrew Luck because the TE8 from 2017 missed the majority of the 2018 season. Jack Doyle is just one year removed from having the 2nd-most receptions and 5th-most targets out of the tight end position. Doyle will be back in 2019 along with, potentially, a new red-zone target for Luck in big-bodied WR Devin Funchess. Don't draft Ebron in 2019 expecting 2018 production. It's not going to happen.

Gary: Jared Cook, NO

I'll freely admit that I don't necessarily have a statistical reason for being nervous about Cook in 2019. He's coming off career highs in just about every statistical category and joins one of the NFL's most potent offenses in New Orleans. But counting on veteran players to post back-to-back career years isn't especially wise, and Cook's going to be hard-pressed to match his target share from last year in Oakland in his new home. Add in that this feels like about the seventh time someone has sad, "No, really ... it's safe to trust Jared Cook in fantasy football this time," and Cook's a good bet to be overdrafted in 2019.

Bogman: Eric Ebron, IND

I'll be the first to admit that I didn't have any respect for Ebron last season, and he was amazing. He had 14 TDs last year, which was more than he had in 4 seasons in Detroit. He was also 5th among TEs in receiving yards, and both of these would be tough to match even if the situation hadn't changed at all. Ebron only played 4 games with Jack Doyle last year, but in those games, he scored 7 of his TDs. The Colts also added Devin Funchess and drafted Parris Campbell. With Doyle healthy, Funchess coming in and Campbell joining the squad, I don't see Ebron recreating his career year from 2018.

Derek: Eric Ebron, IND

Ebron operated as the clear No. 2 option in the Colts passing game last season. That will not be the case this year. Ebron has to contend with the likes of Jack Doyle, Paris Campbell and Devin Funchess for that No. 2 role. Ebron's outlandish touchdown production last year will regress, and now with his target share in question, he is a player that will massively disappoint anyone investing in a sliver of his 2018 numbers.

Chris: Eric Ebron, IND

Touchdowns are touchdowns -- or so they say -- but there's no way Ebron should be drafted as a top-five TE. Do not pay for last season's 14 touchdowns as most his damage came in the red zone and when Jack Doyle was sidelined. Doyle is expected to be ready for the start of the season, and the Colts brought in Devin Funchess (red-zone option) and drafted Parris Campbell. They also have Deon Cain, who failed to play last season due to an injury. I'd be OK with Ebron if he was the seventh, eighth or ninth TE off the board, but that doesn't seem to be the early indication.

UNDERRATED

Quarterback

Joe: Matt Ryan, ATL

In two of the last three seasons, Ryan was in the 5,000 passing yards/35 TD range, yet no one seems to care. He has great receivers, and the running game continues to be suspect. That means more great productivity in 2019.

Jake: Kyler Murray, ARI

Even if Murray merely throws for 3,200/20, the rushing numbers will boost him into the QB1 discussion. Only last year, Cam Newton was QB12 in just 14 games with solid passing numbers, but his value was carried by the rushing numbers. That will be the case with Murray; expecting 600/5 on the ground from the rookie is more than reasonable.

Matt: Philip Rivers, LAC

Rivers is the definition of consistency in terms of fantasy production and reliability. For starters, he hasn't missed a single regular-season game in *13* years. He's also averaged about at least 4,300 pass yards and 30 touchdowns over the last six seasons, and he finished as the QB12 or better in five of those years, while maintaining an ADP of around QB15. Essentially, you're getting a low-end QB1 for free. Let's not forget his skilled supporting cast, arguably one of the best pass-catching corps in the league, including receivers Keenan Allen, Mike Williams and Travis Benjamin; athletic tight end Hunter Henry; and two backs more than capable of catching balls out of the backfield in Melvin Gordon and Austin Ekeler. Rivers might be the best value QB in all of fantasy … again.

Nate: Matt Ryan, ARI

Ryan has been the second-best QB in two of the last three seasons. He has arguably the best WR in football in Julio Jones. I say arguably because I would say DeAndre Hopkins and Davante Adams are better, but that's not what we're here to discuss. The fact is, Julio Jones has 1,400-plus receiving yards in each of his last 5 seasons. No other player can claim that accomplishment. With a weapon like Jones, Ryan should always be in the top fantasy football QB conversations. The fact that you can get him in double-digit rounds in most drafts is crazy. Wait on QB and select Ryan later.

Gary: Ben Roethlisberger, PIT

It's hard to argue against Matt Ryan being underrated -- he's something of a poster child for why it's wise to wait to draft a signal caller. But Ryan's not the only quarterback who finished in the top five in 2018 and is being slept on this year. Yes, Roethlisberger lost Antonio Brown and Le'Veon Bell. And yes, his home vs. road splits are striking. But Big Ben didn't have Bell last year and still finished third at his position in fantasy points, and his ADP is barely inside QB1 territory. He's an outstanding platoon option well worth grabbing just for those eight games at Heinz Field.

Bogman: Kyler Murray, ARI

I'm going to be pushing the chips in on Murray in his rookie season. If this doesn't work well from the jump, it might be his only season, but I'm going to try it. Murray is going to start from Day 1; he has Larry Fitzgerald, Christian Kirk and David Johnson; and the Cardinals spent three draft picks on WRs. I don't care about his height at all; he can make every throw. I'm concerned about his weight, at just a shade over 200 pounds with a questionable OL. *That's* where my worry lies. As long as he's on the field, he's going to produce. You may want to draft someone else, especially in a deep league, in case he can't hold up.

Derek: Matt Ryan, ATL

Ryan has quietly gone from overrated to massively underrated for a quarterback who has been an elite fantasy producer in two of the last three seasons. For a pocket QB, Ryan received one of the best gifts the Falcons could give him: offensive line help in the draft. With a skill position cupboard filled with Julio Jones, Calvin Ridley, Austin Hooper and Devonta Freeman, Ryan is set for weapons. Another top-three fantasy season for Ryan is easily attainable in 2019.

Chris: Josh Allen, BUF

Allen has a solid floor thanks to his rushing ability, and his deep ball provides an intriguing ceiling. Allen finished second among quarterbacks in rushing yards last season with 631 and led all QBs with eight rushing touchdowns. He did that in 12 games and finished first on his team with 21 red-zone rushing attempts. Buffalo has no shortage of running backs, and he may not run around as much in year number two, but the offensive line is improved as are the weapons in Allen's passing game. According to Next Gen Stats, Allen led the league in average intended air yards, average air yard differential and largest completed air distance. Allen also led the league with an 11.2 aDOT and was eighth in yards per completion despite an ugly 53 completion percentage. I believe he'll be able to improve on those numbers, but it's really the rushing upside that has me excited. Keep in mind he broke Michael Vick's record for most rushing yards by a QB over his first eight starts.

Running Back

Joe: James White, NE

The Patriots continue to move the focus of the offense to the running backs, and yards are yards. 1,000 all-purpose yards and 90 catches are well within White's grasp. That's basically what he gave you in 2018, along with 12 TDs. The axiom to "avoid the New England running backs" is a thing of the past. He's a strong RB2 in PPR and a great FLEX in Standard leagues.

Jake: David Montgomery, CHI

Matt Nagy and the Bears already admitted that they like Montgomery more than Jordan Howard and can see a bigger role than Howard had. Even with being merely an above-average running back, Howard still had 270 touches (250 carries). If Montgomery only gets that work, he's at least a top-20 running back.

Matt: Dalvin Cook, MIN

It's almost comical to think you might be able to draft Cook *after* players like Travis Kelce, Nick Chubb and Joe Mixon. An electric and versatile three-down back who's suffered some unfortunate injury luck through his first two seasons in the NFL, Cook was in the conversation among the best and most NFL-ready backs in a 2017 class that included Christian McCaffrey, Leonard Fournette, Alvin Kamara and the aforementioned Mixon. When he's been healthy, Cook has showcased his quick feet and explosiveness on the field. Even in limited work last year (11 games), he still posted over 900 scrimmage yards (including 40 receptions) and four scores. The only thing that was in his way from becoming a fantasy breakout in 2018 was short-yardage specialist Latavius Murray, who left Minnesota in free agency. As long as he can stay healthy, Cook will have every opportunity to succeed in 2019, and his early ADP has him as a third-rounder is an absolute steal for anyone looking to take a WR with their first pick.

Nate: Kenyan Drake, MIA

Last year, I saw Drake's potential as an RB1. Not a popular take, but at the end of 2018, Drake found himself as the No. 14 overall RB in PPR formats. If it weren't for the questionable play calls lending the majority of carries to 85-year-old Frank Gore, Drake would have easily been an RB1 in PPR and potentially .5 PPR formats. Well, Frank Gore is gone, and the Dolphins have a new head coach. If Brian Flores and his coaching staff can't see that Drake is the most talented RB on the Dolphins, then Drake's full potential will be hindered. I'm banking on the Dolphins to do the right thing and unleash Drake in 2019.

Gary: Phillip Lindsay, DEN

Lindsay was a revelation for the Broncos last year as a rookie, topping 1,000 yards on the ground and averaging 5.4 yards per carry en route to a top-15 fantasy finish and becoming the first UDFA in league history to make the Pro Bowl in his first season. Yet despite of those accomplishments, he's viewed as no more than a so-so fantasy RB2 in many circles. No one's doing cartwheels over Joe Flacco, but it can be argued he's a nominal upgrade over Case Keenum, and the Broncos improved the offensive line. Lindsay's a great draft-day target for teams that use their first pick on a wide receiver.

Bogman: Phillip Lindsay, DEN

Lindsay won the job last year as an undrafted free agent *and* made the Pro Bowl. I know the Broncos have been playing musical chairs for awhile at the position, but when this guy runs with the job, the search is over. Royce Freeman was a third-round draft pick and most expected him to take the job, but he's clearly the backup now. Lindsay averaged 5.6 yards per touch to Freeman's 4.1. This isn't close.

Derek: David Montgomery, CHI

Matt Nagy wants a workhorse running back in the worst way. Nagy trialed Jordan Howard in that role last season over the first three games of the season. During that time, Howard out-touched Tarik Cohen 64 to 21 and out-targeted him 11 to 8. After Week 3, Howard saw more than two targets in a game only once. Montgomery can be that three-down back that Nagy wanted Howard to become. Montgomery at his floor should be viewed as a top-20 running back, as Howard was in 2018. Montgomery has the ceiling to be a top-12 running back and a league winner this year.

Chris: Chris Carson, SEA

The obvious answer is Phillip Lindsay, but I'm going to give some respect to Carson since nobody else is. Carson was a bit of an unknown heading into 2018 after he was limited to four games in 2017 due to a broken leg. To say he returned value would be an understatement: He finished as RB15 in .5 PPR leagues. Carson finished fifth in rushing yards (1,151), fourth in rushing yards per game (82) and third in rushing attempts per game (17). It's all about opportunity in fantasy, and Carson's 246 carries were the seventh most last season behind Adrian Peterson and Jordan Howard, who will both see a decline in 2019. Carson also finished seventh in red-zone rushing attempts and rushing touchdowns (nine). Rashaad Penny is bound to take a step forward -- but more so in the passing game. Carson only grabbed 20 balls last season, and he takes a hit in PPR formats, but Seattle's 534 rushing attempts in 2018 were second to Baltimore, and 56 more than the third-ranked Patriots. According to Fantasy Football Calculator, Carson was the 30th RB off the board last season, and he has an early ADP of RB24. It's fine to think Penny will be more involved, but he won't be as productive as Carson. Keep in mind it took Carson a bit to win the job, and when he did, he didn't look back.

Wide Receiver

Joe: Tyler Boyd, CIN

Sure, he's a No. 2, and yeah, Andy Dalton has his limitations. However, with A.J. Green still in the fold, Boyd will once again receive a ton of 1-on-1 coverage. That same situation led to a breakout year from Boyd in which he caught 76 of his 108 targets for 1,028 yards and seven TDs. His knee should be 100 percent in training camp, and Boyd is a great alternative if you end up missing the top WRs in a draft run.

Jake: DaeSean Hamilton, DEN

He already flashed in 2018, and with Joe Flacco (and likely rookie taking over) at quarterback, Hamilton will be relied upon even more in 2019. With Emmanuel Sanders a huge question mark to return to 100% ever again, Hamilton could even be the Broncos' No. 1 receiver and a top-20 wideout in fantasy. The skills are there, and he's the better safety value than Courtland Sutton.

Matt: Mike Williams, LAC

When Williams was given a chance to shine last year, he took major advantage of it. On a Chargers team loaded with talent, the 2017 first-round draft pick was a red-zone monster, especially in a memorable Week 15 game against the Chiefs in which he posted three total touchdowns on nine targets and a game-winning two-point conversion: Kansas City simply couldn't cover the 6-foot-4, 218-pound specimen in and around the end zone. He was one of only three wideouts to score six TDs from inside the 10-yard line (Davante Adams, Michael Thomas) and planted his flag as Philip Rivers' go-to No. 2 receiver opposite Keenan Allen. Williams caught a tough break missing his entire rookie year due to injury but displayed what he's capable of when given the opportunity last season. There's nowhere to go but up for the talented Clemson product, and 2019 could be a breakout campaign. His early ADP has him as a mid-third rounder, a value he should have no problem outperforming.

Nate: Devin Funchess, IND

We all saw what Eric Ebron was able to do with Andrew Luck throwing to him in 2018. Devin Funchess will get his red-zone looks in this offense. Defenses will have plenty to worry about against Luck and his weapons this season, and I believe Funchess will benefit from it. Funchess had an awful year in 2018, but he was dealing with Cam Newton and his bum shoulder all season. That's why Christian McCaffrey benefitted so much as Cam had to lean on dump offs all year. Funchess will have Andrew Luck as his QB in 2019, a night-and-day comparison to Newton, and Funchess should have a night-and-day comparison of his 2018 and 2019 seasons.

Gary: Deebo Samuel, SF

Mind you, this isn't to say that Samuel's going to rampage his way across the NFL as a rookie and finish his first season as a top-10 fantasy option. But I won't be even a little surprised if Samuel's a weekly fantasy starter by year's end and the No. 1 rookie wideout in 2019. Samuel's an excellent route-runner; he's a beast at attacking the football; and calling Samuel tough as nails is an understatement. There's a reason he was the second wideout drafted this year, and I expect Kyle Shanahan and Jimmy Garoppolo to take full advantage of his prodigious talents.

Bogman: Courtland Sutton, DEN

I'm not so sure about Joe Flacco, but I think he's better than Case Keenum. Sutton gets another year under his belt and he should be better this season. Sutton is only in his fourth season as a WR; he was recruited to SMU as a safety and flipped to WR his sophomore season. Emmanuel Sanders is coming off an Achilles surgery from December, and the Broncos are hoping to get him back by for training camp, but he may have to start the season on the PUP. If that happens or if Sanders isn't the same, Sutton could end up being the No. 1 option for the Broncos. At this moment, Sutton is going off as a WR3/4, right on the borderline. He's at least a WR3 with a lot of upside.

Derek: Calvin Ridley, ATL

Ridley finished last year as a top-24 wide receiver. Many will point to his 10 touchdowns as the strength of that finish, and while they are not wrong, that does not mean Ridley can't outproduce last year's fantasy finish in 2019. Ridley's rookie season success puts him among exclusive company. Over the last 10 years, only Odell Beckham, Michael Thomas, Jordan Matthews, Mike Evans, Keenan Allen, Kelvin Benjamin, Mike Williams (former Tampa Bay wide receiver), Julio Jones and Ridley have surpassed 800 receiving yards and eight touchdowns in their rookie season. In that sample (excluding Ridley), five of those eight wide receivers have firmly entrenched themselves as perennial top-12 fantasy options. Dirk Koetter primarily ran his passing offense through his top two wide receivers during his last tenure in Atlanta. Now that Koetter is back as offensive coordinator, Ridley is in for a target bump this season that will compensate and elevate him above any touchdown regression he could see.

Chris: Tyler Boyd, CIN

Boyd set career highs in targets (108), catches (76), yards (1,028) and touchdowns (8). He's certainly capable of repeating those numbers as he only played 14 games last season. Boyd had three 100-yard games where he racked up 32 catches, and A.J. Green played in all of those games. Boyd excelled when

Green was hurt too, but you know A.J. will continue to get top coverage. The Bengals will once again be one of the worst defensive teams in the league which means they'll be a lot of chucking out of the offense.

Tight End

Joe: Eric Ebron, IND

Nate and I will go to war on this one! He's not wrong that Ebron may have a tough road ahead to repeat his 2018 career year. However, at a thin position, to be a TE1 every week all you need is that TD. Even if the TD total falls to the eight to 10 range and his yards stay the same, he'll be right in the middle of the pack, which is where he'll be drafted. That's a good return on investment in my world.

Jake: Hunter Henry, LAC

Sure, Henry is a risk as he returns from injury, but he still has legitimate top-five talent. The Chargers looked for solutions at the position last year -- never truly finding one -- and saw Tyrell Williams leave in free agency. Mike Williams is primed for a huge season, but don't forget about the man everyone was calling a top-five tight end last year before the injury.

Matt: Vance McDonald, PIT

Antonio Brown's 168 vacant targets have to go somewhere, right? Okay, that's lazy analysis, but in reality, those targets will be divvied up amongst Steelers pass-catchers, and McDonald is due to benefit. McDonald established a solid rapport with QB Ben Roethlisberger last season, racking up 50 catches on 73 targets for 610 yards and four scores, marking a career year for the huge, athletic move TE. He's in line to see even more volume in 2019, and early mocks show him going *after* TEs like Austin Hooper and rookie T.J. Hockenson. I'd argue McDonald has top-five upside at his position this year.

Nate: Jack Doyle, IND

As mentioned in the "Overrated TE" writeup on Ebron, Doyle had the second-most receptions and fifth-most targets among tight ends in 2017. That type of production came with QB Jacoby Brissett at the helm. If Doyle can produce those numbers with a below-average QB, imagine how productive he can be with Andrew Luck. I'm not saying Doyle is in line to be a top option at the position; he has to compete for targets with another viable TE. I am saying that you will likely be able to draft Doyle in double-digit rounds or even with your last pick, and he will most certainly return that value plus some at this unstable position. I believe Doyle gets more volume and has a higher ceiling in fantasy football than Ebron.

Gary: Austin Hooper, ATL

By virtue of his 71 receptions for 660 yards and four scores a year ago, Hooper was fantasy's sixth-ranked tight end in leagues that award a point for receptions. Yet he gets about as much buzz in fantasy circles as a potted fern wearing a helmet. No, Hooper is not the first option in the Atlanta passing game. Or the second. Or the third. But he was targeted 5.5 times a game last year and was incredibly efficient turning those targets into catches. Still only 24 years old, Hooper's just now coming into his own as a player -- and he's a solid weekly starter at a position that lacks depth who won't break the bank on draft day.

Bogman: Vance McDonald, PIT

McDonald has never played 16 games, so I understand if you don't want to buy this one. Antonio Brown and Jesse James are gone, and that's 134 receptions out the door. JuJu Smith-Schuster can't add much to his 111 last year; Donte Moncrief had 48 last year and his career high is 64. McDonald is going to be expected see more snaps than the 50% he saw last year, and he could be in for a huge year. He's going off the board at TE14 right now according to FantasyPros, so if you're waiting for a TE, he's worth a shot. If it doesn't work out, dump him and grab the hot hand.

Derek: Vance McDonald, PIT

McDonald will step into an every-down role this season with Zach Gentry as the only addition to the tight end room behind McDonald this offseason. McDonald will be handing out soul-stealing stiff arms with more regularity this year. He will undoubtedly receive a target bump as the Steelers now are without Antonio Brown. The Steelers have no one in the wide receiver room that has shown up to this point (James Washington, Donte Moncrief, etc.) that they are capable or ready to assume the role of the second option in this passing game. McDonald could seize that spot this year, and with it, a top-five finish amongst tight ends is within his range of outcomes.

Chris: David Njoku, CLE

If you're looking for this year's Ebon, Njoku is your guy. I know what you're thinking: Cleveland has plenty of mouths to feed. While that's correct, this team will be one of the better offensive squads in the league. With all of the attention on Odell Beckham and Jarvis Landry, Njoku should inherit some easy completions. He caught all four of his touchdowns inside the red zone last season, and even if that's where the majority of his work comes from in 2019, you should be OK with it, considering the lack of options/production at TE. At least get yourself a TE on a high-octane offense. I usually like to target my TEs near Round 10 or toward the end of drafts where Njoku's going.

Chapter 14

BEING THE COMMISH

Joe Pisapia

I usually put this chapter in every edition of the Fantasy Baseball Black Book, but it's time to bring over some commissioner awareness to the Football Black Book. I've tweaked a few things but the message is the same. So, away we go....

Congratulations! You've decided to run a fantasy league!

Get ready for one of the most thankless jobs, with zero pay and a floodgate of complaints for everything that goes wrong or every decision you make!

EXCITED YET?!

The truth is being the commissioner can be fun with the right group of league mates, so choose wisely. Who you let join the league will greatly impact your enjoyment. Even in cash leagues, you should all have the same attitude: "Competitive but fun" is the goal.

CHOOSING LEAGUE FORMAT

When choosing the style of the league, I suggest being selfish here and pick one you enjoy. You'll be dealing with all the headaches throughout the season, you might as well be enjoying the format. I suggest PPR/Superflex and have a points bonanza, but pick what works best for you!

When you invite owners to join, make sure they are *really* interested. Why run a 12-team league when you only have 10 passionate owners? Those other two teams will turn into ghosts by October. Just scale the talent pool to the number of owners. If you have a small group, consider a 10-team, mandatory 2QB format with 2 flex spots. Go deep into the player pool and challenge yourselves.

All-Pro teams are boring. Get creative! Try IDP even. If you run a quality league, word will get out and you will eventually expand. Host sites for leagues are so advanced, you have no reason not to create a tailor-made experience.

There is also nothing wrong with running a free, fun league either. I am in both cash and free leagues, and they are both super-competitive. It has to do with choosing your league members wisely. You could always spice it up with a silly/ridiculous prize at the end, or get everyone together for a steak dinner and the winner doesn't pay. That is also a fun way to get the group together once a year if you are colleagues, classmates or family.

PROTECT THE LEAGUE

A good commissioner should run a benevolent dictatorship. Leagues with too much democracy can end in chaos.

Rule with a firm hand but not an iron fist. Remember to put yourself in the other owners' shoes when making decisions. A good commissioner can make a real difference in the way a fantasy league operates and sets the tone for the group as a whole. A poor one can ruin the experience for the entire clan. I have experienced both firsthand and learned a lot from those experiences. They have taught me how to be a good league member and the proper way to enter healthy dialogue over a league rule or philosophical difference. I have taken these good/bad lessons and tried to run my own league accordingly.

The first rule of being a commissioner is you must put the interests of the league above any individual interest, including your own. As fierce a competitor as you may be, this may be difficult for you to find a balance between the two. However, it's imperative you not only anticipate problems but also set yourself up for success by keeping your league rules clear, specific and logical.

SAY 'NO' TO VETOES!! ALWAYS!!!

NEVER VETO TRADES! EVER! If you run a system where trades can be vetoed, you are heading toward a dangerous path.

First off, if you're in a league that has owners capable of collusion, you have assembled the wrong group of people. I've been in leagues where collusion took place, and the only answer is to eject the owner(s) involved and immediately refund any money (if needed) they may have used to buy into the league. It may weaken the jackpot prize but will strengthen the league. Plus, you've sent a clear message to your fellow owners that the behavior will not be tolerated.

Unfortunately, there are some owners who are just less skilled than others and they make "bad" or "ill-informed" deals. This is where it gets tricky. Which brings us to …

COLLUSION? OR SOMETHING ELSE?

Value can be in the eye of the beholder and subjective across owners. You also have to strongly consider trades from each team's immediate "needs." It isn't just about talent level sometimes. It's also about keeping water out of a sinking ship or an owner's individual philosophy.

Collusion is a different set of circumstances. You must do everything you can to discern between the two carefully. Once you allow veto power of any trade by any party, you're not only ruining your league's marketplace, but you are also taking the fun and the learning curve out of the process as well.

My strong suggestion is to **never** open Pandora's Box in this manner.

On a side note, I would also suggest steering clear of "Fantasy Arbitration" or "Fantasy Judgment" type sites that charge money for analysis of your league's discord. First off, you never know who's running them in the first place or what their true fantasy knowledge is when it comes to players. Instead, seek out an independent expert of note from a credible website and see if you can get their take on a deal that is "questionable." That's a far better (and cheaper) way to get a second opinion.

Twitter is a great tool for this so use it! And when all else fails, @JoePisapia17 is happy to help out. (Yes, I just talked about myself in the third person, and I'm ashamed.)

MAKE IT A KEEPER!

A good way to avoid the collusion issue altogether is to first make your league a keeper format of some kind.

People are much less apt to get involved in these situations if they are looking forward to next season and building for the future. You can also reward continued competition.

COLLECTING/AWARDING PRIZE MONEY

What do you do with owners who don't pay on time?

First off, you must set a hard deadline for payment and have real repercussions for failing to comply. For example, if an owner is not paid up by draft day, they forfeit their first-round pick. That will get their attention. If certain owners continuously present problems in this vein, simply don't invite them back. If your friendship suffers, consider the fact they didn't respect you enough as a friend to comply with the rules as you do all the grunt work so they can have a good time.

If you run a league involving prize money, always pay out the winnings in a timely fashion. Owners who win the cash put in the effort, and you need to reward them promptly. I also recommend never taking a "commissioner fee" off the top. Some leagues operate where the guy running it gets a cut regardless of performance.

KEEP IT FRESH

If a league has become stale over the years and you feel interest waning, shake things up! Make the draft an auction instead of a snake! Add some keepers! Change is good! Challenge is also good!

Above all else, remember this is supposed to be FUN! If you're running a league and are miserable, consider passing control over to someone else. Fresh blood can also help. Never be afraid of inviting smart, new owners to play. Compete against the best whenever possible. Challenge yourself! If you have owners who've lost interest over a period of time, don't be afraid to thank them for their time and bring in fresh competition.

YOU are the commish! The buck stops with *you,* and *you* control the experience for *everyone* to a large degree. Do all you can to get the most out your league, in the best interest of fantasy football.

Chapter 15

Managing Rosters and Making Trades

Joe Pisapia

For all of the stats, metrics and projections, sports are still incredibly unpredictable. That's why we watch. That's the challenge of fantasy football.

Can we consistently put ourselves in a position to win, despite so many variables? We can, but it doesn't end with the draft. The draft is merely the beginning. You can out-draft everyone in your league and still lose. While this may not seem fair, it's still a fact. Owners who are diligent on the waiver wire, savvy about matchups and willing to take calculated risks often end up winning leagues.

The game will always find a way to be unpredictable. Trends and anomalies will happen, and there's nothing you can do to stop them. However, you can continuously put yourself in a *better* position to overcome these blips on the radar.

The keys are:

1. Having a deep team that can withstand bumps in the road.
2. Being aware of the trends and reacting to them appropriately.

Utilizing Your Bench

Many owners tend to overlook the importance of the latter part of a draft. Some take too many risks, while others, not enough. The second part of the draft often makes or breaks a fantasy team. This is where your knowledge of the player pool pays off, making key selections that have the upside to contribute.

First and foremost, try to acquire talent. This may seem silly to say, but it's true that oftentimes talent eventually wins out over the course of a season. Roles are constantly changing on teams in the NFL due to injury or coaching decisions. Having talent on your roster allows you to potentially make game-changing roster moves or trades during the course of a season.

Handcuffing running backs is sort of an outdated concept, unless you knowingly are investing in a running-back-by-committee (RBBC) system. It's smarter to draft backups who have potential to take over the lion's share of the touches should an injury befall a certain back who's already on thin ice. Drafting the backup of a reliable back is only going to clog up a spot on your bench that could be better served with players you'll need for bye weeks or prevent you from adding waiver-wire talent. In deeper leagues, it's more understandable to use bench spots for backup RBs. The shallower the league, the less important this becomes.

Walking the Waiver Wire

Every year, there are guys who surprise and delight -- players undrafted and left for dead then plucked from the scrap heap and plugged onto what become championship teams. Whether it's a true waiver wire or a FAAB (free-agent acquisition budget) system, I always lean on the side of being aggressive early.

Look at it from this perspective: You have 13-14 regular-season games to turn yourself into a playoff team. How many teams will be out of it after 6 weeks? It's better to be aggressive on talent with the potential to help your roster than to allow them to end up on other teams. Also, just because you're riding high, don't neglect the waiver wire. Keeping other teams from acquiring key talent for the stretch run can turn your great regular season into a first-round ousting in the playoffs.

Why? Because you got lazy! Stay active all year.

MAKING TRADES

Value is in the eye of the beholder. This is the obstacle you must overcome since everyone has different allegiances and opinions on players' values.

Some will work in your favor. Others will work against you. There are some tricks to "the trade." Being able to consistently pull off good deals on a yearly basis is an art form. Much like teaching a young artist to paint, I can give you the techniques, but you must find your own brush stroke and inspiration.

Etiquette

First and foremost, **always** be polite and courteous. You are selling something, after all, and no one wants to buy something from someone who is rude or obnoxious.

Always inquire about the availability of the player you want. You can offer a concise reason this deal would improve their team and yours -- but the key word is **concise**. Don't give a dissertation. It comes off as arrogant and suggests the other owner is ignorant.

You also never want to venture into a deal at the expense of your potential partner. Trying to rip off a fellow owner should not be the goal. Not only will that probably never fly with the other owner, but if it *did,* you run the risk of ruining other potential deals down the road (or annoying the rest of your league). They simply won't trust you anymore.

Also, be sure never to bash your potential trade partner's players no matter how they may have underperformed. It is rude and insulting, and the last thing you want to do is alienate a potential match. Generally speaking, less is more. You should always try to find a positive starting point to the dialogue and try to present a deal that is your common interest.

If they reject your proposal or are "insulted" by the very thought you asked about a certain player, politely ask for a counter from them to see if you can find a middle ground. If they are adamant or even rude in their reply, then just say "Thanks for getting back to me" and call it a day.

DO NOT BELABOR THE POINT! You will rarely convince an owner like this to see things your way. Leave the door open with a "Let me know if there are any deals you might be interested in making surrounding Player X down the line." That way, you keep the lines of communication open for the future. Listen to what they have to say. If they should start a dialogue or counter, that is a sign they are interested and ready to deal. If they become flat-out negative, walk away. Getting into a debate about how *you* see things and how *they* see things will still leave you without a deal. Don't waste your time. That energy can be channeled into finding another solution elsewhere.

It never hurts to inquire about players you think may be untouchable. Every now and then, they may be had for the right price. Most of the time, they will be unmovable. If an owner says someone is off limits, never push. It will be a waste of time and energy for both parties.

Leverage

When making trades, leverage is everything. Leverage is having something the other guy wants … or better yet, needs … or, best of all, simply can't do without.

If a big-time player goes down in your league, be the first guy to offer a solution. Yes, you are a vulture swooping in, but vultures stay full, don't they?

If you are offering a lifeline, you are *helping* the other owner. Don't attempt to take advantage. Instead, devise a strong, simple argument for the offer and preset package of talent (with options and flexibility) that will keep the other owner afloat and improve your roster at the same time. Be creative. Be the solution. Think outside the box and listen to what they have to say. Cater to their needs as best you can, and you may get *your* wants taken care of at the same time. One-sided deals may work once, but you will never foster a long-term relationship of making deals with that partner.

This is where the deep bench comes into play again – sometimes you don't *have to* make a move but see an opportunity to improve your situation. That is the right time to pull the trigger. You should always be looking to get better no matter how many games up you are in the standings. A deep roster maximizes your options. Complacency is death in fantasy.

Still, be careful not to send out deals too frequently. It may also alienate potential partners, and you may come off as too aggressive or unsure of what you are doing. See your opening and strike while the iron is hot. I am always a big proponent of moving young talent in an attempt to "win now" in keeper/dynasty leagues. You'll always get a fresh set of rookies to rebuild your roster, but championships are hard to come by.

Poker Face

Another way to win out on trades is to know your fellow owners' tendencies. Do they covet Steelers because they cannot separate their fandom from fantasy? Do they love young players and collect them like trophy wives? It's a poker game, and knowing their "tells" will inform you of how to approach a potential deal. Exploiting your enemies' weakness is an art form. If you can do this well, you may be shocked what you can get back in return.

Understanding the market for a player is a tough thing. Generally speaking, it is always wise to have more than one dialogue going with multiple teams when trying to make a trade. To play one owner against each other is a dicey business, though. It may put some owners off to dealing with you, so tread lightly. Never grandstand about how much better someone else's offer is. If it was really that much better, then just take it.

If you want to try and improve Owner A's offer, level with them and tell them you have received another strong offer but prefer to deal with Owner A. If they want to go above that, you should listen and give them a chance to counter before pulling the trigger. Courtesy is nice and sometimes surprisingly effective. Even if the offer does not improve, you have shown to be an owner of integrity. That keeps the roadway open for future moves.

Weak and Strong

Every league has strong owners and owners that are not as strong, no matter how expert the level of the league.

Some of the best deals I ever made were with the better, savvier owners in my leagues. I have also taken my fair share of stolen talent from those owners who are impatient or ill-informed. Always be confident in making offers. Before you click send, always put yourself in the other guy's shoes and honestly ask yourself if you would do this deal if you were in their shoes. If the answer is an honest "yes", then send away. If the answer is "no", then work harder, or scrap the trade altogether.

When the deal is done, you want *everyone* to benefit from the move you made together. If it is one-sided, they will be less apt to deal with you again, and you can't survive that way in a league. You need good, solid, respectful relationships that can help advance your placement in the standings.

You should never allow yourself to rip someone off. It is bad karma, bad for the future dealings with that owner, and bad for the league as it will raise suspicions and potentially embarrass the other guy as someone who got duped.

Now, there will always be sour-grape critics. That is a different story. If you know you made a fair deal, then sleep tight. If someone is jealous, too bad! They should have been more active and made their own deal happen!

There is a difference, but always put your best foot forward for the good of all involved.

10133861R00088

Made in the USA
Monee, IL
21 August 2019